15.1

sorption,
roskauer test
fatty acids (
See Vancomy

aring blender-ba
Water, 119. *Se*
wate
Campy
chlor
c

A MARRIAGE
MADE
IN HEAVEN

A MARRIAGE MADE IN HEAVEN

A Love Story in Letters

VATSALA AND EHUD SPERLING

TEN SPEED PRESS
BERKELEY TORONTO

For more on A Marriage Made in Heaven, visit our web site,
www.marriageinheaven.com

Ten Speed Press
P.O. Box 7123
Berkeley, California 94707
www.tenspeed.com

Distributed in Australia by Simon and Schuster Australia, in Canada by Ten Speed
Press Canada, in New Zealand by Southern Publishers Group, in South Africa by
Real Books, in Southeast Asia by Berkeley Books, and in the United Kingdom and
Europe by Airlift Books.

Design and composition by Rohani Design, Edmonds, Washington
Text set in Garamond and Weiss
Edited by Melissa Stein
Photos by Payson R. Stevens (©1996): pages 232–233, 234–235, 240–241, 243,
245, 253, 255, 256

Library of Congress Cataloging-in-Publication Data

Sperling, Vatsala, 1961–
    A marriage made in heaven : a love story in letters / Vatsala and Ehud Sperling.
        p. cm.
    ISBN 1–58008–182–7 (hardcover)
    1. Sperling, Vatsala, 1961– —Correspondence. 2. Sperling, Ehud, 1949–
—Correspondence. 3. East Indian American women—Biography. 4. East
Indians—Biography. 5. Matrimonial advertisements—India. 6. Love-letters.
7. Courtship—India. I. Sperling, Ehud, 1949– II. Title.

CT275.S(Sperling)V+
                                                                    99-055072
                                                                        CIP

First printing, 2000
Printed in Hong Kong

1 2 3 4 5 6 7 8 9 10 — 04 03 02 01 00

त्वदीयं वस्तु गोविन्द तुभ्यमेव समर्पये

שמע ישראל יהוה אלהינו יהוה אחד

To Dadaji Harish Johari and our parents

*Sunrise over the river Ganga
at Varanasi (Benares), India's
holiest city.*

CONTENTS

ACKNOWLEDGMENTS

Swamiji Bhoomananda Tirtha, Rev. Fr. Francis Leonard, Dr. Annamma Varghese, Dr. Saeid Bouzari, Dr. Mathangi Ramakrishnan, Ms. Lissy P. D., Clara James, Seema Joy, Sheela Anand, Shankari Selvaraj, Mr. Venu Gopal, Dr. Padma Priya, Dr. Shyamala Jayamoorthy, Dr. Susan Jacob, Dr. Mary Babu, Dr. Saraswati Narayanan . . . you added special and exotic spices to my life, I am thankful to you all for your trust.

Dana Goss, the very first editor who read our book and said, "Wow." Your positive views and critical comments helped us in shaping this book.

Jeanie Levitan and Cynthia Fowles, your initial reading of the manuscript and your suggestions mattered a lot. Kelly Bowen typed away through the manuscript and all its revisions with a lovely smile on her face.

Pat Young, Deb Turnbull, thank you for helping us in so many ways.

Appa, Anna, Akka, Rajani, Geeta, and Banu, there is no way I can ever thank you enough. You have given me many reasons to live.

Finally, Amma, I wonder if this "marriage made in heaven" could have come down to live on this earth if you had not given me the gift of life . . . for this, I am ever grateful to you, my dear mother.

Dr. Ramakrishnan, his wife Vijaya, sons Kartik and Giri, his parents, his sister and niece Sharada and all the other members of his family who so spiritedly directed and joined in the wedding ceremony.

Thanks to the management and staff of Surya Samudra for being fantastic.

To Payson Stevens, thanks for making the journey with me, providing so many stunning photographs of the wedding, for being my brother and playing the flute so well.

To Ira Cohen for the photo of the great GB.

To Barbara and Peter Theiss for their wedding photographs and their songs and their daughters Sarah and Maria.

To Deborah Kimbell and Leslie Blair, though "a kiss is just a kiss," from you both it is much much more.

To Arthur Jacobs for transcending the systems of jurisprudence and just plain prudence to be with us.

To Phil Wood for turning into an India freak at just the right time.

To Kirsty Melville for giving us a great publishing experience.

To Melissa Stein, the editor-made-in-heaven. It feels good being on the other side of the pencil.

To Michael Rohani, designer extraordinaire capable of participating in the birth of a book and a baby at the same time.

To the staff of Ten Speed Press who got into high gear to make it all happen.

To the Honorable Senator Patrick Leahy for being there for us.

To Donald Weiser, specialist in the occult, orientalia, and philosophy, who instilled a passion for books both rare and wonderful.

To Debby Kanig, who represented our family so beautifully at our wedding.

To Ima and Aba, who are beyond acknowledgment, thanks for the wonderful foundation in principles and values you have given me.

To Dada and his wife Pratibha and son Sachin for creating a safe landing during my many trips to and adventures in Planet India.

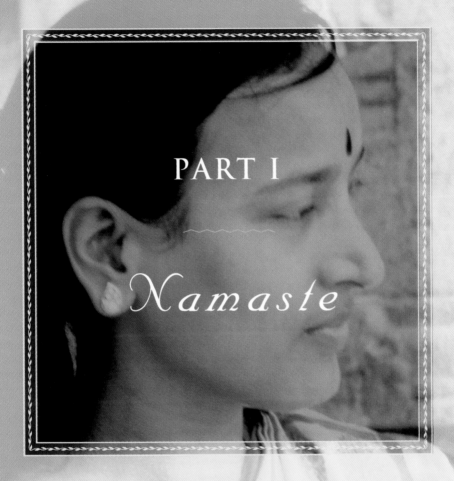

PART I

Namaste

Matrimonial ads in the Hindu, *an English-language newspaper.*

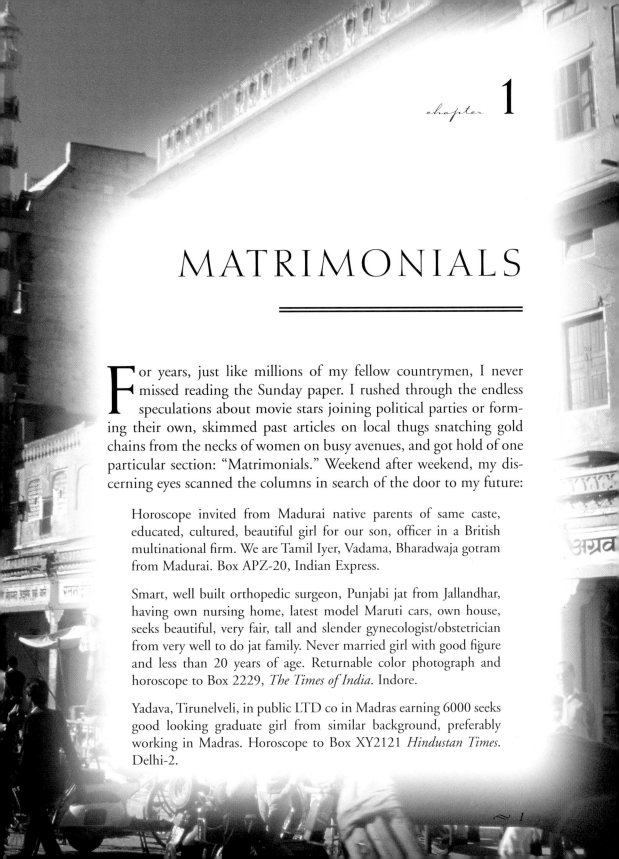

chapter 1

MATRIMONIALS

For years, just like millions of my fellow countrymen, I never missed reading the Sunday paper. I rushed through the endless speculations about movie stars joining political parties or forming their own, skimmed past articles on local thugs snatching gold chains from the necks of women on busy avenues, and got hold of one particular section: "Matrimonials." Weekend after weekend, my discerning eyes scanned the columns in search of the door to my future:

> Horoscope invited from Madurai native parents of same caste, educated, cultured, beautiful girl for our son, officer in a British multinational firm. We are Tamil Iyer, Vadama, Bharadwaja gotram from Madurai. Box APZ-20, Indian Express.

> Smart, well built orthopedic surgeon, Punjabi jat from Jallandhar, having own nursing home, latest model Maruti cars, own house, seeks beautiful, very fair, tall and slender gynecologist/obstetrician from very well to do jat family. Never married girl with good figure and less than 20 years of age. Returnable color photograph and horoscope to Box 2229, *The Times of India*. Indore.

> Yadava, Tirunelveli, in public LTD co in Madras earning 6000 seeks good looking graduate girl from similar background, preferably working in Madras. Horoscope to Box XY2121 *Hindustan Times*. Delhi-2.

Having examined thousands of such advertisements in four national newspapers, I became an expert in reading between the lines. Even though the advertisement consisted of only forty to fifty words, I could almost read the mind of the person who had put in the ad. I could easily classify these advertisers as sex crazy, money crazy, figure crazy, color crazy, degree crazy, status crazy, culture crazy, hypocrite, slave driver, egomaniac, bride killer, and so forth.

Say, for example, a fifty-year-old divorced man wants a twenty-year-old fair, smart, girl with a beautiful figure. He is obviously looking for sex with a young babe and not for a mature wife who might be suitable to his temperament and physical conditions. When the advertiser states clearly that he has many modern houses, agricultural land, and the latest cars, and wants a bride from a similar background, he is not likely to be kind and accepting of someone with little or no money. Next, when an ad states the caste, religion, language, family lineage, and region very clearly, and asks for a horoscope, it means that the advertiser will not deviate from the set pattern and would never reply to a letter from anyone except the parents of the girl.

When I first began replying to the advertisements in an effort to find a husband for myself, I replied—by mistake or by chance—to many such ads. In the majority of cases, I never heard back. In a few cases, I received very negative and highly insulting replies. Thus I learned my lesson, and learned the science and the art of reading the fine print. Most of the ads were placed by people whom I did not care to meet or know because they were, for whatever reason, locked up in their own mental prisons. They were in no condition to see that something good might possibly exist beyond their own set of limits, horizons, and beliefs. Very early on, I decided that I would not spend any time chasing people who were blindfolded.

I was seeking a levelheaded, simple, normal, total human being whose value system was the same as mine, who was not suffering from any manias or phobias. This man had to be focused and successful in his chosen or given mission in life. He should move through his life with a cheerful and generous attitude. Week after week I scanned the ads, sighing, "Oh, God, does such a person exist? Where is he? Can I ever meet him? Oh, dear God, will you please show me the right way, give me courage to reach the goal that you have set for me?"

One Sunday, this advertisement caught my attention:

This was one of those precious Sundays when I was off work and spending time at home with Amma, my mother. She was busy, too, scanning the ads in Tamil-language newspapers. I walked over to her and read this ad aloud. She listened, was quiet for a long time, and then said, "Always be aware, use your common sense, be fair and truthful in your actions, trust in God for guidance, and go ahead without fear. Do what you feel is right."

After listening to the wise counsel of my mother, I read the ad again, trying to visualize the person whose mind worked to put these words together. I did feel that this ad was possibly the one that would take me to where I belonged. After all, every event and every moment in life is always loaded with possibilities, both good and bad. To explore these possibilities we must take action.

Go for your pen, move, get started. I heard these words in my mind and reached for my best pen.

5.3.95

Dear Advertiser,

This refers to your advertisement that appeared in the *Hindu* dated March 5. May I introduce myself? I am B. R. Vatsala, a tall, slim, brown-complexioned woman with well-defined sharp features. Born on 1st January, 1961 at Jamshedpur, Bihar in North India, I moved to Nagpur as a student and spent five years earning a bachelor's and a master's degree in microbiology from Nagpur University. It was a memorable as well as happy moment for me when I received a prestigious Gold Medal from the President of India Dr. Sankar Dayal Sharma for standing first in order of merit at the master of sciences (M.Sc., Microbiology) examination. All through my student years, I received many laurels for academic and extracurricular achievements. Besides studies I have other interests too that include painting, knitting, tailoring, photography, and reading for fun. I enjoy Nature. I also happen to be a health enthusiast and a strict vegetarian, though I learned cooking nonvegetarian food as a student living in a hostel. I have a calm and friendly disposition. I get along well with people and am concerned about their welfare. Presently, since 1991

December, I have been on the staff of a 200-bed pediatric hospital in Madras, working as chief of clinical microbiology services.

As regards my family and cultural background, we are educated, upper-middle-class, Tamil Brahmins, vegetarian, Hindu Indians originating from Madurai. My father worked for TATA Iron and Steel Company for over 45 years. He is a strong, very loud and lively, deeply religious, very honest, and healthy young man of only 81 years. My mother has been a devoted homemaker. In between being a great wife and a mother to six children and eight grandchildren, she somehow found time to maintain a very peaceful, spiritual, happy environment at home and successfully composed nearly 275 original *bhajans*, songs, and prayer chants in Tamil. She has a delicious sweet voice too, and it is a norm in our household to wake up early in the mornings to the sound of my Holy Mother's prayers and music filling the atmosphere. I have one older brother, who works in life insurance, is married to a banker, and is settled in Madurai. My four older sisters are married, have kids, and are living in various parts of India and abroad. All my siblings are college graduates who had responsible jobs prior to their marriages.

I am looking forward to meeting a suitable man with whom to share life and grow, hence this letter. I am enclosing a photograph of myself. I would be grateful if you could write back at your earliest convenience.

Thanking you,
Yours sincerely,
B. R. Vatsala

Ninety-nine percent of the people who scan the matrimonial columns to find a suitable match for their wards would not bother to read this letter. They would consider me a total outcast—a strong-headed, footloose feminist who is out of her family's control and hence has low or no moral character. These moral guardians of my society would not waste their time or stationery in replying to my letter. Such was the mentality of my countrymen, my community, and my culture.

Personally, yes, I have great respect for this cultural rigidity so prevalent in India, and see it as a safety device against the moths that threaten the fabric of our cultural and social traditions. No complaints. I didn't wish to bring about a massive transition in the Indian social code and structure. But as far as my own life was concerned, if I ever wanted to find a suitable man and get married, I simply had to be prepared to be a revolutionary, a warrior. I had to be willing and able to be sure of what I wanted, to know how to find it, and to lose no dignity in charting my own path.

Well, my dear, it was one woman against an entire country—against thousands of years of established cultural practices.

To 'bring back Indian culture'

Samya Sarma speaks to Ehud C Sperling, chief of Inner Traditions, who was in the city this week

PRADEEP CHANDRA

EHUD C Sperling is an optimistic man with big plans. A US-based businessman, he was in Bombay this week to discuss plans for a tie-up between Inner Traditions — of which he is president and publisher — and India Book Distributors to print and produce volumes in India at amazingly low rates.

The volumes will be printed "most likely" at the Thompson Press, the authors involved in promotional activities such as those they would experience in the US. The publications will be priced between Rs100 and Rs595, "depending on the book, half or less than the US cost," and will be "more affordable to more people."

TOUCHDOWN

Inner Traditions produces "works representing the spiritual, cultural and mythic traditions of the world, focussing on inner wisdom and the perennial philosophies."

These, generally-biased as 'coffee table' tomes in this country, are usually available locally only at "outrageous" prices, affordable only by tourists and "out of reach of the people responsible for the material in the first place," says Sperling.

Also, there are "no indigenous publications in this area of interest, and no contemporary practitioners" of the issues discussed, he believes. His deep interest in India has led him to note "an erosion of Indian culture in our times."

Sperling feels "aspects of Indian culture are dying," citing the example of a hakim in Bareilly — "he is the last of a 600-year lineage and I visited him in a street in Bareilly famous for Ayurveda and Unani. He started when he was six and he has in his pharmacopocia remedies that are 150 to 200 years old. Ayurveda and Unani will be taught in universities, but what happens to the oral tradition?"

It is partly this concern which has encouraged Sperling to work out the tie-up with IBD, which has been in the pipeline for about two years now. "Our primary motivation is not economic" he insists, "It is to bring Indian culture back to India. Part of my job is in preserving that culture through publications."

His own entrance into the country and its cultural environment was encouraged by one of Inner Traditions' authors, Harish Johari, who "was feeling bad as an Indian, a Hindu, writing on Indian mysticism and not being available in India."

But will he find a market here? Sperling believes so — "The fact that an American publisher publishes Indian books is a validating point" of his acceptance in this country. And, once the desired level of quality is achieved, the books will perhaps be exported to the US, where it all began.

If his venture is successful, would that not open the floodgates for a deluge of similar books from Indian-based publishers? Sperling is not worried. "I don't believe in the competitive model," he says, "I am unique unto myself, as is the company.

One thing he is sure of, that with liberalization, which made the tie-up possible, India now has the "opportunity to build a competitive and successful print industry — the technology is universal, the labour and education are there. All that is needed is the will to pull together to make it happen."

More interestingly, Sperling believes in "commerce from a familial point of view. It is a commerce of brotherhood, a kinship model — real business goes on because of that. That is the tone which sets the community going," he says.

After all, he realises, if your employees are happy, they work better, and then you are happy!

Dear Ms. Vatsala,

I am Ramakrishnan writing to you in connecti with your response to the matrimonial advertisement in the *Hindu* inserted on behalf of our family friend Ehud Sperling of the USA.

Some preliminary information about Sperling and a photograph are enclosed.

My idea is to pay you a visit sometime in the course of this or the next week so you can quiz m informally and I can meet you in your home environment. My visit will be purely exploratory, and there will be ample time later on for you to get acquainted with Sperling when he visits India. Please treat my visit as an interesting and a necessary procedure before an intercultural alliance can be decided on. If for any reason you don't wish to go further in the matter, just call me and tell me so. I am based in Delhi and at the moment am holidaying in my ancestral village of Trivandrum. Thank you, and hope to meet you in Madras.

Yours sincerely,
Ramakrishnan

Above: *A letter sent to me by Dr. Ramakrishnan accompanied by an interview of Ehud in the* Metropolis *(left) and by a photograph* (right).

chapter 2

REACHING

OUT

So I must deal with this Mr. Ramakrishnan before getting to know who Ehud Sperling was. It did not bother me not to have a direct connection as yet with the advertiser. After all, in my scientific inquiries, I had gotten used to trying and trying again until I found the answer I was looking for. Six years of intensive academic drill with my Ph.D. thesis supervisor had filled me with plenty of high-powered gasoline for long and difficult drives. Happy journey, Vatsala; go on, have courage, and don't give up your search.

I read the clipping from the *Metropolis*. Though Ramakrishnan's letter said nothing about Ehud Sperling, the interview clipping, biographical sketch, and accompanying photograph gave me something to think about. Here was an unusual man! I replied to Ramakrishnan, thanking him for his letter and telling him that my mother and I would be delighted to meet him at our home.

One afternoon my mother was taking her pre-lunch nap on the living room couch. Hearing the doorbell, she woke with a jolt and approached the door with unsteady steps. "I am Ramakrishnan," said a gruff male voice with a strange British accent. Amma gaped at him in astonishment, wondering who he was. I came to the door and greeted this tall, distinguished, neatly dressed man.

He came in and immediately began to look for a telephone. On finding none, he exclaimed, "How do you live without a phone?" Having ingested his immediate shock of not being recognized by an

old lady and not finding a phone, he rolled his eyes in all directions trying to assess the living facilities of our household. Soon I noted a sense of relief on his face, perhaps because he did not have to deal with stinking rich people with a fortress for a household and an army regiment for a family.

We soon got into the usual conversation. He said he liked my smile (this compliment wasn't new), and he was impressed to find that I was balanced and stable, and did not get excited at the prospect of dealing with his highly esteemed American friend. On my part, no, I did not specialize in getting excited without a tangible, genuine cause. And even when such a cause came my way, I was always aware of the transient nature of everything, and that helped me maintain a balanced approach to people and events. Ramakrishnan asked me to get my photograph album and fished out a few pictures of me that he liked. He then scribbled down a name and an address, and told me to get in touch with Ehud Sperling at my earliest convenience. He wished me the best of luck and made a quick exit without finishing the cup of coffee that I had offered him.

Amma and I stared at the name and address for a long while. "Good for you, go ahead and try. Maybe something good is in store for you," Amma said, trying to break the silence that descended on our household after this sudden coming and going of Ramakrishnan.

Dear Mr. Sperling,
Namaste.

Intercultural alliances sound great. They are great if by the grace of God, things go well and people find the happiness they have been searching for. As best as I can think, I do not know what means other than letters exists for getting to know a person who lives on another continent. Yes, phone and fax do help, but the good old letters in which for a given length of time the writer "talks" about something are still the best. So let us see where these letters take us.

Two days ago, your friend Dr. Ramakrishnan called on me at home. We had a pleasant exchange of news and views. He gave me your name and address and asked me to write to you. Hence this letter.

May I tell you something about myself? I am B. R. Vatsala, a tall, slim, brown-skinned woman with a "good smile," to quote your friend. In fact, he left my home with a series of strongly positive observations about me. Instead of quoting them, I would prefer if with passage of time people who are concerned about each other make genuine efforts to *discover* and *understand* each other on the basis of their own observations and interactions. This is more scientific, right?

By training and profession, I am a clinical microbiologist. Besides bugs, many other topics interest me deeply. My present job in a hospital is challenging and stimulating, and quite often it jolts me severely about the role of God in our lives.

I am positively looking forward to meeting a compatible gentle-man with whom to grow and share life. I do cherish family life. It instills a sense of belonging. In the future I envisage myself as a competent homemaker (a good wife and a good mother to kids). I have a great deal of energy which can also be utilized into shaping a career in the practice/teaching of clinical microbiology.

Enclosed please find a few pictures of me. Some of these were selected by Ramakrishnan. Also, I apologize for writing to you by hand. My handwriting is not one of the very best. I could use the computer terminal in my laboratory, but it is connected to the main computer in the hospital and it would be possible for anyone to get the file name, get a printout, and enjoy finding out whom Dr. Vatsala is writing to. You know curiosity is an incurable disease. It affects everyone all over the world.

Then may I look forward to receiving a reply from you? I have enclosed my office phone number and the time I am around, so you could call, if you feel like it, that is. I think it would be interesting to hear your voice.

With best regards,
Sincerely,
Vatsala

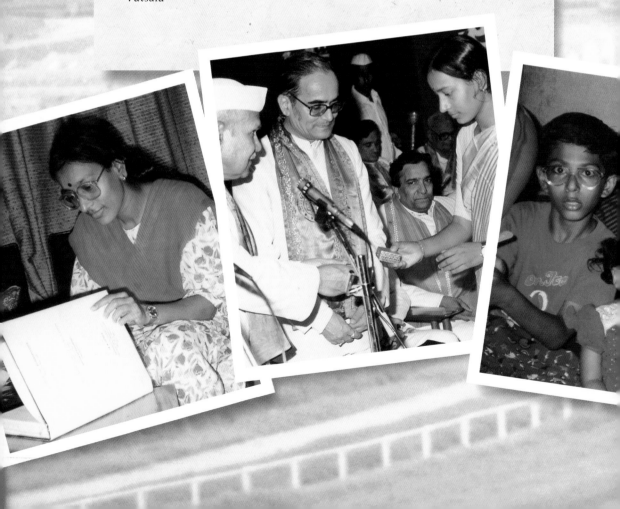

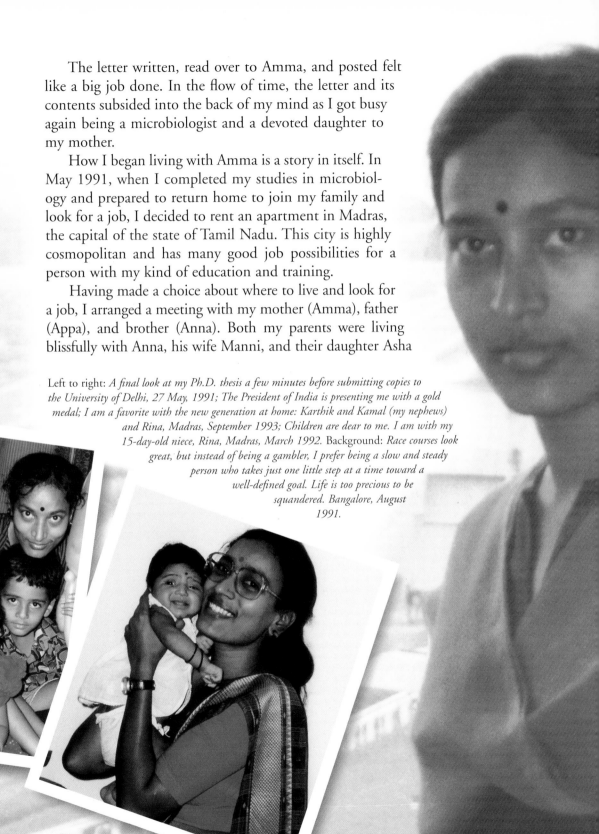

The letter written, read over to Amma, and posted felt like a big job done. In the flow of time, the letter and its contents subsided into the back of my mind as I got busy again being a microbiologist and a devoted daughter to my mother.

How I began living with Amma is a story in itself. In May 1991, when I completed my studies in microbiology and prepared to return home to join my family and look for a job, I decided to rent an apartment in Madras, the capital of the state of Tamil Nadu. This city is highly cosmopolitan and has many good job possibilities for a person with my kind of education and training.

Having made a choice about where to live and look for a job, I arranged a meeting with my mother (Amma), father (Appa), and brother (Anna). Both my parents were living blissfully with Anna, his wife Manni, and their daughter Asha

Left to right: *A final look at my Ph.D. thesis a few minutes before submitting copies to the University of Delhi, 27 May, 1991; The President of India is presenting me with a gold medal; I am a favorite with the new generation at home: Karthik and Kamal (my nephews) and Rina, Madras, September 1993; Children are dear to me. I am with my 15-day-old niece, Rina, Madras, March 1992.* Background: *Race courses look great, but instead of being a gambler, I prefer being a slow and steady person who takes just one little step at a time toward a well-defined goal. Life is too precious to be squandered. Bangalore, August 1991.*

in Madurai, a city in Tamil Nadu, where both my parents have ancestral roots and connections going back many generations. Since both Anna and Manni held full-time jobs, my parents gladly babysat their two-year-old daughter.

In this family meeting I explained my job preferences and living-facility options, and I stated in very clear terms that I had already spent over twelve years living in hostels as a student and certainly did not now wish to join any working women's hostel in Madras. I needed and wanted to set up a home. Since Indian society does not look very kindly upon an unmarried girl living in an apartment all by herself, I needed my mother to stay with me while I held a job. This would give me a home atmosphere to return to after work and would provide me with security and freedom. Also, in some way, I would be able to make up for the twelve years when I had missed the love and sacred company of my dear mother.

My father and brother understood the intensity and the genuineness of my request. Very graciously, my father agreed to continue babysitting my brother's daughter—both my parents hated the idea of abandoning their little granddaughter to a paid babysitter—and he very kindly let my mother set up a home with me in a small two-bedroom apartment. Now, even at this old age, when each of my parents was trying to hold on to the wrinkled, shivering, and weak hand of the other, they sacrificed their precious time together to help their children.

The reason I became a spokesperson for myself has a lot to do with my logistic placement in the family. Being the last born, during my growing up years I enjoyed total and absolute attention from my dear parents and all my siblings. Yes, a very happy, contented, loving, and celebrated childhood. But when I completed my studies and returned home, the people with whom I had begun my life had gotten married and had moved away. My parents were eighty-one and seventy-six years old; they were in no physical or mental condition to arrange a marriage for me. As far as my siblings were concerned, no matter how much they loved me, their priorities had changed and their spouses and kids were at the top of the list. Since I did want to get married in due time and I didn't have relatives to take the initiative for me, my only option was to find a man myself through the matrimonial columns, make my own decisions, and then initiate the wedding procedures.

Though in this case I was taking an unconventional approach—pursuing a relationship all the way across the globe with a person with whom I didn't have any apparent compatibility—I was still deeply rooted in my traditional culture, and wanted an arranged marriage based on shared values. What I had in mind was exactly what was approved in Indian society, but in the absence of family leadership, I simply had to take charge of continuing the thread of cultural and social practices.

Let me tell you, it is not the thing done in India. These arranged marriages, even when initiated with the help of modern-day methods like a newspaper ad, do not begin with the prospective bride writing the first letter of introduction.

It is well known that India's cities and villages contain over 900 million people. What is not known about the country is how she works—my personal opinion is that it is a great mystery and an unexplainable grace of God that India is able to function at all! On the political map, India is divided into twenty-one states and a few union territories. Almost every state has its own language. These languages have very distinct accents. Many of the Indian languages—for example, Bengali, Oria, Tamil, Gujrati, Telugu, Kannada, and Malayalam—have scripts quite different from one another. Food habits, dress codes, festivals, celebration of rituals, mythological beliefs and stories, climate, cultural etiquette, facial features, skin tone, physical build, the impact of imported religions like Islam and Christianity . . . all these variable factors divide this country into clearly defined ethnic groups. Add to that the very alive, functional, and elaborate caste system which partitions Hindu ethnic groups into still smaller groups . . . the division goes on and on and on.

Despite such ethnic diversity, throughout India the family is considered far more important than the individual. Each family believes that *grihasthashram* (family life) is a practical and very potent route to salvation, and tries its best to nurture and perpetuate its cultural heritage. Children are raised according to the eternal tenets of the Hindu religion, which encourages austerity, obedience, self-discipline, respect for the parents and all the elderly, and respect for religion and God. All of these qualities are essential for proper and healthy functioning of the family unit. Raised in such an environment, children learn to trust their parents' judgments and happily accept their small and big decisions, including the choice of a mate for marriage.

Even though elder women in the family have some say in matters concerning marriages, it is the patriarchs that call the final shots. Parents begin looking for a suitable match as soon as their children reach their mid- to late teens. Word buzzes around in the community, and all relatives and a professional matchmaker are alerted. They come forward and make their recommendations. These candidates are scrutinized by means of direct and indirect personal interviews, and inspected for various social, moral, financial, and health qualities. The families and the relatives of the bride and the groom are also investigated thoroughly, including their ancestry and present state of affairs.

Sometimes families make concessions about the region and language of the prospective bride or groom. For example, a Tamil boy born and raised in the United States may not know how to read or write or speak Tamil, but a Tamil girl born and raised in India and proficient in this language could be married to him. However, many families try their very best to stick to caste compatibility. This system came into existence in Vedic times when people were categorized according to their occupation: those concerned with the learning of Vedas and the performance of prayers and religious ceremonies were known as *Brahmins* (priest caste); those concerned with running the political and military affairs of the country were known as *Kshtriyas* (warrior caste); those concerned with business, trading, and commerce activities were known as *Vaishyas* (business caste); and those concerned with maintenance and cleanliness of human habitats or with handicrafts such as weaving, leatherwork, etc., were known as *Shudras* (smaller caste). This livelihood-based caste system has long vanished from the Indian scene because the modernization and industrialization of India has brought about a massive transformation in lifestyles and professions. For example, a Brahmin may find employment as a weaver in an urban knitwear factory and a Vaishya may become a professor of *Vedanta* and Hindu religious studies in a university. While Brahmins still tend to be more orthodox or rigid, many Indians are adopting open-minded attitudes and are trying to relax this requirement of caste compatibility in arranged marriages.

After intense investigations, horoscopes are acquired and tallied. These horoscopes were cast soon after birth using time, day, date, and place of birth as basic data for determination of the position of various components of the solar system: sun, moon, Mars, Mercury, Jupiter, Venus, Saturn, Rahu, and Ketu. The location, angle, ascent, descent, duration, and combination of these nine celestial bodies, if interpreted correctly, can give fairly accurate predictions about health, body type, possible diseases, mental state, personality type, possibility of progeny, wealth, job, name and fame, stability of family and spousal relationships, death, major accidents, and so on. When a man's and a woman's horoscopes are matched with a view to marriage, a comparison of thirty or so criteria is made. When about twenty-six criteria of one horoscope favor/support the other (and vice versa), the horoscopes (and hence the persons whose horoscopes are being tallied) are declared compatible.

Only when astrological, social, financial, and cultural factors have been found compatible is a marriage formally announced. Marriage thus arranged is regarded more as a wedding of families than a wedding of individuals. Around this bond of matrimony the entire kinship structure of the two families undergoes a reshuffling. Marriage per se is a social, festive, religious, and cultural event conducted at great expense to the girl's family, and the celebration goes on for at least two days (abridged version) in the presence of hundreds of guests and relatives. There is no paperwork or marriage license, but a Hindu wedding conducted according to cultural and religious practices is considered a union of souls for the next seven incarnations and is a final binding of two people and their families.

This form of conducting marriage is considered the moral and social responsibility of the parents and older siblings and other relatives. This tradition has been handed down over thousands of years, fosters a deep sense of family values, and is a time-tested, sure-shot method for continuation of cultural, social, and traditional practices. Even today, about 90 percent of marriages in India are arranged. The young people who are about to be married do not know each other, do not go on dating and mating experiments, and do not form premarital friendships; they trust the wisdom and the judgments of the elders in the family and agree to marry a total stranger. This system works perfectly well for youngsters who have energetic parents with plenty of money and social contacts.

Not long ago, India was a quiet country with an agriculture-based economy. This profession bound people to their ancestral land, and it was common for several generations to live together in joint family households. In the expensive, crowded industrial cities that have since arisen, this age-old tradition could no longer be sustained. Following a natural course, city-based, wage-earning nuclear families underwent a painful process of alienation from the joint family system, their community, and their ancestral roots. Fortunately, this trend of immigration to cities and the exposure to modern lifestyles has not made people forget their ethnic roots completely. The masses have discovered to their utmost delight that newspapers can very successfully convey the signals regarding a suitable candidate for marriage. These newspapers, which reach almost all corners of the country, happily accepted the role of matchmaker fifty or sixty years ago. Presently all Indian newspapers of stature and consequence devote several pages in their Sunday special editions to carrying hundreds of thousands of these matrimonial advertisements.

Some newspapers have gone quite far in serving their customers: they methodically group the ads into categories like caste and subcaste, religion, food habits, educational level, language, physical traits, and employment. They also carry separate columns for those living/working abroad and those who are open to marriage to any Indian from any ethnic background. While this kind of classification system may give the impression that India is a prejudiced country, in fact, this apparent bias is the only device left in the armamentarium of the city-dwelling Indian who is cut off from his ancestral foothold and is still trying to preserve, maintain, transmit, and nurture his ethnic roots, originality, and diversity in the face of the so-called modern winds of industrialization that have blown over the vast Indian soil.

Presently, millions of concerned mothers, fathers, brothers, sisters, aunts, uncles, cousins, and grandparents—whoever happens to take the responsibility and the initiative for the marriage of his or her ward—get serious every Sunday, spending hours reading the fine print of these advertisements, selecting the ones that match their requirements, and replying to the appropriate box numbers. In this fashion, five marriages have successfully been conducted in my own family as per the cultural and religious modalities handed down to our family over generations, and I have many friends whose marriages have been arranged this way as well.

In making up my mind about finding my own husband, I realized that deep inside me there was no hatred for the established norms. Perhaps this seeming rigidity was the formula which had assured a continuity of Indian culture, society, language, and everything else that makes India what and how she is despite thousands of years of rule by the bandits who invaded the country. Some foreign values were imbibed, but they could not replace the Indian value system completely. No matter who attacked, India was always successful in retaining her immense cultural and material richness.

I have always nurtured a great deal of emotional love for my country and everything that she has given to me. As an Indian woman, my cultural inheritance is my identity. And the richness that I was blessed with by my birth in this great country is something I live with happily and pass on generously. Even if I chose to deviate from the established path and chart my own course in my individual revolution, my ultimate goal was good. This reasoning filled me with ample courage and confidence.

As I reread the advertisement I had chosen to respond to, it was quite apparent to me how different the advertiser and I were. He was Jewish (I was Hindu), white (I was brown), a businessman (I was a research scientist, salaried professional), internationally traveled (I had never been outside of India). I was intrigued by the word *Jewish*. In all my life I had never met a Jewish person, never seen a synagogue or a rabbi, never encountered Hebrew script, and never heard the language spoken. I had read a little about Israel (in the context of its ongoing military love affair with Palestine, as reported by the Indian press). I also knew a little bit about Nazi Germany and the killing of six million Jews in Hitler's concentration camps, and had heard that nearly two-thirds of all Nobel prizes in science and medicine were won by Jewish people. Otherwise, I knew nothing about Jews. Ehud was the first Jewish man I might meet. So to begin with, I was contacting a person from another religion, another country, another culture, another language, another color, and no caste at all for a possible arranged marriage.

Could there be an inner thread that connected religions, cultures, ethnic identities, and lifestyles? Could I arrange a marriage without the normal signposts and road maps that guided my Indian brothers and sisters? I would try. Certainly, this advertisement was the most unique and original that I had ever seen. I wondered what door it might open. Would this Ehud Sperling even write back? What would I do if he did?

chapter 3

MUKTA

=======================

April 19, 1995

Dear Dr. Vatsala,

Thanks for your charming letter and the enclosed photographs. Having the postman deliver our missives is certainly appropriate. Developing a relationship through correspondence may be old-fashioned, but it seems a lovely and fitting means for getting to know each other. I'm using my computer and "password protecting" the contents of this letter, as the desire to gossip is as strong here at the publishing company as I'm sure it is at your hospital. As your pen-manship is superior to mine, I trust you won't be offended to receive my letter in type—you'll find it much easier to read in this form!

I'm glad you had the opportunity to meet Dr. Ramakrishnan. When I spoke to him on the phone the other day he reaffirmed his favorable impressions of you, but I don't agree with him: you don't have a *good* smile, you have a *great* smile. It was wonderful receiving so many photos and getting a glimpse of so many aspects of your life. Unfortunately, as an avid photographer myself, I am rarely in front of the camera and often behind it. I am searching through my slides to find a few of myself and I'll send them along. I do photography as a creative outlet, but it's now turning semiprofessional, as my work's been published on a number of occasions.

I've recently been introduced to Hi-8 video technology and have taken to it. I have marvelous footage from my trip to India, including the wedding of a dear friend of mine, and some footage of Mr. Desikachar, son of Krishnamacharya, one of our authors, at his yoga school in Madras.

This past September I took a trip deep into the Amazon jungle, spending time with the Shuar and Achua people. I filmed my experiences down there, and they've recently been shown on television here in the States. One of the wonderful things about shooting these videos is the opportunity to share my experiences with my friends and colleagues.

I understand from your letter that you're a lover of nature. So am I. I moved my publishing company from New York City to the Green Mountains of Vermont in 1986 so that I could be surrounded by the pristine beauty of the mountains, lakes, and rivers. My practice is to rise before the sun and take a walk with my dog, Ngurra (Noogie for short) in the mountains. This morning I saw four magnificent white-tailed deer only a few yards from my home. The excitement and intimacy of a moment in communion with nature in its wild state is continually uplifting and nourishing.

I especially appreciate the tranquillity of nature now, given the hectic pace of my office, which, especially at this time of year, is extremely demanding. Tomorrow I leave for a meeting in New York where I'll be giving a lecture, to be immediately followed by our annual sales conference, where we'll launch our 20th anniversary publishing program. Shortly after that, I travel to Chicago with members of my staff for the annual booksellers' convention, and then move on to California. Consequently, do not take it amiss if it takes a week or two for me to respond—this is not an indication of any lack of interest on my part. To the contrary, I am delighted to receive your letters and will always respond, if somewhat tardily.

I agree with you—let's exchange a few letters and get to know each other better, at which point we can arrange a time to speak on the telephone. Please send me your birth date plus birth time in your next letter and let me know something about your family and your childhood. I will be happy to respond in kind. I have given you some insight into my daily life, and I look forward to hearing about yours. Until then, I send you my best wishes and remain,

Yours truly,
Ehud C. Sperling

Thus began our first exchange of letters. I was pleased with what I read. So this Ehud Sperling was in no hurry to arrive at a quick decision based on phone calls and faxes; he was prepared to spend an extended period of time in correspondence in an effort to know me and educate me about himself. He was an active photographer, loved India and other ancient cultures, shared his home and experiences with friends, loved nature, loved dogs, was busy in his profession, was interested in astrology, wished to know more about my lifestyle, and, well, he also happened to like my smile. My intuition told me that I could invest my time and energy in trying to find out where our correspondence might take us.

2.5.95

Dear Mr. Ehud Sperling,
    Your letter of 19.4.95 has arrived. Thanks. I did enjoy going through it.
    "Password protection" must be such a fantastic invention. This privilege is, however, not available in my computer. I, therefore, just have to write my letters by hand. Since you find the writing acceptable, it tells me not to worry about technology and just stick to handwriting. I am sorry my English is not as crisp and compact as yours. Mine is an Indian version of English and inadvertently I commit spelling mistakes, for which I do apologies.
    How did you like your trip to the Amazon? Was it a guided tour or were you on your own, exploring and learning from one step to

the next? Yes, I would like to be in touch with nature, but if left alone in the deep jungles, wild rivers, rough seas, and rugged mountains I guess I would be very simply frozen dead out of sheer fright. I feel at home amidst gentle, mild, and well-tamed nature, where I can feel like a part of it rather than an inquisitive and yet frightened, defenseless intruder. Being in touch with nature reaffirms my deep faith in a power that is more creative, wise, thoughtful, considerate, and competent than man can ever hope to be. In my day-to-day life, well, I do have to put up with polluted city life, swallow dust, get deeply sunburned 11 out of 12 months in a year, and bear all this (and much more) with a wide grin. Is there any other way?

My day begins at about 5 A.M. After finishing a quick round of cleaning, cooking, and sitting quietly for a few minutes, I run to catch a bus that takes me in 20 minutes to a stop near my hospital. During the 10-minute walk to my hospital every morning, I am totally relaxed. I am in the department by 8 A.M. I spend my first couple of hours reporting on the cultures. Thereafter, I speak with my clinical colleagues on the phone clarifying their doubts about culture reports, if any, or returning their calls. If any patient has an infection and my opinion about isolation or specimen collection is desired, I visit the wards to see the patient and suggest to the attending doctor how to proceed further. Afternoons are spent reviewing and analyzing antibiogram and laboratory statistics, reading, or accumulating and analyzing data for some of the research programs in hand. Administrative meetings, management conferences, and the continuing medical education (CME) lecture series, as well as occasional microbiology lectures to doctors and nurses, are all scheduled for the afternoon hours. In between, I meet company representatives who come to promote their products. A few anxious parents like to talk to me about the condition of their children, long-term outcome of infection that their child seems to have, precautions to be taken, etc., and I meet them on a priority basis. Meanwhile, I do grab a few moments for lunch (which I bring from home). Though officially I am expected to be here till 4 P.M. only, I invariably pull on till 7 or 8 P.M.—what I begin, I must complete. Nothing should be pending and postponed to be done next day. This keeps my colleagues on their toes. They know by experience that when it comes to commitment and work, there is no fooling around, I mean business (in the politest manner possible for a boss).

Shankari, Sheela, Lissy, Clara, Seema, and Venugopal . . . all these youngsters in their early to late twenties are my immediate colleagues. With them, I share an intense relationship of love, trust, friendship, goodwill, and acceptance. Our friendship is so alive and deep that we can't stand the weekends and rare holidays that interrupt our daily meeting and working together. We have great fun working together, we share our meals, tea, and snacks, celebrate birthdays and festivals in the lab, occasionally get together for shopping or movies, visit one another's families, and exchange gifts. This whole network helps us feel connected, part of a family or a community. I hired them and have worked with most of them for nearly four years, training them in the science and arts of diagnostic clinical microbiology and turning them into very capable research assistants. The way we interact with each other always brings out the very best of human nature in us. I have learned very good lessons from these youngsters . . . politeness, humility, helpfulness, patience, and nonstop hard work, never grumbling at the numerous resource crunches faced in our department, but always making the best use of daily situations and emergencies. I count myself very lucky to have the privilege of working with such nice people.

Left to right: *Kannan, myself, Clara, and Lissy at the Childs Trust Hospital.*

A few days in a month, I do manage to get back home early. These days, I take my mom out for a walk through the neighboring park, or to the sea beach. She also likes to go to temples. Dinner is a simple affair by 9 P.M. after which we both read something—a newspaper is a must. Amma often watches TV, but I don't. I simply do not have the aptitude for becoming a couch potato. Mom and myself are best friends. We chat about every topic under the sun. We call it a day by 11 P.M.

The best aspect of this job is that it lets me do what I like doing—using my time, training, and energy in helping the sick overcome their sickness, and working for children, trying to make them smile. Another good aspect is that it gives me no time to brood and grumble over the pay, which is shamelessly low. Yet another good aspect is that this job as chief of clinical microbiology services makes me a thankful, grateful person and never lets me take anyone/anything for granted. It continuously reminds me to be humble and bow with reverence to the creative power that is within and beyond man—call it God or anything you like. All these were not mentioned in my service contract, therefore I consider them bonuses and perks that I generously receive apart from my pay.

My date of birth is 01.01.1961. Sunday, 8:20 A.M., place Jamshedpur in Bihar. This is when and where I was welcomed by my dear parents into their loving fold where they already had four daughters and a son. My childhood memories are good. I have been loved, wanted, and superbly cared for by my parents and all my senior siblings. My father never regarded money as something that should be earned, accumulated, and invested. He worked very hard, earned very little, and spent all of what he earned in helping anyone who was ever in need and approached him. He never anticipated or hoped for anything in return for his Good Samaritan deeds. He is a contented man, now 81 years old, and is as enthusiastic and energetic as a healthy man in his middle age. My mother is a gentle, warm, caring, and very affectionate woman. She taught us the value of education, freedom, and discipline. She never raised her voice or used even the mildest of physical punishments to straighten out any one of her six boisterous, energetic, mischievous children. She never ever lost her patience in raising us. But ever so gently, efficiently, and firmly she conveyed to us that we could not fool around and waste our lives. She gave us a sense of purpose, an urge to set a goal and reach it, and she made us work with dignity to improve ourselves and our lot in life. She has a creative urge springing forth deep from her consciousness— she has composed hundreds of original Tamil songs, prayers, and hymns, all devotional, and she has also composed music for them. She sings them in her own melodious voice. She simply is a genius.

My dear parents are approaching their 51st wedding anniversary. We have planned a prayer meeting, followed by distributing food to needy, poor people who have nothing to eat, and then a small gathering of friends at home. Anna and his family are coming to join us. All my sisters and my brother are moderately educated, married, and have reasonably good lives. We meet rarely nowadays, as everyone is busy in running their household and raising their kids.

As a little girl I was quiet, made very few friends. But I was almost a minicelebrity at schools because in every public event I always had a couple of lectures to give and a couple of prizes to receive for studies or extracurricular activities. My family was always encouraging and supportive. They celebrated with me when I won and loved and supported me even when I lost, but it was my mother who taught me the futility of the rat race. She often says that even if you win a rat race you remain a rat. She encouraged us to become lions and not rats.

The picture that you get after reading these lines is that the correspondent of this letter is a person from a family with a somewhat light purse and an unusually deep sense of human values. This is my inheritance from my parents, and I am proud of them. The values that I grew up with are still with me. I do feel I have strong and deep roots and therefore I have the faith and confidence in myself that I can reach far and wide without losing track of who I am, without getting lost. I will remain levelheaded and never lose my identity.

From the interview of you in the *Metropolis* entitled "To 'bring back Indian culture,'" I particularly recall one line: "After all, he realizes if your employees are happy, they work better and then you are happy." This is a rare breed of employee-friendly businessman who believes in "commerce of brotherhood, a kinship model—real business goes on because of that." I am impressed and amused. It would be interesting to get to know you because other than the TATAs, my father's former bosses, I have heard of very few employee-friendly, humanitarian businessmen. In the world of commerce, business sense and humanitarian view appear grossly incompatible—this is how it looks.

Next how is Noogie? Is Noogie he or she? What color and breed? Friendly and gentle or ferocious and violent? In your reply you could also tell me about Noogie. I hope your busy schedule ahead gives you satisfaction and peace of mind (most essential requirements for a happy life). I also hope you will get time to write back. Please take care. With regards and best wishes,

Sincerely,
Vatsala

May 22, 1995

Dear Dr. Vatsala,

Greetings. Thanks for your letter of May 2nd. You certainly come across as a dynamic and talented woman and it's a pleasure getting to know you.

I traveled to the Amazon with my dear friend and author, John Perkins. John did volunteer work in the Peace Corps in the Amazon 20 years ago and, with my encouragement, he's returned to the Shuar people of the Upper Amazon Basin and is writing books about his experiences. This was the second time I've been to the jungle with him; this time we went to an outpost on the Pastaza River. This is a very remote and inaccessible region of primary forest. The people here first made contact with the modern world only some 20 to 30 years ago and it is a difficult and challenging environment that very few people from the outside have ever entered. The reason for going down here was the request of two of our friends in Ecuador who are looking to do a project with the people of this area to help preserve the jungle from the inevitable exploitation which will come. It is a restricted area and we were given special permission to visit it by the

Minister of Health and Education. Since our visit, John has taken it upon himself to raise money for a forest preservation project that is now in its initial stages of development.

I'm sure you would find this environment taxing, as I did. However, the environment of my home is much more as you describe and more in keeping with the sentiments expressed in your letter. The mountains that nestle our village are covered in exquisite hardwood and pine forests; there are lakes, rivers, and streams every-where; and I've recently started horseback riding again, which gives me a wonderful opportunity to enjoy the countryside.

We're in the height of spring now and everything's bursting to life with incredible fragrances and colors. It is difficult to be inside at this time; Noogie and I take every opportunity to be outside with nature.

Being very hardworking, committed, and conscientious myself, I marvel at the sentiments you express about work in your letter. Rarely today does one find someone with such a creative and positive attitude about the work they've been given in life. Personally, I'm very grateful and I feel privileged to serve in the capacity I do at my work. Along with the creative and business responsibilities come the demands of encouraging the development—both personal and professional—of the people I work with.

Being the chief executive of the company means that I must constantly be helping my staff realize their goals and expand

Left to right: *Me with my one-month-old niece Sara; I am with my nephew Michael and my dog Noogie; Noogie's arrival, summer 1992; With Dada Harish Johari at Rishikesh.* Background: *Sacred waterfall of the Shuar people, Upper Amazon Basin.*

their horizons, and must give them a creative, moral, and ethical standard that is fitting for a company that publishes books on spirituality and health. I don't see any point in publishing books on these topics if we can't function together as a team of high-minded and healthy people, and have some fun doing it.

We recently set up a food co-op so our staff can have organically grown and healthy food products delivered to our office at a lower price than that of a store. One of the greatest pleasures I receive in my work is seeing my colleagues realize their own potential. This shouldn't sound like philanthropy or some kind of saintly endeavor; rather, I've seen this attitude of mine engender loyalty and commitment to me and the company on the part of my staff, and it provides a warm and happy atmosphere to work in. You could take the point

Left: *Noogie and I. Summer 1994.*
Below: *Relaxing at home.*

of view that this is the ultimate selfishness, i.e., that I treat everybody well and I get treated very well in return.

I'm delighted to hear about your fondness for and your warm relationship with your parents, who both sound like remarkable people. So many people these days suffer from low self-esteem because of a lack of warmth and support from their families while they were growing up. I can see that that's certainly not the case with you, and it is not the case with me, as I also enjoyed a loving and happy childhood with parents who cared for me, nurtured me, and supported my enthusiasm and endeavors throughout my youth. They continue to be interested and involved in my work; my father maintains a library of every book we have ever published and keeps scrapbooks of the clippings and articles that appear about me and the company. Next week, they will travel to Chicago to be my guests at our 20th anniversary at the American Booksellers Convention. They will attend all the dinners and events as honored guests; it will also be my father's 75th birthday. Like your parents, my parents just celebrated their 51st anniversary last month and I was pleased to be present on that occasion.

Given your very close relationship with your family and the obviously important work you are doing at the hospital, how do you think you would feel about adapting to a life in a small town in the United States, away from your family and a job you clearly love? Certainly, there would be many advantages and positive aspects in finding a rewarding relationship, raising a family, and living in nature. However, it would be quite a radical change from the life you are now leading. I'm sure you've given this some thought; I'd be interested to hear from you on this subject.

I can't close this letter without responding to your questions about Noogie. The Noogman is ferociously friendly, and a gentle and loving being. His experience with humanity has been one of constant love and affection and he gives the same in return. I often think of what an extraordinary life experience he's having, one in which he feels that all humanity is his friend. We should all be so fortunate.

Noogie is a German shepherd, born and bred to be a Seeing Eye dog for the blind. He comes from Fidelco, one of the 10 not-for-profit Seeing Eye dog schools in America. All of the dogs are bred with the goal of becoming a companion to a blind person. However, the larger, more "alpha" dogs are allowed to be adopted, as they are too active and independent to be good at this work. Their breeding makes them very sensitive and friendly toward people, courageous, and highly, highly intelligent. When my one-year-old niece came to the house, she was going through that phase where she would avoid contact with anyone but her mother. However, Noogie came charging over to her, licked her up and down, and, rather than being traumatized, she is now a devoted dog lover—just show her a picture of a dog and she goes crazy. Noogie weighs almost 100 pounds and as you'll see from the enclosed pictures, he's primarily black in color. He's with me 24 hours a day, coming to the office every day, as he has since he was eight weeks old. He's an absolute delight and I hope someday you'll have a chance to meet him.

I am enclosing a selection of pictures, which I hope you'll enjoy. I'm off to Chicago next week and will be gone until June 12th. I send you my very best wishes and hope to hear from you soon.

All the best,
Ehud C. Sperling

30.5.9

Dear Mr. Ehud Sperling,
Namaste.

Your letter plus the copies of the snaps have arrived. They are quite a treat. Thank you. I have gone through the pictures. You look good.

In your letter you have raised a point regarding my adaptation to life in a small town in the U.S., away from my family and job. Call it sixth sense or anything, while writing to you about my job and family, I thought you might wonder how I'd feel about relocating. This is in fact a sensitive issue. I have been thinking about it for quite some time. In this letter, maybe my ideas and thoughts will not come to you in a logical sequence. I do hope that you can get what I mean to convey.

I do cherish my family ties. Loving my family does not block me from starting a new chapter in my life. With growth, branching out and making an independent existence is inevitable. While pursuing my studies I lived away from my family for almost 12 years, seeing them only during vacations. There was a purpose to that separation. Now, too, I am free to move away, as there is a holy purpose to it, and its name is marriage.

The best feedback parents like yours and mine can hope to get from their kids is to see for themselves that their children have grown up into responsible adults who can share life and love with their new families. I do not want to let down my parents in this regard. They have had such feedback from all my senior siblings and they are holding their breath to have the same from me. This is my motivation for reaching out with a view to marriage. It is a mission: reaching out, praying to God to bring me in contact with a compatible person, working together on making my marriage a strong base and foundation for a healthy, normal family.

Besides, I have no intentions of being a nun. I am a domestic woman to the bone. I do have normal, natural views on marriage, kids, family, and all the commitments that come along as a package. I have given my prime years to studying and making a microbiologist out of myself. In this long, drawn-out process extending over several years, I watched my friends and foes dating, mating, and procreating. Since my involvement with studies mattered more than anything else, I barely had time or mood for any serious or light diversions. In those years, if a prince charming had tried tempting me, he would have encountered not just cold but deep-frozen shoulders.

Again, in this job, which is my first one, I have put in my best efforts, thereby earning a stamp of recognition, trust, dependability, quality, and highly professional standards for the department that I lead.

All along I have been growing up. My attitudes have been through a process of change. This process of growth, especially if you happen to think, analyze, observe, and understand, brings in a kind of mellowing, smoothening of raw, rough edges. I have been mellowed too and have learned to take a complete picture of life, to see myself as a total person of whom "clinical microbiologist with a busy, upwardly mobile career" is just a small aspect. There is more that goes into making a total person. Having been involved in science and research, I have come to the conclusion that in the vast world of science I am very much dispensable, and so is everyone else. This has made me a free person. I never did, nor do I now entertain a crazy idea that the research and clinical microbiology services in this hospital are resting on my strong shoulders. Today it is me, fine, tomorrow it could be someone else better than me. Why should I think that the show would not run if "I" am not there, anyway? This says that my total commitment to doing my job to the best of my knowledge and ability is backed up with a sense of total detachment. This is my career in microbiology, the way I see it.

Next, about me, the woman. I am aware of a deep need in me to share life, warmth, and closeness, to develop dependable, solid, genuine relationships, and to share love, share the experience of life, reciprocate human feelings. *Sharing* is the key word. Just being alive, just being a woman who can think creatively with compassion, affection, and concern, is a great feeling. I need to bring out my complete potential as a human being, as a woman, and share these profound feelings with another human being who feels the same, whose needs are same as mine.

Have you known any education, any career, any job that can take the place of a human being? Commitment to a job is different than commitment to a human being. The former, maybe, boosts the ego and helps in making a larger-than-life picture of an achiever, but can never satisfy the need for human touch. In simpler words, playing with a cute Barbie doll and cuddling a live baby create two different sets of reactions. Even Noogie can tell the difference, considering what a loving fellow he is.

Precisely because I have grown to understand the difference between the two types of commitments, I am not pathologically pos-sessive and crazy about my present career. It can only fulfill certain needs. Some other needs and the fundamental need of sharing life can only be fulfilled in close association with another human being. By God's grace, if and when the time comes for me to make a transi-tion from a hard-nosed career woman to a loving wife and a doting mother, this will be done smoothly, with a full understanding of the meaning and purpose for which such a transition is being made. I am sure of myself that when eventually I meet Mr. Right, I will not regret the change. I will take to it as happily as a fish takes to water.

To your one-line question I have given quite an essay as an answer. I couldn't help it. I needed to tell you how I look at what I am doing now and what needs to be done. Now you see that I have given quite some thought to the question of the change in lifestyle. On examination, my needs appear to be the typical needs of any other person. I am looking forward to change, to marriage, and to the commitments it brings along. For me marriage is not just a social institution. It is a challenge that calls me to bring forth the very best of my human qualities, for the happiness of another person. If it also includes relocating to a small town, why make a fuss about it?

Have you ever wondered why I am opting for an intercultural, interreligious relationship? Whenever such a question comes to you, please do not hesitate to ask.

Your trip to the Amazon with John Perkins must have been quite thrilling. Depending on what the future has in store for us, that is, you and me, I suppose I would like at least once to venture into pure wilderness. I do appreciate your sense of commitment to your work, company, and employees. Since the company is your brainchild, I find that you see it with a lot of affection. Also I could see your attitude to people as a form of ultimate selfishness. But, Mr. Ehud, is selfishness a bad attribute? Thinking about this word can take us to a very primitive concept about God and man. Who invented whom? But not for the awareness of self, man could not have had the cognitive power to feel his own self and nonself. Even awareness about God or something akin to that comes primarily because of realization of self. This awareness, thus, gives a point of reference. To me selfishness does not seem something to be shunned. It is a very fundamental awareness and if it is directed, focused, and utilized for a good cause, the effect explains itself. For example, treat others well and get treated very well in return. This is a simple formula for successful business interactions. This is also common sense. I wish more people practiced it—at least those who have some capacity to bring a change.

My mother, Amma, with whom I'm sharing the news about my correspondence with you, is delighted to know that your parents have also completed 51 years of marriage. She thinks they have good reason to be proud of you and cherish your work. She also finds you good-looking (I don't disagree).

Coming to Noogie, from what you have told me about him, I'm beginning to like him. I am not used to moving closely with pets. When Noogie meets me in person and in a bid to strike friendship decides to do what he did to your one-year-old niece, it will be quite a "culture shock" for me. In personal encounters, I will take time to adjust to Noogie, and can do so in small single doses, one at a time.

Here the latest news is that I have just started a short-term research program in collaboration with Dr. Mary Babu, a very dear friend and a respected senior colleague. She has three postgraduate students in her lab for summer training. I am introducing them to basics in clinical microbiology, giving them exotic bugs from my lab to work on. We have planned to study molecular weight profiles of outer membrane proteins of *Klebsiella pneumoniae* isolates from neonates with bacterial septicemias. The hospital is just as usual. Many consultants have gone away for their summer vacation. I intend to stay on and complete some parts of my research work before the nasty, dirty monsoon begins in Madras.

At home, Amma is fine. I am fine too. Amma, my brother Anna, my sister-in-law Manni, and their kid Asha came home for our parents' 51st wedding anniversary celebration. A few close friends from the hospital came over for dinner. I presented Amma and Appa with sets of new dresses. My sister Geeta and her family from Muscat are planning on coming here for a long holiday.

Then is it possible for you to drop the prefix and call me "Vatsala" at least on the inside of the envelope? I am a "Dr." only to people with whom I interact in formal, official settings.

I wonder when it will be possible for you to visit India. Letters are fine, but they take ages to travel, and such a long wait to get a reply is quite agonizing. I am looking forward to your reply. Tell me something about your beliefs. Are you a very religious person? Do you like Indian food? I do hope the 20th anniversary celebrations go well and mama and papa Sperling are able to enjoy themselves fully while participating. Take care of yourself and Noogie. Who cares for Noogie when you travel or go out of town? Does he have a regular babysitter? Do you take him for horse-riding too? Could you please send your reply letter to my office address? In our apartment the letter boxes have broken down and gone for repair. As a result the postman simply dumps all letters in a basement corner. I do not want to take any chances with your letters. When the repair work is over, I will let you know and then you can send your mail again to my home address. Thank you.

Yours sincerely,
Vatsala

I posted this letter and, as usual, began looking forward to Ehud's reply. When conditions are normal, airmail from India takes no less than three or four weeks to reach the United States. The mail from the U.S., however, takes only about ten days to reach India. I thus figured that a reply from Ehud would not come sooner than a month, or the end of June.

From the letters I had already begun forming a mental picture of this person. He did appear to be friendly and interested in hearing what I had to say. And I had a lot to say to him! I often wondered about his question about my leaving my family and career to live with him in the United States. Was it a genuine and honest inquiry into my adaptability? He must be concerned that his future wife should not nurse any regrets about moving away from her Indian scene. Or was it a trap meant to trip me? If I faltered and hesitated and mumbled with indecision, would he write me off and continue corresponding with other girls? After all, an advertisement such as his would get responses from hundreds of highly accomplished girls (or, more likely, their families) who were reaching out to other shores.

What I knew with total certainty was that I must write only, exactly, and truly what I felt. I must not varnish my words or tailor my sentences to please this man.

Dear Mr. Ehud,

Namaste.

It is some time since I heard from you. It requires lots of patience . . . just to wait for so long for a letter to reach you and then get a reply. Cable News Network claims to have converted the world to a global village but the post and telegraph departments don't accept this fact. They are intent upon proving that India and America are indeed quite far apart.

Recently I drew a cartoon picture of you and myself and wrote my thoughts on "searching." Since I was not sure how you'd react to humor in cartoons, I did not post that letter. I need to know you more to share humor with you.

Something happened here. My father, Appa, was taking a walk to a temple in the colony where he lives. A cabbie did not see him crossing the road and hit him from behind. Dad got his kneecap and tibia broken. He was operated upon for setting of broken bones. Presently his leg is in a cast and he has been advised total bed rest for six weeks. We have retained a nurse attendant to take care of his requirements. He is at home and is in a positive frame of mind. So far no complications. I took Amma along and we stayed at Anna's home where Appa lives. I cared for him as well as I could during my stay. Though Appa never said it, I could feel that he would be happier if Amma stayed back, boosting his morale. I am back to Madras sans Amma and have rejoined duty.

I am not at all happy to be "home alone." Looks like I have forgotten all cooking. Simply no mood. I mostly survive on sprouted beans, nuts, cheese, milk, curds, fruits, and raw vegetables that can be eaten without elaborate cooking. Well, it is a nutritious diet: high fiber, high minerals, low fat, live vitamins, proteins, and enzymes. It however does not give me the joy of cooking for another person, sharing the food, and then reading from her face if the food was awesome or awful. Mom never criticizes my cooking, but the minute she puts the first spoonful of food in her mouth, I learn what she feels about it. Since I consume raw material (my friends get a hearty laugh when they hear about my menu), no time is spent in cooking and, well, that leaves me with more time in which I do not know what to do.

Days at the department are as busy as ever, thank God. In the evenings the very thought of returning to an empty house puts me off. I do return anyway, to find everything as I had left it. The "untouched look" is hard to digest. When Mom is around I get special smells and sounds from the kitchen. She is always full of surprises. The best thing in the life of a working person is to get back home in the evening and see that the kitchen is active—warm food (oh, anything, a little snack, a warm cup of tea) is waiting and with that there is also a person very or most important in your life. With Mom I could unwind over a cup of tea. Then we could talk on almost any topic under the sun. She is well read, well informed, curious and eager to learn, attentive, intelligent, and a good listener. I have an engrossing style of narration that is sprinkled generously with hot-and-sweet Indian humor. Thus we two have enjoyed many evenings going over the events of the day. Now that she is away, I wonder what and how much to read, say from 6 to 11 P.M. Long hours. TV is simply as boring as ever. Well, choosing between TV and a book or newspaper, I go for the latter and bury my nose in it till my eyelids get glued with sleep. Simply in no mood for indulging in any other hobby, not that I don't have any. I am missing my Mom badly and am longing for her to return home again.

Worse still, I am wondering why I still do not have a family of my own—a home that does not just have me as the only occupant, but has a man and a big bunch of kids. I have seen men and their junior descendants giving women the worst time of their lives, yet I think marriage is an experience that no woman should die without having. With my mind busy with being the woman of my family, it will be easier for me to adjust to staying away from Mom. She will be happier to see her last born, at long last, on her own.

This brings to my mind a question about what we mean by the word *independent*. Well, for all practical purposes I am very independent. I can get on in life and be myself. Beneath this charming mask of independence lies the natural and real face of vulnerability and dependence. As human beings we need to depend on other human beings, interact with them on an emotional level, speak to them with the language of the heart, and not simply rush through life with a Swiss-clock precision and a mechanical timetable. Basically as human beings we need to share feelings, no matter what the feelings are. In my view a family gives (or should give, but may not always give) the best possible environment for this kind of expression, i.e., people tell about their feelings and understand others' feelings. That is being dependent despite being independent. Staying alone deprives a person of this unique privilege of exchanging feelings. I can't possibly exchange feelings with the walls, the ever-stupid TV, or with thousands of printed words. They are not human beings. Nothing, never, ever, can take the place of a human being—for good or for worse.

You know, Ehud, I have been thinking of you. With plenty of time in hand, the frequency of thinking about you has obviously gone up and I have been wondering what is the likely future of our contact. I do very much hope this does not end up as the "Hi, how are you, fine thank you, how about you, bye" sort of interaction that does not take anyone anywhere, which does not mean much on the surface or in depth. If, God willing, our contact leads to a serious encounter, I want both of us to be enriched by the experience. It simply has to be a two-way traffic. In giving ourselves—our concern, time, and energy—to making a relationship, we should be able to experience the joy of giving and the joy of knowing that what we give is needed and welcomed warmly. A relationship is stronger, more full of life and energy if we approach it with a "giving heart" rather than with a begging bowl sans bottom.

Well, I do need a lively, warm, and deep relationship based on total trust, confidence, love, acceptance, and very genuine interest in the person. When I know my needs so specifically, as a habit I also conduct an elaborate, conscientious session of soul-searching. Am I capable of giving what I need? If I search for something because I do not have it, on finding the object of my search, I might devour it without the slightest consideration and regard to the feelings and needs of the person who is giving. On the contrary, if I am searching for a person because I have something that I can share, on finding such a person, *sharing* becomes the key word. In giving what I always had with me, I would like the person to feel the same bliss. In order that my resources do not dry up, I would need the other person to maintain a regular feedback.

Do you think such expectations are the influence of the mass media, or that they are more idealistic than practical? The hard realities and colder-than-ice facts of life may soon teach me not to have such expectations from any relationship, including one with the spouse. I don't know how you look at these issues. I would be grateful if you could share your thoughts with me. Let all contacts—no matter heading to what—be an education.

I am writing this letter from home. It is 11:45 P.M. already. I had better close this rambling and convoluted letter right now if I intend to catch up on some sleep. I need to stay fresh tomorrow, as I am expecting a busy day. Lastly, Mr. Ehud, tell me—do you feel lonely too? What do you think of this syndrome? My recommendation is "share life, be true and genuine in your sharing."

Take care, best wishes,
Vatsala

Usually I did not mail my letters right after writing them. I didn't want to rush Ehud, nor did I want him to feel that he was being chased or sought after. This was the last thing I ever wanted to do . . . throw myself in anyone's way and seek to be lifted by him. I was more inclined to stand firmly on my own two feet and to be myself, unashamed to admit my true feelings and reactions to this relationship that was blooming via mail—no matter where it ended. Since I could write to Ehud freely at my own pace, and without fear or any kind of compulsion, I could simply express myself as and when I felt the need to. If he wrote back and told me that he was keen on getting to know me more deeply, I could post him all the backdated letters. After all, the letters did not seem to have an immediate expiration date. I also had another reason for delaying my letters: airmail was expensive, and the hospital pay did not leave much scope for this extravagance. But this shortage of funds did not kill my instincts for communicating with Ehud, especially when his reply arrived so quickly.

June 23, 1995

Dear Vatsala,

Namaste.

Thanks for your recent letter. I've been traveling and have just
now returned to Vermont. The 20th anniversary booksellers' conven-
tion went beautifully, and my parents had a great time sightseeing in
Chicago. They also joined me in all my dinner engagements, getting
an opportunity to mingle with my colleagues and members of our
staff. It was a very different experience from their everyday life and
one that they enjoyed.

I've come back to an extraordinary amount of work. We're building an addition to our office and, as you might imagine, it requires a
great deal of my attention in terms of both aesthetic decisions and
technical matters. They'll be putting the roof on the building next
week, and we're hoping to move the staff into the new facility in
August. Everyone at the company is very excited about the building
and seeing it appear before their eyes.

Experiencing the boost in morale and excitement around this
building project has led me to reflect on the social and community
issues around architecture. I can really understand more fully how the
ancient cultures of both East and West engaged in mammoth building projects with a religious emphasis, and how those projects must
have affected the emotional and psychic climate of the people at that
time. If this little project can have such a felicitous effect on my staff,
you can only wonder at the experience of the people building the
great temples of India, Egypt, and Greece. Add to this the inclusion
of sacred proportion in the architecture, as well as the application of
the sacred canon to the imagery and sculpture on those buildings,
and the effect—which still can be felt today—must have been monu-
mental on the populations of those eras.

You see, you are not the only one who can ramble on, with colorful language and imagery. I am not always concise, as you will learn.
And my staff will quickly tell you that my spelling is atrocious.
Luckily for me, this computer has a Spellcheck function that catches
most of my errors.

I really appreciate your opening up your head and your heart on
the matter of marriage and a change of life. It gives me a lot of

insight into who you are as a person. It strikes me that your name fits very well with the sentiments expressed in your letter. You certainly express yourself as a loving and affectionate person and it is somewhat serendipitous that you work in a children's hospital, as one of the Sanskrit definitions of *Vatsala* is "child-loving."

Certainly, the relationship between a man and a woman embodies the whole mystery of creation and the meaning of life. Marriage takes place not only in this world of comings and goings, but on a deeper, more mysterious plane. A healthy, loving, and positive relationship between husband and wife is one of the most important goals we can aspire to.

I'd certainly be interested to hear why a woman of your background and cultural upbringing would entertain a relationship with someone from another cultural and religious background. For my part, there is only one religion: that is the religion of truth, and wherever I've encountered it, whether it's been in a Hindu, Jewish, Buddhist, Islamic, or Shamanic form, I've recognized it as beautiful. The religion of words spoken by the hypocrite and the egotist is for me uninteresting. Let me know them by their acts, not their words. If someone is acting well in relationship to his fellows and to himself and reflecting God's beauty, then for me, this is religion.

As to my own personal journey, it has been heavily influenced by the Hindu tradition. This has happened spontaneously and mysteriously.

Renovation and addition to the Inner Traditions house.

At one of the most challenging points in my life, a time when I was filled with despair, a Shri Mahant of the Anand Akhada appeared, moved into my home in New York (where I was then living), and pulled me out and up. Ganesh Baba was 92 years old at that time, a mendicant with only the clothes on his back, and one of the most unusual and extraordinary men I've ever met. Whenever I'm in India, I try to visit his *samadhi*.

I've published many books on Hinduism and have among my best friends devout Hindus. In fact, I'm very much looking forward to my annual visit from my dear friend and author, Harish Johari from Bareilly (you saw his picture in the selection I sent you). He'll be staying with me later this summer, as he does every year. We'll be cooking up big vegetarian feasts, all prepared according to the principles of ayurveda, and having many friends and colleagues over to dine. (I guess this answers your question about whether I like Indian food. I love it, and in fact, my regular diet includes Indian dishes prepared from Harish's cookbook.)

Please send your mother my respects and warm regards, and thank her for her flattering comments (and yours, as well). I hope to be able to meet her on my next trip to India. I'm looking into the possibility of making a short trip there in October (monsoon season, I know!). I'll be in Germany for the book fair, and will come if my work permits. Otherwise, I will definitely be in New Delhi on February 3rd for the book fair there, and will visit Madras shortly thereafter.

I understand and appreciate the frustration in simply corresponding when a meeting would help accelerate matters. However, I

Ganesh Baba's samadhi, a simple stack of stones. Baba told me, "leave only one footprint behind."

think we should try to take pleasure in what is turning out to be a marvelous exchange of views and ideas. It's the first time I've ever had such an interaction, and I've been thinking about it in relationship to how I've gotten to know other people. In most cases, when you meet someone, you have to react to and assess the packaging before you get the opportunity to find out what the contents are all about. In our case, we have the good fortune of being forced to explore our inner natures with each other as a prelude to meeting.

As with my last letter, I can't close without a word on Noogie's behalf. *Ngurra*, which is his proper name, means "a sense of place" in an Australian aboriginal language. It is used often to mean "simpatico," i.e., you're both in the same place emotionally. Noogie is definitely true to his name and both receives and gives affection lavishly. I'm sure, given your namesake, that you would be able to find a common ground on which to meet and become good friends. Yes, he does come horseback riding with me, often doing 10 to 20 miles of running. When I'm not home, he goes to the Sawmill Kennel, where he spends time with his friends and the owner, who adores him as he does her. So he's a very lucky guy, leading a truly blessed life.

I look forward to your next letter and until then, wish you,

All the best,
Ehud C. Sperling

Dear Ehud,

That came to me as quite a surprise: you telling me the meaning of my name in Sanskrit. I have yet another name at home: *Mukta*. Now it is quite a quiz for you to say if I am Mukta, a liberated woman. My concept of liberation is different from the freedom to stroll on nude beaches and purchase drug-induced nirvana at the pseudoreligious and pseudospiritual headquarters of cult figures. The world is full of such hypocrites.

Ehud, I just had to open up my heart and mind or else there was no method available by which I could tell you what I am all about.

To understand each other we simply have to do surgeries on ourselves and be true in presenting our various aspects—no masks, no pretensions, please. I have been thinking deeply about the role of astrology, psychology, culture, religion, color, language, and social norms that give identity to a person. My ethnic definition is "Indian, Hindu, Brahmin, brown-skinned woman speaking Tamil and Hindi." I live in an urban, middle-class locality. Born under a set of lucky stars, I happen to have a strongly creative, multifaceted personality and goat-like perseverance in reaching my goals. A psychiatrist might find me deeply affectionate, too forgiving and nonaggressive, no other phobias or manias that affect the loonies. Likewise you too have an ethnic definition of yourself that gives you your identity.

What happens when we take ourselves and our ethnic definitions very seriously to the extent that we exclude anything and anyone outside of them? This is a pathological condition, this is excessive obsession with oneself, and this is the starting point for a sad process of decay. I firmly believe there is more that goes into the making of a human being than just his ethnic/cultural/religious/social background and inheritance. These are the trappings one has acquired from birth, and who could ever choose where and to whom to be born? That choiceless, formless spirit of life that yields itself to the guidance of the power of life and takes a visible, live form is the very basis and origin of man, and is the point of reference from which we need to draw our strength. All other visible, earthly aspects of man are acquired in this world and will be left behind in the same world—with or without his choice.

With this deep-rooted belief about what in a human being is real and what is acquired, I have learned that my passion is for the real. It appears childish to see and judge a man from what he has acquired. I'd rather seek humanness, strong commitment to honest living, good thinking, better actions, and deeply compassionate and kind love in a person than take him on the merit or demerit of the circumstances of his birth, or whatever external factors that have made him what he appears to be. This is the motivation that has made me reach beyond ethnic boundaries and definitions. No one is a better human being just because his ethnic definition is the same as mine. No one is bad just because he happens to be an ethnic outsider.

When I am searching for certain "human qualities" in a person, I simply need to have an unbiased, random search mode, to be prepared to cross the static ethnic barriers (if need be) that have done more damage than good to the collective human psyche. It simply doesn't matter to me that you look different, are from a different country, or have a different religious and cultural identity. If I am lucky to find those human qualities in you, everything else, all our very obvious differences exist, too—but only to nurture, synchronize, and harmonize our relationship, not to play havoc with our foundations.

I am watchful of the world scenario. Many human tragedies could have been avoided if we were all better human beings. It hurts me deeply to see people killing each other, fighting endless battles and purposeless wars, and trying to commit genocide, annihilating those who do not fit into the politico-religious ideologies of the powerful ruling class. Is this why we are born? Just to kill, kill, and kill others and get killed? Is there no better purpose to life than to bulldoze mosques, set temples on fire, kill the marchers in the Tiananmen Square, drop napalm bombs, stuff people into the black hole of Calcutta, drop atom bombs, and create concentration camps? Is there no better ambition in life than to create political famine and use children for mine detection in wars? Why is mankind getting mad? What has gone wrong? Where are we, the human race, heading? Is this visible madness an expression of internal chaos in the minds and the priorities of mankind? Is this madness an expression of a strong obsession with one's own self to the total exclusion of everyone else?

Single-handedly one cannot change the fate of the human race (or can he?). What can he do? What can I do? What should be my way of bringing about peace and oneness? In my small capacity, I hold a white flag—a flag of truce, peace, and acceptance of others as equals, as human beings. I refrain from causing further damage to the already wounded human race. In my capacity as a human being I try to rise above the limitations set on the man, by the man, for the man, and try to see the total picture from the eyes of a person who is on a peace mission. That is why, in my search for a whole and true human being, I need to look at a person much deeper than the few millimeters of his dermis and epidermis, and instead study him in the light of only one culture—the unbiased culture of a genuine, truthful human being. In this search I have met you (actually, yet to meet you in person) and in my search for the core, the icings of the cake don't matter at all. Are we searching for similar things?

Enjoy your Indian guests and Indian food. Do you cook? It is little difficult for me to imagine you amidst pots, pans, and Indian curries. Well, Ehud, if we become "Man and Wife," I would like you to leave the kitchen to me. I would much appreciate a kind and helping hand once in a while, but it would still be my singular privilege and pleasure to cook what you would like to eat. And I may not much refer to Harish Johari's cookbook. The necessary recipes are in my head, and with the right ingredients available (an appreciative, adventurous, and hungry husband included), I can invent new dishes too. Joy of cooking gets killed when people do not enjoy eating or are very critical.

I am beginning to look forward to October and hope you will come to India then and again in February '96. Madras in October will still be hot (when is it cold anyway?). I'd not like to cause distraction in your work and insist that you must somehow come in October, but if some-one asked me what my single secret wish was I would say aloud that you should be able to come; if work does not permit, you make the work to permit you. If you find time to come to India in October, we will meet, you can meet the rest of my family, and then we can decide whether our relationship can be accorded the honor of marriage. Ehud, it is simply my feminine instinct that tells me to tell you not to put off your visit. Shall I tell you a confidential joke? If we decide positively, we could well be on our way to bringing Junior Ehud by then. As much as you know me, it is not a joke. I am quite serious about chil-dren. I am sorry if it seems that I am encouraging you to hurry up. Please don't be offended, but don't you think that at my age and your age, we have already spent half of our lifetimes and haven't yet known the taste of a blissful married life and the taste of having kids around?

Feel free to comment and tell me to my face if you feel I'm hurry-ing you up—that is one more added privilege of correspondence that we share: we can say what is in our mind without the fear of offend-ing the other (because we do not intend to offend).

Bye for now . . . .
Vatsala

Dear Mr. Ehud,

I have just returned from a trip to my family in Madurai and am glad to tell you that they are doing well. During this trip, I was musing over your letters. Somehow I feel you are still a distant, aloof, and detached person, whereas I am warming up beyond my own expectations to these developments in our relationship. Are you always like that? Well, my enthusiasm and warmth are quite infectious, watch out or else you might be infected too. Better for me, I will gain a more open, informal, warm, and lively friend to exchange my views with.

Ehud, what were you going through in New York when Ganesh Baba pulled you up and out? Do you mind (if you are willing to) sharing this with me? That will help me to know you better.

Back to duty, it was a busy and long day at the hospital. Amidst all this running around I thought of you in unusual places like flying up and down the staircase, while in a cab commuting in the city . . . I was gripped by an acute communication syndrome of sudden onset. I thought of sending you a fax, even dialing your number to try speaking to you . . . You must be wondering what on earth is this syndrome? Well, I needed to make a decision regarding switching my career. An offer came by for a lecturership. For slightly better pay, it involves traveling 20 miles up and down from home, and teaching microbiology to undergraduates. No possibilities for research, but regular teaching work with the opportunity for a promotion from lecturership to professorship. Initial tenure of one year will be revised and renewed if my work is found satisfactory. So I was thinking whether or not to switch to teaching. At this juncture in my life, getting married to a compatible person and beginning to raise a family is my only priority. If you and I are likely to make a positive decision regarding getting married, I need not enter into this one-year teaching tenure. I can continue to be where I am and try finishing the projects in hand. Also, I am happier working for children if I have to work at all. Accepting a teaching tenure, getting married in the middle of the contract, and disappearing from the country would be unfair to the students and to the new employer. If I do accept, I must complete the tenure. With these arguments for and against the two careers, I decided to stay put where I am till some sort of magic moves me from here.

I would have much liked to know your views and hear what you have got to say about this. Actually, maybe I was swaying with indecision and needed a second person to help me decide.

But presently the moments of indecision are over. I am feeling better. No regrets, no remorse or sense of loss. Instead, having decided to stay put, I feel a stronger sense of belonging and commitment to this temple-of-health-for-children.

This morning, Dr. Ramakrishnan called and said he would like to meet me on Wednesday, 12 July. He asked if I have been corresponding with you, and if so, how things were. I told him that I have been writing to you religiously and things were fine, to which he gave a small laugh that told me he knows exactly and much more about what is happening between us than I ever could or would care to tell him. He wanted to see me at home, which did not seem practical considering that Amma is away and I am all alone. I have invited him to the hospital and he has accepted. I hope he does not mind the horrible canteen coffee, exotic bugs, their offensive smells, wailing kids, and the continuous nuisance of phones ringing. I am getting a little restless about Dr. Ramakrishnan's visit. What is he seeing me about? Something like a pre-examination tension (which I never really had during any of my academic exams) is gripping me. God, for good or for worse, please be with me.

I wonder when you and I are likely to speak. Will it be as far away as in October or February? In my correspondence I have painstakingly been maintaining as much clarity as written language permits me. If a day comes for me to speak to you, I think I will really not plan on what to say. I will just be myself . . . easier on me. And then let the bridge come and I will cross it.

Vatsala

chapter 4

LET THAT BE

12.7.95

Dear Ehud,

Dr. Ramakrishnan came to the department this morning. We chatted and soon my pre-examination tension vanished. We spoke about you and he said that you have been telling him about my letters. He said that you are a shy person. *Is it so,* I wondered. I had presumed, looking at your pictures, that you took time to warm up to people, to a concept, but once you get warmed up you can get right to the heart of the matter, no fuss, not shy or afraid of anything. When he told me you are a shy person, I was quite surprised, but I accepted on the grounds that he knows you more than I do and for a longer time. He came back again in the evening and he wanted me to have a chat with you on the phone . . . God, there I was thinking of October and February and the moment is right here . . .

Ramakrishnan spoke to you first and then handed the phone to me . . . I was slightly nervous and a little embarrassed. I know the phone booth attendants very well, as they handle all my faxes to our collaborators in Denmark and phone calls to and from my sister Geeta, who lives in Muscat. While he was speaking with you he did so loudly, and went on describing me to you, recommending me with his approval and then telling you that I was aware of all the ifs and buts and you can make your own decision at your own pace and time . . . I would have given anything to run away . . . This is a set of two male friends each describing me, approving and disapproving of me in his own way. One I could hear and the other I could not and to the one whom I could not hear, I had so meticulously given a first-hand biopsy report on "ME." It was embarrassing, very much so. I would have preferred if you two had spoken in detail about me in my absence. But then people don't marry only the mind, which is what so far you had known about me; they marry the whole package, and that includes height, weight, vital statistics, color, breed, chemistry, likes and dislikes, and whatnot . . . and since we have not met in person so far, you have no idea about the rest of the contents of my package. In the complicated world of very complicated human interactions, my simplistic approach to a person might at best be outdated.

However, while speaking with you I felt much at ease. You did sound friendly, not cold and aloof and indifferent (which I am not either). It did feel nice speaking to you though at times I could not understand what you were saying and had to ask you to say it again. Similarly, forgive me, I might not have been all that clear to you. Worry not, we will improve . . . It is just a game of accents. After Dr. Ramakrishnan spoke to you again, we took a quick walk to a nearby cool drinks shop. Dr. Ramakrishnan was genuinely pleased with this development, and, as he has been saying repeatedly, he would much want you to get married to me because he thinks (for reasons best known to him) that I will make a good wife. That is what he meant by his strong recommendation, he clarified.

Well, Ehud, from the medium of letters we have graduated to the medium of phones. And God willing, you might even decide to come to India in October. While I have been optimistic about our relation-ship right from the moment I posted the first letter to you with a bunch of photographs, I have accepted that the hands of God pull the final shots. Optimism is one thing; practical consideration and expectations are another.

In a fairytale manner, in our October meeting we simply might like each other and go ahead with a positive decision. Or, as Dr.

Ramakrishnan put it, in case we do not like each other, we can tell him separately and he will take care of how best to tell us. Well, on my part, if I had not liked you, and liked what I am doing, you would not have received these many thousands of words from me. So you can be sure that a walking back would not be staged by me. I am sure of this. However, as is natural, you have the freedom to judge and decide for yourself. And if for some reason you feel/think that I may not be the right person for you, courtesy Dr. Ramakrishnan I will receive and accept the news. No fuss. No accusations. Better not to make mistakes than to make them and to try to rectify them later. It is another story to learn from one's mistakes, in which case, an attempt is being made to derive objective lessons from our errors. But trying to rectify a mistake means that one is trying to live with and adjust to it to suit the resulting situation.

What happens after a disaster is actually the story of progress of the human race. Resilience is the essence of life. If everything works out as I have been hoping, well, I move on with you, and if it sours, well, then I move on with my routine of bugs, sick kids, and research, and you too move on with your work . . . and we both resume a renewed search for a suitable companion. This is what Dr. Ramakrishnan also advised me: "Keep an open outlook, accept what comes naturally." And think of it, we are not left with much choice than to accept what comes to us naturally.

While I was speaking to you, Dr. Ramakrishnan went on prompting me, "Speak something interesting . . ." He is a cheeky, naughty man and I guess you two are quite sure of what interests the other. Well, to conclude, Ehud, I liked speaking to you. I hope you too liked speaking to me. I might even be tempted to call you again. But I will check my temptation . . .

Bye and wishing you the best,
Vatsala

July 14, 1995

Dear Vatsala,

It was lovely speaking to you on the phone, if only for those brief, awkward moments. The telephone only reproduces a small portion of the audible frequencies of the voice, so you never really get anything but a truncated, minimal part of the full spectrum of expression that's possible between human beings when they are in the same room. I'm taking very seriously your request that I appear in the same room as you in October and am looking into arrangements. As I'm sure you can appreciate, there is considerable expense involved, as well as time away from the office during a very intense and busy season. Nevertheless, I'm going to try to make it happen, and will let you know over the ensuing weeks.

I'm planning on writing you a longer letter, responding to many of your queries. Right now, I'm caught up in a number of events around guests and work. This is really highly unusual, as in the summer, I customarily am able to take it a bit easier, but this year, a number of events have converged and I've been going nonstop.

Your recent letters are quite beautiful and engaging and I want to reflect upon them and give them my full attention and a considered response. That will happen shortly. For now, I'd like to ask you to have your horoscope done according to the *Bhrigu* system. It should be sent to me within the next couple of weeks, if possible. I'm not sure how much it will cost to have a computerized horoscope done in Madras, but since I'm requesting it, I'd like to pay for it if you'll permit me.

Sorry for the brevity of this note, but I trust you'll understand that my request for your horoscope is an indication of how deeply I've been affected by your letters and that I am indeed moving forward in considering a future for us.

All the best,
Ehud

He wanted my horoscope. This letter from Ehud said one thing to me: our friendship would reach its positive or negative conclusion depending on the location, compatibility, and effects of the heavenly stars and planets. My spirit sank into a deep abyss. Having grown up in India, I had a pretty good idea about the game of hypocrisy and money played around horoscopes. I was a little apprehensive, a little upset, and, yes, a little angry too. If he was so keen on getting our horoscopes matched, why didn't he ask in the very first letter, the way it is done in India when families try to connect through the matrimonial columns? Why did he write to me, receive nearly four months of letters, and only then decide that he needed to get our horoscopes matched? Having written to him in so much detail, with so much truth, honesty, and passion, I would feel like a fool if now he found that since our horoscopes did not match, he was not interested in pursuing our connection any further. Thinking about this abortive possibility filled me with rage, and I lamented over all the time and energy that I had spent writing with such devotion.

That evening after work I waited for over an hour at the bus stand. It was past 7:00 P.M. and darkness was gradually descending on the crowded city. The bus never arrived, prompting me to walk the six miles to my home. A wry smile came over my sweaty, dust-covered face.

The bus was not supposed to come, so it did not come. And I was supposed to walk six miles after a full day's work, so I am walking . . . why get annoyed over what has to happen? As I talked to myself, the Sanskrit word *tathaastu* came into my mind again and again. This word, translated roughly, means "let that be." When priests utter blessings and best wishes in a chorus, one of them says "tathaastu" at the end of each blessing.

I watched my mind trying to get over the rage of not getting a bus, and the rage of being asked by Ehud to provide my horoscope. I watched my mind calming down, feeling peaceful, and praying to God for help and guidance. It occurred to me that this business of horoscope matching is God's wish too. This has to happen. This will happen. Let that be. Fear and rage are not necessary. What is necessary is to feel deep down in my heart and mind that only that happens that has to happen. If it is destined that I have a future with Ehud, all hurdles both earthly and heavenly will move away, clearing my path leading to him. If it is destined that I have no future with him, then we will continue to go our separate ways.

I saw the entire pattern and progression of my life as a manifestation of God's wish. I had no ways or means to prove this belief but had learned as a little child to submit myself to that wish and accept what came my way without placing blame on myself, on others, or, for that matter, on God or my destiny. And whenever anything good happened to me, I gave total credit to God and saved my own ego from inflating to the limits of bursting.

These beliefs seated deep in my psyche prompted me to regain balance and stability, get over my initial negative reaction to Ehud's request for my horoscope, and reply to his letter.

22.7.95

Dear Ehud,
Namaste.

Your letter of 14 July is here. Thank you. I'm glad to know that this letter from you is simply a prologue to a more detailed letter.

I too loved talking to you. Here comes another compliment: I liked your voice on the phone. You did sound warm, friendly, and in control of yourself, not distant and uninterested. Moments were awkward, yes very much so, for me too. Would we feel the same when together in person for the first time, hopefully in October? I don't know, but I think feeling awkward in physical proximity will be there, naturally. Despite awkwardness and embarrassment, the human sense of fondness is a strange feeling. It may develop instantly, but "seasoning" is what gives fondness the depth necessary to make it lasting and meaningful, and this seasoning (and aging) alone can differentiate it from infatuation. Now, if you ask me whether I am continuing to be in touch with you because of fondness or infatuation, I won't be able to answer convincingly. I am sure that infatuation has got nothing to do with my correspondence with you. Fondness . . . well, I am looking forward to feeling the first warm glow, and for sure will tell you exactly when that happens. Presently, I like being in touch with you. I do hope God will bless us with a future together, and in that future, I will pray to God to let us feel the entire range of human emotions, right from fondness unto a complete acceptance of each other as a total person, and a very complete and deep sense of love and belonging.

I am relieved to know that you found my recent letters beautiful and engaging. Once I wrote them, I agonized over editing them to a suitable, readable size, so that they wouldn't demand much of your time. Then it occurred to me that abridged versions often lack the flow and essence of the main text. Thus the main versions escaped being edited and were sent to you. Also I thought if there is to be a future to our contact, it is better if you know me just as I am . . . why bother with cosmetic surgery?

Regarding your request for a horoscope, Ehud, I must work in this direction because I care for and respect your wishes. Do you have one for yourself? Where, how, and by whom will you get it compared? I am beginning to be much troubled by a very annoying question: what happens if our horoscopes don't have the desired degree of compatibility? You alone can put my mind to rest regarding the possibilities.

In India, especially in the weddings that are initiated, organized, and performed by the parents, the moment horoscopes don't match, the proposals—no matter how good they are in all other aspects— are dropped like hot potatoes. All negotiations come to a grinding halt, and people who were considering getting "related" go their separate ways, searching for more favorable stars and planets. Human feelings are reduced to nonexistence because a person is totally characterized as per his/her stars in the horoscope. In the pre-Vedic and Vedic times, when astrology was beginning to germinate as a science, people had deep knowledge about the planetary powers and weaknesses. Also, in those times, the practitioners of these great sciences were wise and spiritually evolved people who would not base their astrological readings and predictions on the amount of money to be earned in the process. Their knowledge was not just information; it was wisdom seasoned with compassion for their fellow human beings. The present-day scenario is shockingly different. Astrology can be studied in universities or even by correspondence courses. Many call themselves astrologers as soon as they have finished reading a few cheap, borrowed, or stolen books. And in this country, where actions are strongly influenced by religion and traditional culture, and people tend to faithfully believe anyone who claims to be able to match a horoscope, greed and lust for money can change the predictions to suit a rich client. Totally mismatching horoscopes can be declared matching if the fee to the astrologer is raised by a few rupees. Such is the decline in the manner in which the great science of astrology is approached in present times.

Presently it appears that in this Indian way of arranging a marriage with you, I still have to pass the acid-test of horoscope compatibility. In this tricky and sticky situation, I just have to do my best to keep myself indifferent, detached, and aloof. In India, if horoscopes match, parents go to great lengths discussing an exchange of money called dowry. And besides female infanticide, in India, dowry-related deaths of women in "kitchen accidents" (read *murder*, mostly by husbands and in-laws) is yet another policy adopted by the literate as well as illiterate masses in keeping the population explosion under control. God . . . you alone can save and redeem my beloved motherland, which is being ruined by misinterpretation of its original, wonderful, and mysterious culture.

Do I take your request as an indication that if our horoscopes do not match, we go our separate ways? Or will you bravely consider marriage even if the horoscopes do not match? Will you feel comfortable going against what the stars foretell? If you intend to marry me anyway (to be decided after a personal meeting), then why bother with horoscopes? These questions have come to mind and have upset me to some extent. I am attempting to see this whole business of horoscope from your point of view so that I can understand and appreciate your reasons. Ehud, forgive me, I am very sorry if my outlook on this topic sounds very negative. Please bear with me and please for God's sake do not be offended. All this has got to do with my firsthand observation of some unfortunate women in India. I have seen many good, efficient, competent, warm, caring, educated, beautiful women with/without money and with perfect anatomy, physiology, and endocrine systems reduced to dysfunctional ghosts of their brilliant selves, just because their horoscopes were not found to be compatible. In these cases men, and the society that permits such strong exclusion and segregation criteria, cared for only the planets. They never really cared for human sentiments and feelings. They never cared for the alive person who should be treated with love and dignity, and who could create a happy home and a wonderful life together if given the chance. Despite all the so-called progress being made, the highly traditional and conservative Indian community does not offer a healthy and clean atmosphere for men and women to interact as responsible, sensible adults. And these unfortunate women die a lonely death without ever knowing what a man's simple touch feels like. I strongly sympathize with such women, who have been caught in this star war for no apparent reason or fault of their own.

As we cannot choose to whom to be born, we cannot choose under which planetary condition to be born. This is the ultimate and ever-unsolvable mystery of human birth, and the cosmic reason behind each such birth. When God simply has not given us a choice in these aspects, why condemn a person, why avoid him for reasons beyond his mortal control? I do consider astrology and astronomy as wonderful, mysterious, highly mathematical, and hence predictable sciences. I have great admiration for them for purely academic reasons. Similarly, I have much regard for the scientists who invent great weapons and bombs. They have great brains, yes. But I have scant regard for the politician who orders an army general to use the weapons on the unsuspecting, innocent people of a so-called enemy country. The scientist discovered the weapons because of his excellent research skills. The army general used it because he is employed and paid to do his job. What the hell is the role of the politician who exploits the scientist as well as the duty-minded, patriotic army man in order to strengthen his own political clout and position? Isn't he a self-serving, egotistical scum?

As life influences matter, so does matter influence life. All is interrelated. Everything exists for only one purpose: sustaining life. Once we try to learn how to see the mechanism of the universe, the cosmos, we learn to appreciate the vastness, the endlessness of the entire creation. I do think about these aspects. I wonder about the truly endless universe and the great cosmic forces that maintain order on this earth and also in outer space. The whole mechanism puzzles me deeply. My thinking apparently comes to a standstill, Ehud, and it invariably turns toward thinking about a mind that must be behind all this endless, nonstop drama of life and of matter. Is this mind what we call God? Or is this simply the creative power and expression of nature? Is nature the other word for God? And when I see the same mystery of outer space confining itself into the DNA molecule inside the 2×3 micron bacteria, I simply become numb. What is DNA but a highly mathematical arrangement of oxygen, hydrogen, carbon, sulfur, phosphorus, and nitrogen atom? And it seems to give all the intelligence the bacteria needs to survive and live on. I am amazed beyond limits.

What wide range of power God/nature has . . . In my frequent, deeply meditative and contemplative moments, be it while hanging on for my dear life during the overcrowded bus ride to and from the hospital, or during the rounds of the water treatment plant on the seventh floor of the hospital, where, in between work, I steal a few quiet moments to stand still and gaze at the drama of life and death unfolding seven floors below, I reach only one conclusion . . . that no matter how unscientific, undefinable, unattainable, invisible, and highly controversial the concept of God is, I have a total, unquestioning, complete, and deep faith in Him, His power, His wishes, and His ways. (Don't ask why my God is He and not She. I don't know. But I've often wondered if God could be She or It. Why we assign the male gender to God, I simply don't know.) With that total faith I have learned to be as flexible to the wish of God as is humanly possible and accept what comes with balance, grace, equanimity, and gratefulness. I could go more into it, but it is high time I came to a conclusion and told you that my faith in God is stronger than my faith in planets or in a man's or a woman's ability to interpret the intentions or effects of the planets. I will therefore tune my mind to maintain a total calm. I will definitely respect your wish and send you a copy of my horoscope. May I also request that you not bother with the bill? It is not likely to cost a fortune, anyway! And I will wait to hear from you until horoscope compatibility results are available.

If you find it fit to go ahead and get married, well Ehud you will find a nice Indian bride who is capable of lots of love for her man and who is keen on filling his home with kids. I hope this event will come true. And depending on the compatibility reports, if the verdict is unfavorable and you decide to call it quits, then, well, I will be hurt and feel lost, but I will learn to live with it, get over it, and go ahead in life, accepting it as what else but a wish of God. Left to myself, I will not accept a man simply because his horoscope is compatible with mine, and also I will not reject him simply because the planets didn't agree. For me, a man means more than his birth chart. He is a human being in whom the power of God very much lives as it surely does in everyone else and everything else.

I'm very sorry, Ehud, for this outburst, forgive me, and please do not take it as if I'm overly critical of this ancient science that is woven intricately into the fabric of Indian culture. Misinterpretations by self-serving people have ruined many otherwise perfectly nice people, and despite my sympathy for these victims, I do not wish to and am not prepared to join their league. I really want to live a full, complete, and meaningful life, not just exist like a vegetable (even plants feel something, don't they?). I do not know how you will react to this letter and whether you will find it as beautiful and engaging as some of the previous letters. God knows! But I would request that you not get offended. I thought that instead of complying to your wish mechanically, I would learn to genuinely respect your wish and, at the same time, without hurting your feelings and beliefs, would try telling you my views and ideas on this particular topic of horoscope.

I guess in our marriage (that is, if the stars permit us to marry), if we keep a tradition of respecting each other's feelings and sentiments and, at the same time, use with economy and prudence our right and freedom of self-expression, we could be an enviable, happily married couple who do disagree occasionally but are wedded to the cause of happiness and will survive occasional disagreements because love is the equation that keeps them bound. Shall I say that I am thankful to you for seriously considering a future for us because you have been touched deeply by my letters? Just this very moment when I am about to close this letter I am in a prayerful and serene mind, Ehud. I do wish you happiness and I do ask God to show you and lead you on to the right goal through the right path. May God be with you always. It is 1 A.M. and I think a scrawling handwriting is natural.

Best wishes,
Vatsala

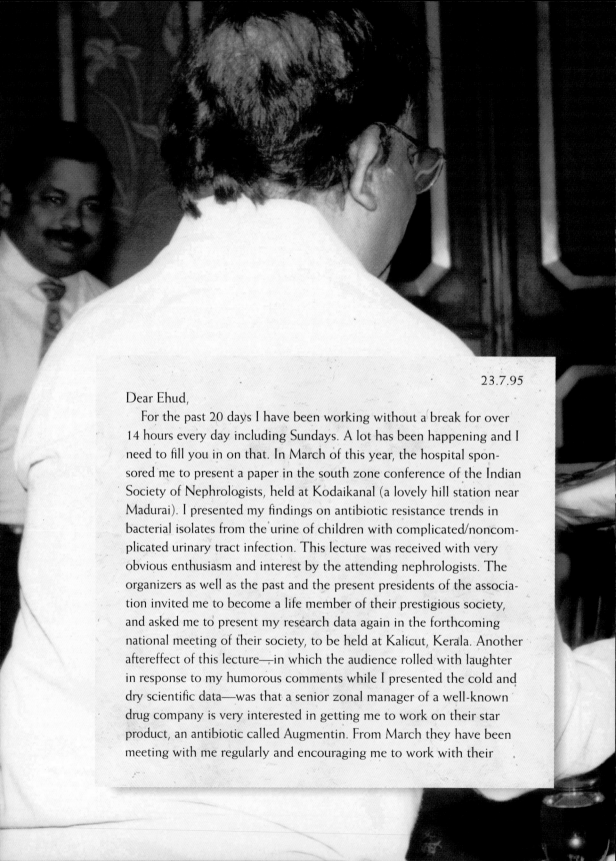

23.7.95

Dear Ehud,

For the past 20 days I have been working without a break for over 14 hours every day including Sundays. A lot has been happening and I need to fill you in on that. In March of this year, the hospital sponsored me to present a paper in the south zone conference of the Indian Society of Nephrologists, held at Kodaikanal (a lovely hill station near Madurai). I presented my findings on antibiotic resistance trends in bacterial isolates from the urine of children with complicated/noncomplicated urinary tract infection. This lecture was received with very obvious enthusiasm and interest by the attending nephrologists. The organizers as well as the past and the present presidents of the association invited me to become a life member of their prestigious society, and asked me to present my research data again in the forthcoming national meeting of their society, to be held at Kalicut, Kerala. Another aftereffect of this lecture—in which the audience rolled with laughter in response to my humorous comments while I presented the cold and dry scientific data—was that a senior zonal manager of a well-known drug company is very interested in getting me to work on their star product, an antibiotic called Augmentin. From March they have been meeting with me regularly and encouraging me to work with their

Background: *I am welcomed with a buke of flowers at the beginning of my lecture.* Below: *Lecturing at a conference of the Indian Society of Nephrologists.*

product, dropping very obvious hints that I was on the list of their top-priority scientists. Well, we could learn from drug companies how to find and cultivate a good catch.

They arranged for a meeting on 21 July with leading pediatricians from across the city and invited me as Chief Guest to deliver a guest lecture on my findings with their drug. They treated me very well and made me feel like a queen. They introduced me to an audience of over 60 top pediatricians and in very glowing terms highlighted my achievements as a microbiologist. The lecture lasted for a full half-hour followed by a 45-minute question-and-answer session. I did well, wasn't nervous, displayed amazing levels of self-confidence, charm, and ease. Later the drug company executives gave me feedback that the pediatricians had known me as a microbiologist-par-excellence and had happily rescheduled their evening appointments to be able to attend and listen to my lecture.

It was a great moment of gratification and pride. I felt good and realized that my hard work has not been a waste. It has gotten me a name as a leading clinical microbiologist in the city and the pediatricians look upon me with respect. The organizers of the meeting were extremely happy with this very successful outcome. They have asked me to prepare an article on "the growing problem of bacterial drug resistance" and publish it in the science and technology section of our national newspaper the *Hindu*. Also doctors at the railway hospital Perambur in Madras are very keen on having me give the same lecture in their auditorium. It's the first time a nonclinical doctor from my tiny hospital has been invited as a guest lecturer at this very prestigious railway hospital. Also, the drug company people are asking me to accept lecture tours to nearby cities and assure me that they will sponsor each trip, including airfare, hotel accommodation, and safe transport to and from home. I have accepted the request because it is a good opportunity to come up in my career and it is good to be known for the quality of work one performs. Also it is a great honor for the hospital and my department. The hospital is feeling proud of me, and in turn I am feeling good and useful.

Ehud, this whole experience is very intoxicating, just like the cocktails they served (relax, I do not take liquor!). But I am totally in control, I have my priorities in perfect order, and I regard this good fortune as a spell of sunshine that nature gives during lingering, cloudy monsoon months, just to keep our chins up. Isn't it strange that I should earn more name and fame than money in my chosen profession?

While being the star performer of the grand evening, while being in the limelight, while being showered with praise, admiration, and recognition, Ehud, I felt terribly alone, as alone as a lost child could feel in a crowd. While the auditorium reverberated with the sound of clapping at the conclusion of my speech, I closed my eyes for a moment and wished that Amma were with me. And at the very same moment I wished you were with me too. I could imagine you and Amma sitting in the audience, encouraging me to go on. Isn't it strange, amidst this admiring crowd, I missed having Amma and you here. Amma is my nearest and dearest darling person. I wonder how and when you walked in so close that in the same breath as I missed having her here, I also missed having you here. I wished like hell that you could be here with me.

If you asked me the reason and the logic of why I missed you at this brilliant moment, I wouldn't be able to answer with conviction. Maybe I am looking for something deeper, stronger, and more durable and real—affection from one person. A crowd's cheering and admiration is just as unstable as a layer of mist when the sun finally shows up. The affection and love that I am so honestly and truly looking forward to giving to and receiving from a man, in my imagi-nation, is not as light as a mist. Since the beginning of our contact, I have been thinking of you quite a lot, and probably my poor mind thinks you could possibly be that one person.

Well, Ehud, take it easy. I just told you what was on my mind and how I missed you. But I have quickly put that emotional pang under control and have become my usual self again.

After the evening's dinner, I was escorted back to my home. Again I felt terribly alone, as my home was empty. I walked into the prayer room and amidst streams of tears thanked God for being so kind, generous, loving, helpful, and supportive to me. But for God's grace, what could give us the happiness we seek?

Vatsala

Celestial observatory built by the maharaja of Jaipur.

chapter 5

DOS AND DON'TS

Madras summer was still at its peak in August. I had not received a letter from Ehud in a few weeks. While getting steamed and boiled in the humid heat of this city, I wondered if he had rejected me because of my horoscope. Would I get a neat little note from this American man saying, "Dear Dr. Vatsala, thank you for your horoscope, but sorry, it is not compatible with mine." Would he take his note a little farther on humanitarian grounds and say that as per his astrologer's suggestion, I could take certain steps to pacify the bad planets in my chart, and then he could consider communicating further?

Well, he might reject me, but I believed nevertheless that how we conduct ourselves is of equal or greater importance than the stars and planets. While musing about the power of personal conduct, I started on my next letter.

Dear Ehud,

Namaste.

Since I began trying to locate and meet a person with a view to marriage, I have been observing married people both old and young. What makes them click? Do they enjoy or just tolerate each other? Is there any spark of passion and romance alive in their physical relationship? Do they exist together simply because they have no means of getting away? Are they compatible in terms of physical and mental makeup, energy, and presentation? Do they clash often and try proving their supremacy? Who wears the trousers at home—the man or the wife? How does/do their child/children influence them? Which spouse is competing with the child? Is there any indication of friendship, simple humanly love and affection between them, or is the only thing that ever brings them close an intense physical urge felt only once in a while? Is their relationship healthy and deep? Are they cold and dying? Are they warm and alive?

I am by no means a psychologist or psychoanalyst going around meeting people and asking them to fill out questionnaires. I observe and try to assess their chemistry. My observations may be called more intuitive than scientific but I believe they are based on detecting small changes in cardiac and encephalic electric wave patterns that bring about very slightly perceptible changes in the facial muscles and body language. An ECG or EEG machine is not necessary. All that is needed is concentration and compassion for the subject of observation.

So far my readings have given me interesting and reliable clues to human behavior. Once a close friend suggested that I try chucking the bugs out the window and take up marriage counseling as a profession. And for all the real-life counseling that I do as an amateur, I could make a lot more money than I make as a microbiologist. This idea did not (and will never) appeal to me. I observe because I am a student of life; I want to learn and improve and, whenever necessary, correct myself. Preaching and correcting others is definitely not my piece of cake. This yearning for learning and improvement is because *if* and *when* I meet a man I have been searching for, I want to make him absolutely happy, giving him no cause to grumble and regret his decision. He must feel at peace on meeting me and being with me, or else the entire purpose of the meeting and the union is defeated.

I believe in the saying "Never cease seeking light till you become light." As human beings, we are born with and acquire several factors that might make us offensive and undesirable. Should we not make a willful effort at continuously weeding out the bad so that the good in us can multiply and outshine the bad?

I have learned from my observations so far that what makes a couple blissfully happy is treating the spouse as equal; being considerate in thought, action, and speech; being courteous and kind; never trying to win an argument for the sake of winning, but trying to hold a sensible, logical conversation that gives a fair chance for the right party to win; and, finally, accepting a person totally. What happens, you may ask, if these efforts at being oh-so-good are purely one-directional and the other person is totally inert in the face of these life-saving remedies? God save them, in the USA they go their separate ways. In India, where legal help is scarce, they continue to exist without living.

Do you know, Ehud, what my fears are? I'm afraid of meeting a person who is insensitive to these life-saving remedies. I'm afraid of waging a lonely battle to keep a relationship alive. I'm afraid of meeting a man who is a monster in every way except having two horns, sharp claws, prominent incisors, and bulging, bloodshot eyes popping out of their sockets. Since my fears are real to me, I am almost always in a prayerful mood—*God, please do not let the holy energy of life be wasted; keep me in your grace; help me find a person whose needs and expectations from life are the same as mine; let there be reciprocation, warmth; equality, peace, love, and simple and pure friendship; let there be a spark of humanity always alive in us; let us not become senseless, mindless monsters.*

God helps those who help themselves. And prayers alone never accomplished anything in the absence of determined, focused efforts. To help myself, I have been thinking about some *dos* and *don'ts*. I am practicing them in my day-to-day interactions with people. I intend to practice them in my relationship with my spouse because I want my marriage to be secure, solid, and full of peace and love, and I want above everything for my would-be spouse to be happy and at peace.

DOs and DON'Ts

1. Be straightforward in your approach.	1. Don't be piercingly sharp; it hurts.
2. Speak the truth.	2. Don't use hurtful, humiliating language while saying the truth.
3. Be soft, gentle, polite.	3. Don't get trampled.
4. Try to forget and forgive.	4. Don't be revengeful.
5. See good in a person.	5. Don't preach. Don't remind people of what is bad in them.
6. If possible, try acknowledging the good.	6. Don't flatter. It stinks of self-interest.
7. Tell clearly what you do not like.	7. Don't grumble. Don't nag. Don't hate a person for what you don't like in him/her.
8. Talk sensibly.	8. Don't argue.
9. Listen with compassion and sensitivity.	9. Don't be a dumb doll.
10. Reach out, touch.	10. Don't encroach on personal freedom and privacy.
11. Accept your faults. Admit when you've made a mistake.	11. Don't try to cover the wrong with excuses, sweet talk, and exercise of authority.
12. Tell clearly what you want, wait for your turn.	12. Don't grab. Don't be greedy.
13. Say "sorry."	13. Don't use "sorry" as a quick way out of a messy situation. Don't say "sorry" without presenting a corrective measure.
14. Say "thank you."	14. Don't say it without feeling thankful.
15. Be grateful.	15. Don't take anyone or anything for granted.
16. Learn to respect and reciprocate small gestures of concern, kindness, compassion, and humanity.	16. Don't be heartbroken if you don't see them in a relationship.
17. Children are God's best gift to mankind. Love them without spoiling them with too much or too little attention.	17. Don't use children as a means of breaking an adult.
18. Learn to understand quietness.	18. Don't consider words as the only and ultimate means of communication.
19. Do your best to help.	19. Don't be hurt if help is unwelcome. Maybe it was not needed.
20. In being good . . .	20. . . . don't forget, like everyone else, you too are a human being and are likely to falter.

Ehud, are you wondering why I'm telling you all this? Well, my interest in material possessions is very limited. I do not love poverty, but I can be quite happy with small things and live with minimum facilities without grumbling or dissatisfaction. I do not find pleasure in the common pursuit of women: proving that they have the latest in fashion and style. What can really make me glow with happiness is finding a man with whom I can practice the reformative and constructive measures, because our beliefs are similar. With this man it will be my pleasure to belong to him, be there for him, and raise my family with him. Can you do a thorough soul-searching and tell me if your beliefs are similar too? It is important for us and I hope you will find time. If your answer is yes, then I will consider my search complete and wait patiently for you to have the same confidence. Then I'm sure a life of togetherness will be truly meaningful.
May God bless you . . . . . .

Sincerely . . . . . .
Vatsala

July 31, 1995

Dear Vatsala,

I find it hard, if not impossible, to reject or deny a sincere and heartfelt request. Consequently, I'll arrive in Madras either October 18th or 19th. What are your plans for the Festival of Lights on the 20th? Is it possible for you to leave work and travel to Delhi on either the 25th or 26th? The reason I ask is that I'm trying to arrange to meet with Harish Johari and his family at that time and I would like you to meet them. If this works, can you come? My plan would be to come down to Madras, spend a couple days with you and your family, then move on to visit Ramakrishnan and his family, then back to Delhi, where hopefully I'll see you again. We can work out the details at a later date.

It was good to hear about your visit to see your parents. I think you'll be interested to know that I refer to my mother as *Ima* and my father as *Aba*. Those are the Hebrew words for "mother" and "father," which I have retained since my childhood in Israel. The phonetic similarity to your Appa and Amma are quite interesting, and further confirm my belief that the fundamental expressions of mankind are universal.

The decline in spiritual values and focus in society also seems to be universal, although its forms of expression are many. India loses babies to contaminated water; the U.S. loses them to crack cocaine, handguns, and random violence. Here, politicians and scientists study the "problem," looking for the "solution" in a dispassionate analytical mode, as is the practice in the western scientific model. However, it is my belief and conviction that these problems will never be solved with this approach. The only "cure" is a fundamental re-envisioning and a new imagination or dream, if you will, for society, based on a spiritual impetus. Having said that, I also recognize that the human experience is the human experience and the cycle of time that we're currently in needs to be played out. Let us be sons and daughters of the moment without worshipping at the altar of the church of progress. All this progress brings a reduction in human values and qualities. As we externalize an inherent quality or power, we lose it within ourselves. As the computer's memory expands, mankind forgets its stories and its past. I'm sure you can see this happening in front of your eyes in India; your parents must be experiencing quite a different India from that of their childhood.

You say that I appear to be detached, distant, and aloof. Well, I'm certainly distant from India and yourself at this moment. However, I've decided to remedy that. I think you're taking my high-mindedness and idealistic nature and translating that into aloofness. I think you'll find when you meet me, and certainly my friends will tell you, that I'm anything but aloof. My horoscope also indicates (and I can't remember the Sanskrit term) that I'm a person who is "for the people" and that my sentiments lie with the people rather than the ruling oligarchies.

When I decide that I care for a person and that his or her life, feelings, and concerns are important to me, I throw myself completely

into the relationship. I'm an all-or-nothing person and am there intensely for my friends and those I care about. So, deciding whether a person is indeed someone in whom I want to invest my time, love, and emotions is a serious and deliberative process. This is why it's important for me to remain somewhat detached at this time. This is not to say, however, that I'm not feeling the content of your letters and recognizing my own growing involvement and appreciation of who you are. You are a remarkable and loving person, and this comes through very clearly in your correspondence.

You have asked me about Ganesh Baba and the circumstances of our meeting. When I met Ganesh Baba, I was going through an extremely difficult time in my marriage. It was the first time I had encountered a problem in my life where I had no idea of the remedy, no approach to solving it. I was extremely unhappy. I had lost my sense of certitude and was falling into despair. Baba appeared and proceeded to transform the situation, reconnect me with myself, and

Sri Mahant Ganesh Baba (GB for short) with his favorite herbal remedy.

help me move forward. At the same time, we had an absolute blast together. He was, at 92, one of the most fun and exciting people to be with. He was an ocean of knowledge and love, and we shared an incredible time together. He's certainly the most extraordinary person I've met in my life.

Baba was definitely on the wild side, being a *Naga*. He was of course a *ganja* smoker and was uncontainable in his ecstatic and unconventional expressions of wisdom. He also had degrees in physics and mathematics, spoke five languages, had worked out a unified field theory as an extension of Einstein's work, and was on an intellectual level above anyone I've ever met. He was indiscriminate in his love, giving it as freely to the virtuous as to the bandit. This was really a test for me, as he could relate and interact with people whom I only wanted to get away from and take a bath to purify myself! Baba was able to exhibit compassion and a level of tolerance I've never experienced in anyone else. Add to this his incredible sense of humor and his perfect diction and command of the English language, and you have some impression of why he's such an important figure in my life.

Somehow I have a mysterious connection with Baba and his Akhada. Quite independent of Baba and without his knowledge, I met Harish Johari (whom, since he is like an elder brother to me, I call *Dada*). It turned out that they were both from the same town, that Dada grew up around Baba, and that Dada's teacher Dat Giri was Baba's guru-brother. When I visited the Anand Akhada they knew who I was and of my relationship with Ganesh Baba. Keep in mind that all of this happened without me trying to make it happen or inviting it to happen. It just happened. Life is far more extraordinary, unusual, and unconventional than one could imagine or expect it to be.

Your letters have brought up a lot of questions and I'd like to respond to them. Please don't think me abrupt, as I will just skip from topic to topic.

I'm enclosing with this letter a copy of our most recent catalog to give you a sense of the books we publish. As you rightly say, my work is full of purpose and direction, and integral to my life. Our wild and eclectic collection of books reflects my own interests and tastes. However, now that the company has a number of editors, there are titles in the list that are not necessarily my personal prefer-ence, but reflect other people's interests and tastes. Why don't we save the longer discussion about my publishing activities until we meet, as it would take too long to answer your questions here.

I have a love of Indian art, music, and culture, not to mention the cuisine. I have quite a collection of Indian art at home, gathered from many parts of the country.

I do need a lot of stamina for my work, but happily I have it, due to a healthful diet, the clean air and water that is so abundant in Vermont, my yoga practice which I do each morning before work, and my walks with Noogie through the woods and mountains, a minimum of an hour to two hours a day. I've also started horseback riding once again (I had my own horse for many years, but she died five years ago). I try to get out three times a week for a two-hour ride. As you can tell from the above, keeping physically active and fit is very important to me, and I wish to find a life partner who also gets enjoyment from these activities and is committed to keeping physically fit.

Clearly you are a strong-minded and accomplished woman, intel-lectually free-spirited and open, so given the cultural context of women in India, I suspect you would definitely be regarded as liber-ated from some of the more conventional and dogmatic confines and strictures of the Brahminical tradition. Beyond that, I'll have to wait to meet you to find out how liberated you are.

You should know though, that I've had a wonderful time on nude beaches all over the world. When I travel to Germany, the conven-tion there is for men and women to take saunas in the nude, and I find it quite humorous to be in the hotel lobby where everybody is dressed up in their suits and ties looking quite serious and sophisti-cated, only to find them naked at the sauna in the health club minutes later, along with their children and grandparents. I have no problem with the physical form, covered or exposed, young or old. I do feel that it is important to respect the body and to keep it fit, clean, and in shape. Before the "advent of civilization," humanity by the very nature of its lifestyle maintained its physique well into old age. Now we must work at it.

I've traveled through many cultures and cultural modalities and have a great deal of respect for the use of psychotropic plants in an appropriate cultural context, whether that's *auyahuasca*, the "vine of communion," in the jungles of the Amazon, or the ganja of the sadhus of India, both of which I've experienced and appreciated. Used appropriately and respectfully, they can yield important progress in the paths of liberation and healing. Used inappropriately and out of context, these plants can become the messengers of death and destruction.

I've seen both manifestations in my life, and look for the meaning and metaphor in them. For example, the coca leaf, which has been used for millennia by the people of the Andes in a very positive and helpful way, in the modern world becomes the cocaine that has enslaved and is destroying the fabric of European culture—the very culture that suppressed and exploited the Andeans. It is the shadow side of our culture emerging. The repression of these plants and the people that grow them is now coming out in a dark and destructive way. Similarly, tobacco, which was used as a sacred plant by the Native Americans, is now the cause of a great deal of disease and unhappiness in the culture of their oppressors. It is my view that it is only by getting over the denial inherent in these contradictory relationships that there's any chance for healing. It is, as you say, the hypocrisy around what is moral and correct that is the real destroyer in all these things.

I'm glad to hear that you are an accomplished cook, as I'm helpless in this area and rely on Sue, my housekeeper, to prepare my meals each day. I would be more than happy to turn over to you authority for all matters involving food and the home. I've put a lot of energy and creativity into my home, having recently redesigned my kitchen, bought new furniture in India and had it shipped here, and put in extensive gardens and stone paths and walls. I have a highly culti-vated sense of aesthetics, which is translated into furnishings, fabrics, and the other accoutrements of a warm and welcoming home. My greatest pleasure is in sharing my home with others. For myself, a bed, a chair, and a table would suffice, but for the wife, guests, and friends, much more is needed.

Your desire for children is very exciting to me. I'm completely in accord with your sentiments about a happy home and family life and feel it is time for me to give back some of the good fortune that has come to me. I've been given the privilege of a birth and feel that I should extend that privilege by bringing my own child or children into the world.

I am hardly ever lonely. I live a very intense life, full of people, places, and activities, and find myself enriched and extended by them. I truly like and love myself and consequently when I find time to be by myself, I'm happy with who I'm with. However, I do really miss the companionship, sharing, and happiness that can only—for most people—come from a committed, loving, and giving life partner. There is simply no substitute for it.

I believe that your idealism around marriage is correct. The problem is that people are imperfect; many, particularly in the West, bring baggage into the relationship that contains a lot of dirty laundry. In most cases, this baggage becomes the stumbling block to a happy home life. This has been my own direct experience and it's one of the reasons I've turned to the East in search of a life partner.

If our relationship proceeds to marriage, then certainly we should strive for its highest manifestation. I believe that can only be accomplished by a clear understanding of the different and complementary roles of a husband and wife, and a deep respect for those roles and for each other—a respect that is reflected in speech and actions. There must also be a deep sharing and companionship that cannot be upset by the vicissitudes of life and the ups and downs of one's emotions. Ultimately, the marriage should reflect the spiritual ideals of that greater marriage between the masculine and the feminine. The man must worship the goddess in his wife and conversely the wife must see her husband as her god. We are just reflections of the beloved, striving in our imperfect way for union and liberation. Marriage should be the foundation that helps us achieve those goals.

The problem, Vatsala, is that if you talk about it, you gotta do it. So I now need to see your cartoon to see if I get as big a laugh as you do out of it. Please send it to me with your next letter, which I hope will come soon.

All the best,
Ehud

Dear Ehud,

I am withdrawing my statement. You are not distant, detached, and aloof. I am definitely looking forward to meeting you and discovering that my observations were wrong and that you are very much a people's man. Thanks for the compliments about me being a loving person, but remarkable . . . I do not know. God only knows. If you are beginning to feel the contents of my letters and are recognizing your own growing involvement and appreciation of me—the woman—I feel blessed and feel happy about both. Thank you, Ehud, for beginning to respond and reciprocate. Like you, I am more or less an all-or-none person. Either I put myself totally into a relationship or I don't go anywhere near it. Half-hearted hobnob is not my forte.

While going through the catalog I did recognize a growing sense of respect for you and what you have achieved in your profession. For a person of your merit and accomplishments, I have very mixed feelings—one is of awe, wonder, and very deep respect (which is for you, the achiever), and the other is of course of affection and love (which is for you, the man). It will be an education for me to understand your commitment to your work, to see it the way you do. My desire is to learn about the complete man, and that means all aspects of you, including the one that runs the publishing company. When we meet, you can of course tell me all about how you have grown with the company.

Physical exercise interests me a lot. My current lifestyle, however, leaves no scope for any kind of workout—aerobic or indoor. No time and no atmosphere. I am, however, considerably fit (though not an athlete) and can take up any exercise schedule. Yoga is too serious a science to be toyed around with. If you have learned it the right way, I can learn it from you, or else I would not venture near it. Horse riding, my God, what if the horse decides to throw the rider down? I have seen them do that in the Hindi movies. Ehud, if God-willing we marry, it will be a marriage and union for all purposes (common exercise sessions included). In school, I was on a volleyball team for a few months and I did well, as I was taller than most of my teammates. With practice sessions and study time clashing, I scored near-failing marks in the subject that I do not like at all: maths. That was the end of my sportswomanship. Next, from 1976 all the way to 1985 I have been a bicycle rider. Two to three miles of fun ride was always on the card. I have the highest regard for the humble bicycle, as it happens to be the only non-polluting mode of transport. Even though I have an apparently sedentary lifestyle, I have not put on layers of fat in all the wrong places, and am slim (as per Indian vital statistics, mind you, and that happens to be very different than western vital statistics and beauty concepts). I can never imagine feeling at home in the common saunas and beaches you have mentioned. This is because of the environment in which I have grown up so far, and also my belief that the human body is indeed a temple; it is not for public display and amusement. And also there is this deep-rooted concept of Indian womanhood, that what I do have and am blessed with is for one man—my man. No one else can take a look and try his luck. If this concept of privacy and individuality appears to you as outdated and outmoded, well, I would try talking to you and making you see the logic in it.

Ehud, have you personally used the products of psychotropic plants? God, I am amazed. How you could stay without getting stuck to them? I would do anything to avoid getting addicted to even tea or coffee, and therefore I take them with moderation, no fixed timing or interval, may or may not take a cup of that in a day.

If by God's grace I am destined to join you as your wife, we could send Sue on a brief vacation away from the kitchen as I love cooking (as well as eating) and minding home. It would indeed be my pleasure to take charge of your gastronomic department and home ministry. I would love to do both.

In Sanskrit, there is a saying *"Atithi devo bhava"* that means "Guests are equivalent to God." Extending a warm welcome to guests is becoming a dying art. Hosts do grumble about inconveniences and expenses. Guests too behave without any consideration to the hosts. In this present-day scenario, your attitude toward friends and guests is very refreshing.

I am very very happy to know that my desire for children excites you. Ehud, let us mainly talk in terms of "children," not "child." I have often thought about the possibility of life with you and the juniors around. Shall I tell you that not even once could I think about only you? Do not feel hurt and neglected. Whenever I thought about a family with you, it was always with kids. That is my strong premarital maternal instinct. I can't help it, nor do I want to.

Ehud, whereas sibling rivalry is a much-discussed subject, have you heard about rivalry between the children and spouse to get the attention of the other spouse? In a home setting, a man may subconsciously compete with his son to get his wife's attention. A wife may likewise compete with the daughter to get the attention of her husband. This can lead to much unrest and hostility at home. In our situation I don't anticipate such rivalry because I am absolutely clear about the fact that my husband is going to be the only and topmost priority of mine. Children come subsequently. No matter how dear they are to me, they will be made to understand that their father happens to be the axis around which the family globe revolves.

Relax and rest assured, the damage suffered by western women has come nowhere near me. And the sole credit for this goes to my Holy Mother (Amma). She has shaped me into the woman that I am. I am confident that the light that she has given to me, I can safely carry to brighten the home and the family that I may be blessed with.

This brings me to the last paragraph of your letter (which I so much enjoyed reading). Yes, if our relationship proceeds to marriage, we certainly should strive for its highest manifestation. I do fully understand the difference between man and woman and do realize that they have distinct and different roles to play. How would you feel if I asked you to consider a theory of mine, "interaction without interruption": a wife interacts with her husband on all issues related to their life and at the same time leaves enough scope and freedom for him to be the man of the house. Similarly the man lets her be the woman of the house, treating her with all dignity and grace. There is no crisscrossing, messing up of roles. They are together in everything that they do but they do not try impersonating each other. In other words, the man does not try wearing a skirt and the woman does not try wearing trousers.

I am happy, Ehud, very happy indeed, to know that your expectations from and ideas about marriage are the same as mine. That answers my query . . . are we searching for something similar? Now read the accompanying picture and the letter of 2.6.95 (that I did not post before, as I did not know how you might react). The cartoon is actually not intended to make you laugh. It is simply a two-dimensional, linear representation of a thought/concept that has been expressed in written words. Tell me what you think.

Yes, if you talk about something you have got to do it. What I have been talking about in all my correspondence with you can be done only if we do marry. These assumptions/presumptions/theories/hypotheses/ideas can be proved/disproved in only one sacred laboratory, and that is called *home*.

Having read your letter again, Ehud, I think I am beginning to become fond of you, and am amazed to note that your views on guests, home, personal needs, kids, and marriage are so deeply influenced by the philosophy of Hinduism, which is getting to be grossly out of fashion among many Indian men and women. They are busy following the footprints of culture imported into our country, and have bought wholesale the concept of instant self-gratification based on *ME . . . NOW . . . HERE* ideas. If we do marry eventually, I will consider myself a lucky woman and be grateful to you for the type of man you are, and be grateful to God for having put refined thoughts in your mind. I will ever and always be aware that you have in you the germs of Vedic times and teachings and are more truly Indian in your mind, thoughts, and actions than many Indians can ever hope to be . . .
Bye . . . . . .
Vatsala

Dear Mr. Ehud,

Think of it, how incredibly true it is, all of mankind is involved in some kind of searching. The search could be for as abstract a concept as "peace of mind," or as mundane an object as a "piece of bread." No matter what is to be found, the search is always on. Extrapolated into an extreme, imaginary situation, if all the little and big searching expeditions indulged in by mankind can somehow be brought to a halt, the world as it is would become a different place. It would resemble the mummies and pyramids of the great Arabian deserts. Objects just staying put, never raising a finger in any kind of search.

Incidentally, you and I belong to the live and pulsating mankind that is dynamically and eternally involved in some kind of search. This very action of reaching out, enlisting Dr. Ramakrishnan's help in running an ad, urging him to make an exploratory visit for locating compatible people with whom contact can be made, shows you are involved in a search. On my part, priming my mind to swim through all the barriers of distance, culture, and whatnot, sending thousands of words to tell you of my existence, says that like you and every- body else, I am in a search too. We are aware of what we are searching for. As time moves on, as we get more confident and com- fortable communicating to each other at all levels of consciousness about every aspect that can ever be communicated, we will learn about each other's search. The final outcome of our efforts, the fruition of our searches, depends on whether we are on the lookout for something similar. If that is so, a natural, spontaneous process of "bonding" is bound to occur. This, in other words, is also called matching of chemistry, feeling some kind of peace, assurance, and calmness. Should we rush into things, or should we let time take its own course, let the process of searching, learning, and finding go on at their own pace?

Line drawing on the left side is a cartoon picture of yourself—a smile that is always there in all the pictures you sent me, curly hair, strong nose, solid jaw lines—holding a biconvex magnifying lens in hand . . . searching . . . On the right side is me, forever looking through a microscope, sometimes at bugs, sometimes at life, at people . . . but always looking and searching. And in the beginning

of our respective searches, I am wondering if we are looking for something similar. Hope you are not offended by this cartoon of yourself. I have a keen sense of humor. I always manage to see some funny aspect even in the most grim situation and can take humor sportingly. The sensitivity to feel the pulse of the situation is always there and I do love a hearty laugh. If you are offended by this picture, my apologies. Also, I hope that you will think over this concept of searching and let me know how you feel about it. If this idea does not amuse you at all, then I don't know what to say.
Well, bye.

With best regards . . . .
Vatsala

Your search &

my search

are same ... ?!

Dear Ehud,

Namaste.

I have yet again read your letter of 31.7.95. Would you like to
know how I look at two or three important issues? About decline in
spiritual values, yes, the cycle of time we are presently in needs to be
played out. You have put this concept beautifully. In thinking about it
further, I find it to be true. Like individuals, collective mankind also
has got its own cycle of rise and fall, of happy times and moments
of despair. Is it in anyone's control? If the unhappy event occurring
at a given moment is simply the way it has to be because it is as per
the design of a greater mind, this explains why, on occasion, well-
intentioned efforts at helping to relieve suffering and stress look
like mockingly insufficient patchwork that does not really solve the
problem, only covers it up for a while. Here comes the importance
of maintaining an inner calm while being in a turbulent external
situation. I do think about my immediate and distant environment
and watch the suffering borne by man. In my meditative moments,
I have never asked for an answer or an instant-shortcut redressing
of individual or collective human grievances. Since I see the whole
drama as a wish of God for man, instead of imposing my likes and
dislikes I ask my mind to be in the scene and yet remain detached,
accepting what comes with grace and with the faith that only that
happens that has to happen. This training of mind takes a big burden
off my shoulders. People nurture a false idea of being in control of
everything and everyone else. But people are only instruments,
pieces on a chessboard. This thought makes me cultivate a humane,
sympathetic approach to issues that affect people . . .

I am touched deeply by what you are looking for in a marriage.
Rather than generalizing the subject, may I take you to the specific
issues that can precipitate a mini-war in a household? I have seen
them happen, and I have thought about how they can be avoided or
solved so that nobody is hurt. For example, take things like volume
of the TV, responsibility for household chores, types of food, types
and number of guests, reading habits, manner of using the bathroom,
beds, and cupboards, and also whether the light should be on or off
when people go to bed . . . all of these issues can spark arguments

and fights and nurture divisive, negative attitudes in relationships between people living in a household (also add extra- and premarital affairs to the list). Do you think any of these issues can be solved by the use of physical force, violence, heated arguments, total withdrawal, criticism, or hurtful comments? I don't believe in these methods, which are the products of negative emotions. They at best can complicate a situation. My way of approaching each of these issues will be to make you feel free to express yourself, make you feel welcome in doing that, avail the same freedom for myself, and, with your active participation, work out the correct possibility that suits us both. Mutually suitable possibilities are not impossible to find if you and I are prepared to adjust to each other, rather than trying to change each other as per our likes and dislikes. Adjustments can often be made simply because there is a strong current of love between people, whereas the tendency to urge total or partial change is based on the presence of such factors as "might is right" or a general sense of disliking anything beyond the self. I might go to great lengths to accommodate all your whims and fancies, and you might do likewise, provided the relationship that binds us is based on trust and love. In the absence of that, any request for change might be perceived as a threat to individuality and might be met with revolt.

You might feel relieved to learn that I don't suffer from depressive mood fluctuations, don't brood, and don't indulge in crying fits to find my way around an issue. This is because I understand that these strategies don't help, and in my body, mind, and soul I have been blessed with good health. I do my best to maintain peace using all available methods. My own fear of hurting anyone is so big that I constantly keep vigil on all I do, say, and think such that I can curb hurtful tendencies. Finally, I have been loved a lot by my family despite my shortcomings, therefore I have, in gratitude, learned to make peace and give back love in abundance.

I am by nature a logical, careful, cautious person and I never abuse my body or mind, either internally or externally. I believe in and practice patience and moderation. I do not suffer from hypochondriac tendencies and do not use ailments as a means of drawing people's attention to me. A balanced way of life in tune with nature is a key to good health. Good health is the natural state of being.

I believe that illnesses—accidental/acute/chronic—indicate deviation from natural order and harmony. Once in a while it is natural, too, to become ill, and one must learn to cope with it and accept it gracefully. During any illness, when a person concentrates his energies on well-being, balance, and harmony of nature, healing comes naturally, requiring less external intervention. With these views, I see an ill person as someone who is off-center and needs to be brought to the center such that his body can recover and bounce back to its original state. And accidental illnesses appear to be nature's effective speed breakers— they tell us to look around, slow down, look inward, relax, rebuild our reserve, and then go on again with renewed vigor and vitality.

If God and the stars let us have a future together, I can assure you that I will ever and always be for peace and goodwill such that our relationship can survive the test of time. As they say, the proof of the pudding is in eating it. All that I appear to believe and claim has no meaning if I do not get an occasion to prove it. Shall I add that with all my patience I am waiting for that moment of action when I can demonstrate all that I have been telling you all through these days. Have no fear Ehud, we will be blessed.

Bye, will write later . . . .
Vatsala

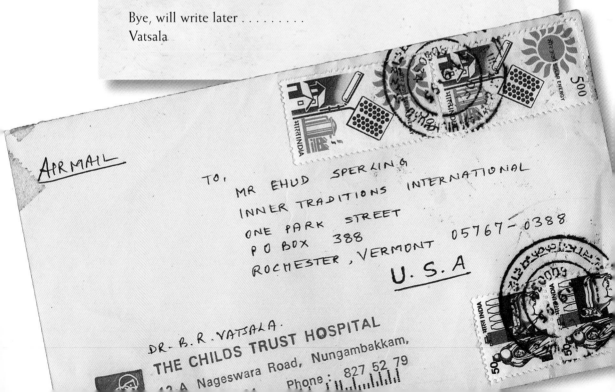

APR MAIL

TO,
MR EHUD SPERLING
INNER TRADITIONS INTERNATIONAL
ONE PARK STREET
P O BOX 388
ROCHESTER, VERMONT 05767 - 0388
U.S.A

DR- B.R. VATSALA.
THE CHILDS TRUST HOSPITAL
12 A Nageswara Road, Nungambakkam,
Phone : 827 52 79

Dear Ehud,

I am realizing again the value of the time we have spent in writing each other. It is "getting to know" in small, tolerable doses, in "privacy" but without the hazards of getting to know in private. If our friendship takes the shape of a durable relationship, I might type out all that you and I wrote to each other and read it in leisure, just to see how we educated ourselves about each other. How and exactly when the warm glow of appreciation, love, and acceptance made its presence conspicuous in this journey of two minds crossing the globe and reaching out to touch each other. How many time zones, cultural and ethnic differences, and how many countries this journey has crossed. Strange are the ways in which human interactions occur and I never cease to wonder whether it is God alone, man alone, or both God and man who are responsible for what happens to people, what goes on between them . . .

Did Dada come to you for the holidays? What happened with the horoscopes? Did he say nice things about our birth charts, or something that you found disturbing? Our future, present, and past are the product of what is called destiny or fate, but much of it depends on what we do with ourselves and with our potential as human beings.

Then before I forget, let me tell you that recently during my visit to the neonatology ICU, I saw a set of triplets and also a set of twins. Triplets each weighed around 900 grams and were absolutely cute. And the parents must be quite sporty, as they had brought colored booties, caps, and gloves for the three babies. However, the outfit was so oversized for the babies that one of the gloves could have fit three tiny hands at the same time. Incidentally, the babies were fine. After being delivered at home by a midwife, the mom and the bunch of kids were brought to our hospital to be looked at by the doctor. Well, in addition to the customary look by the doctor, which cost thousands of rupees for the family, the babies also got long, admiring stares from the in-house microbiologist (for free). I just could not help cuddling them. They just escaped getting kissed because I did not intend gifting them with bugs from my department.

The twins have a different story altogether. Their mom delivered them and dumped them in a waste bin. The babies were picked up by a passerby who brought them here to our hospital. Nurses had a hell of a time removing all the ants and dirt from the ears, mouth, and rest of the bodies of these babies. Presently both the kids are quite sick but it is hoped that they will be well soon, and will go home to the social welfare organization that takes in abandoned babies. Looking at these two little girls brings tears to my eyes, and I wonder if becoming a mother and feeling like a mother are the same or different. They must be very different . . . I understand so because the first one is a physical, physiological, anatomical, and hormonal accident or incident in the body. These events need not involve deep feelings, thoughts, and mind. On the contrary, feeling like a mother need not involve any of the aforementioned accidents or incidents in the body, and it is simply a state of mind in which the heart reaches out to anything/anyone, including all babies that need love, care, compassion, and protection. Shall I tell you that I have more respect for people who feel like mothers than for people who become mothers and ruthlessly dump their babies in the waste bin (for whatever reason).

If I were a married woman, I might have simply brought the kids home (to hell with society and people and their opinions). These children need homes to grow up in and learn that they must refrain from doing what their biological mother did to them. You can ask why I did not do it now? Well, at the moment I am willing to take on, but not fully prepared for, this commitment. I am very likely to do that—and for very many kids—if I remain single and reach my 40s. In my hospital a person can meet every year about 20 to 25 ready-made babies with no tags from the manufacturers. This is a very sad statement, but is true. And it says that the sociological problems of unwed mothers and orphans are present in India too, even though the culture and the religion boast of family values, respect for character, and chastity and respect for women. Add to that the stigma attached to the female child. No families come forward to adopt a female child who has been abandoned. If it happens to be a male child, there is a long queue of childless couples coming for adoption. That is being beggars as well as choosers, though the two are mutually exclusive.

I have grown to realize the numerous privileges that I have been born with. Instead of asking for more, I feel content just in thanking God for all His kindness and for all that I have been given and others have been denied.

May I close for now, and hope that you will find time to write back soon?

With love and best regards,
Vatsala

Dear Vatsala,

The air is beginning to cool, and the last rays of the sun are moving through the canopy of trees as we gallop past the meadows and streams of North Hollow. I'm riding Willow, a seven-year-old Arabian that has come to me untrained and inexperienced. She shies at the slightest provocation: a log on the ground, a change in the contour of the land, a sudden movement by a rabbit or squirrel. My riding partner and I are galloping through a wide and open field and for no reason whatsoever, Willow throws out her front legs and comes to a screeching stop. I go flying over her head and land on the ground, rolling. I immediately rise to my feet and lunge at her. She runs off at a frightened gallop. Ngurra and Morgan (a Belgian shepherd friend) do the most amazing thing. They run after Willow, approaching her left side, and force her into smaller and smaller circles, shepherding her to me. Thanks to Noogie and Morgan, she's now standing in front of me. I mount and we ride off. Noogie is loving our two or three rides a week. He runs 10 to 20 miles alongside me, and is becoming stronger and more powerful all the time. Gradually, Willow is also becoming quite a reliable, if a bit challenging, horse. She's learning to trust me and has started to become really affectionate, rubbing her nose on my back and shoulders after we've ridden, and no longer shying and spooking at the least provocation. We have a wonderful terrain in which to ride, with open meadows, deep forest trails, and unpaved roads. Willow is the fastest of the group of horses that go out with us. I ride with as few as one other rider, and as many as four others, most of them quite experienced and expert riders and well-trained horses, Willow being the exception.

That's news of Noogie. More news of me—and a longer letter—at another time. However, I do want to put your mind at ease about the influence of astrology on my life. The stars impel—they don't compel. When we breathe our first breath, we draw in the influences of the moment and fix our natal picture. However, it is my view that it is up to us to make the most of the pluses and minuses, the good and the bad, of our birth moment. The horoscope is a road map, indicating what we may expect on the journey. It is not, however, the journey itself.

I'm going to ask Dada to look at our compatibility when he visits me. He's uniquely qualified to do this, as he's known me for close to 20 years, has married off three daughters, has a thorough knowledge of the occult sciences, as well as the modern sciences, and is a traditional Hindu with a vast experience of the West. We'll look together at the horoscopes and our compatibility in an effort to see the problems and the strengths of an alliance. But I would *never ever* leave a matter of such great importance to only one of numerous considerations that would inform a decision of such magnitude. Our horoscopes are just one piece of the puzzle that would make up a satisfying, successful, and rewarding marriage.

So please don't be worried about this. In fact, you should be feeling quite good, as your assessment of me is definitely more on target than Ramakrishnan's. Shy? I don't recall ever being described that way and can't imagine what he was thinking of. You've described me as I am, which is a credit to your astuteness. I'm glad to hear that the stars are favoring you in work and your profession. I look forward to seeing their glow reflected in your eyes in October. Until then, I remain,

Yours truly,
Ehud

*Noogie and the horses love to frolic
in the White River, which is close to my home.*

Ehud, my dear,

I'm absolutely relieved to learn from you that "stars impel, they do not compel." With this mention of how you look at astrology, you have definitely put my mind at ease. I wish I could convey how happy I'm feeling at the moment, and how grateful I am to you for considering the horoscope as a road map and not the journey itself. You have, with your brief and warm note, taken a big worry off my shoulder. Thank you so much, Ehud.

When I wrote to you about how I felt regarding horoscopes and the great Indian fixation that ruins many lives, I just did not know how you would react, nor could I make any learned guess. I felt that my interactions with you were not a game of chess where calculated moves assure victory. In interacting with you, in reaching out to you, I would rather stress a spontaneous, natural approach, because I am not interacting with you to win or lose. It is an action of reaching out and trying to touch you with a far greater purpose . . . that is, if God wishes, to belong to you totally and have the honor and pride of you belonging to me. In this belonging, winning and losing have no place, as it is a total assimilation of one person into the other. When you requested my horoscope, I asked my mind to learn to respect your wish, but not to comply mechanically with your request. In doing that, my views on this star-studded road map came to you with all their spontaneity. They just had to, without the fear of losing or winning.

Ehud, shall I repeat that I am immensely thankful to you for taking a worry off my head? I appreciate your views in this regard, and my respect for you has definitely registered an all-time peak (there are many more peaks yet to come, as I am sure the more I learn about you, the more I will discover reasons to respect you). I will never ever worry about stars. Yes, you did make me feel quite good with your reassurance and with your strong compliment about my assessment of you. I did not know I was so near the target. Well, that is one example of intuition.

Your description of horseback riding . . . it is sending a chill shiver up my spine. You appear like a hero out of a Hindi movie . . . full of superhuman stunts . . . riding the horse, flying off her head and landing on the ground, rising again, lunging at her . . . my God, this is wild adventure for me . . . something like car racing, paratrooping. I am beginning to get concerned about your safety. I hope you will take all precautions in this wild game. News about Noogie was nice. Give him a huge bear hug for me. For Madam Willow, I only hope that she will learn to trust you completely and will stop throwing you off her back (for my sake).

Now that you have put my mind at peace, I am glowing with happiness and will wait patiently for your longer letter and then for you to arrive here.

With best wishes and with earnest prayers for safe horseback riding,

Yours sincerely . . . .
Vatsala

P.S. Ehud, would you like to know one aftereffect of your letter of 7.8.95? It has made me ecstatic for God-knows-what-reason, and as a result I am just not able to concentrate on my work. I have spent quite some time thinking about you and writing this note to you. I intend to post it right this evening. Considering that I do work hard as a habit, taking time off working hours to focus on you does not bother my workaholic conscience. It is 3 P.M. I am rushing to the post office to send this letter and will get back just in time to go for my NICU rounds. I can always put in extra hours of work to compensate for the time used up in thinking about you and writing to you. Well, you are a distraction, and the beauty is I do not mind being distracted at all—rather I welcome it with all my heart.

Left to right: *Me with my younger sister Debby and my mother Ima against a backdrop of Lake Champlain at sunset; Me and my father, Aba, before the boat set sail; You are asking, "Why is he holding that twine? Have someone's pants fallen down?" Actually it was given to me just as I stepped up to the podium, as the twine is made of 100 percent hemp and we are publishing a book on the subject; From left to right: Bob Amberger, art director and photographer; Annabelle Westling, one of my closest friends in Vermont. She works with emotionally disturbed people and has a wonderful and generous heart. Robert Williams, Annabelle's husband and my architect. He designed both my home and the addition to our office. Sharyn Amberger, Bob's wife and a great dancer. Me. Doon Hinderyxck, the biking Viking. He runs Green Mountain Bikes, a bike shop in town, has a degree in fine arts, and is the local pied piper—all the children in town follow him. Below: My staff and I. Yes, there are a lot of good-looking women, but have no fear, they are all married.*

chapter 6

MITZVOTH

September 11, 1995

Dear Vatsala,

Your letters arrived, along with 150 people (including my mother and father, and my sister and brother-in-law). I took them all on a cruise on Lake Champlain in celebration of the 20th anniversary of Inner Traditions. We were quite concerned, as the temperatures have been falling and we had a number of chilly nights before the party. Fortunately, it warmed up that day and we had a balmy night on the lake, cruising around to the sounds of Mango Jam (a local band) and eating dishes prepared out of our books *The Healing Cuisine, Mostly Macro*, and *Fruit Sweet and Sugar Free*.

The party was a great success: everyone thoroughly enjoyed themselves and I got to dance for two hours nonstop. It was a truly exhilarating evening. I honored my parents, as well as colleagues who have been with the firm a long time, with a speech that was short and well received.

I'm enclosing some photos so you can join in the party, at least a bit, from a distance.

The next day, as soon as all the guests left from my house and the partygoers traveled back to their homes, I got a phone call from Patty Harvey, my vice president of operations, telling me that John Baker, the husband of one of our oldest and most-loved employees, Priscilla, had died. Just like that, at 51 years of age. This was a great shock and loss for all of us. Priscilla and John were an ideal couple, married for 28 years, parents of two sons who turned out really well, and still, after all these years, very much in love and the best of friends. They were an example to all of us.

When I went to visit with Priscilla the next day, she said to me that if there was any solace to be taken out of this, it was that she and her husband spent their last night together cruising hand in hand, watching the sun set at our 20th anniversary party, and that he died in her presence, without suffering and without lingering. Four days after the party, our whole staff and close colleagues were again all together, but this time at John's funeral. The church was packed, with standing room only. We heard a eulogy from John's boss, and then the minister asked if anyone else wished to say anything. I thought to myself, *Well, I had best get up and say something*, and in the moment that I was collecting my thoughts, up to the podium stepped Deborah Kimbell, who, unbeknownst to me, had decided on and prepared a eulogy for John. (Deborah basically runs Inner Traditions, is a very close friend, and is the only person with whom I've shared our correspondence. She's been telling me since the beginning that you were the one for me . . .) Deborah spoke with extraordinary eloquence, capturing all our sentiments about John and Priscilla in a way that was heartfelt and genuine. There wasn't a single dry eye in the church.

Later on, at the gathering after the burial, I was talking to Deborah's husband, Steve, and commenting on the eulogy Deborah had delivered. I said, "Boy, you're a lucky man." His response was "Well, so are you. We share her, don't we?" I thought to myself, *How extraordinary, how self-possessed and self-aware. He has no doubt about the love and commitment of his wife, and consequently can take pleasure and pride in her accomplishments and relationships with others*. I told him how I had grown to feel a great deal of affection for him, even though we had not spent much time together. This was due to what Deborah felt for him; her feelings had permeated my feelings. What's so special to me about Steve's reaction is how unusual and unlikely the "normal, healthy, positive" reaction is.

As I and my company have a strong presence and dynamic influence on the women who work for Inner Traditions, this is often threatening to a husband, or the husband will wish to ignore or deny our importance in the life of his wife. So how fantastic, how refreshing, when a healthy and secure man happens to be the husband, and also happens to have an uncomplicated and, as Deborah would say, "perfect," relationship.

The day after the funeral, Harish Johari and company arrive. Dada comes with his two old friends, Carmen and Mavis. He says, "Ehud, I am the host now and you are now the guest." So they cook up a storm, and people show up from all over the place. A friend from Bareilly who now lives in Montreal appears, other people are coming and going, lots of food is being cooked, and I get to simply enjoy.

I sent Dada your horoscope prior to his arrival in Vermont. He took time to convert your chart into the system he works with and to do numerous calculations, and soon after he arrived, when everyone settled down, he and I sat down in my study to discuss the

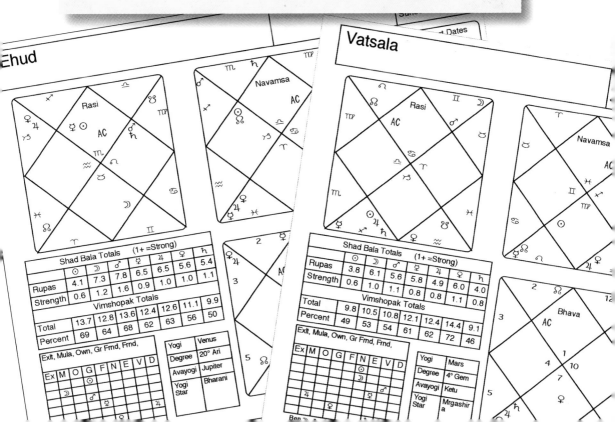

Ehud

Rasi

Shad Bala Totals						(1+ =Strong)	
	☉	☽	♂	☿	♃	♀	♄
Rupas	4.1	7.3	7.8	6.5	6.5	5.6	5.4
Strength	0.6	1.2	1.6	0.9	1.0	1.0	1.1

Vimshopak Totals							
Total	13.7	12.8	13.6	12.4	12.6	11.1	9.9
Percent	69	64	68	62	63	56	50

Exlt, Mula, Own, Gr Frnd, Frnd,

| Ex | M | O | G | F | N | E | V | D |
| | | | | | | | | |

Yogi	Venus
Degree	20° Ari
Avayogi	Jupiter
Yogi Star	Bharani

Navamsa

AC

Vatsala

Rasi

Shad Bala Totals						(1+ =Strong)	
	☉	☽	♂	☿	♃	♀	♄
Rupas	3.8	6.1	5.6	5.8	4.9	6.0	4.0
Strength	0.6	1.0	1.1	0.8	0.8	1.1	0.8

Vimshopak Totals							
Total	9.8	10.5	10.8	12.1	12.4	14.4	9.1
Percent	49	53	54	61	62	72	46

Exlt, Mula, Own, Gr Frnd, Frnd,

| Ex | M | O | G | F | N | E | V | D |
| | | | | | | | | |

Yogi	Mars
Degree	4° Gem
Avayogi	Ketu
Yogi Star	Mrgashira

Navamsa

AC

Bhava

AC

horoscopes. (Take three deep breaths, slow down your heartbeat, have courage, and read on!)

It turns out we have very compatible horoscopes. In the category called *gunas*, or qualities, where the compatibility scoring is from 1 to 30, we achieve a 26. The compatibility is very good for home, wealth, and progeny. My house of romance is in your house of children, so my romance with you will be around children. There are chances for three to four children, two boys and one girl being the most likely. The best period for conception is the next two years.

Our horoscopes say that our bodies will like each other and that we'll make good bed partners. They also indicate that your mother and I will become good friends and have a close relationship. There's more, of course. However, I'll leave that for you and Dada to play with when you meet in October. As far as Dada's concerned, a marriage between us is now a fait accompli. He said he does not even need to meet you; just based on the horoscope, your photo, and reading a little bit of your letter, he is certain that a marriage would be successful.

You must be asking yourself, How is Ehud taking all of this? Well, it all seems quite extraordinary, given my background and upbringing in the West, where the development of this kind of relationship simply doesn't exist, where people don't engage in marriage discussions until well after meeting and (in most cases) sleeping together. The usual scenario is: boy meets girl, they fall in love, they make love, they move in together, they live together for a period of time, they decide they're compatible, and then they get married.

So I, as someone coming out of this culture, am taking a big departure and a step in a very different direction. Everything on paper seems quite perfect: the shared goals and values, the intelligence that shines through your letters, the commitment to virtues that I am also committed to. It is all quite remarkable.

The Hindu tradition and the Jewish tradition share many fundamental values. They are both highly focused on the family, children, education, tolerance, a universality and acceptance of other points of view. All of this feels very good and proper. I've also learned in working with so many women over so many years that you really do grow to love the people who are close to you and share your goals, aspirations, and values. I can honestly say that my capacity to love has been expanded in my relationships with others, and that that love has not been limited or restricted by gender, or economic circumstance, or social, cultural, or religious background.

So in me is the capacity to make this decision and move forward in this way without fear or hesitation. Doubt does not enter my mind. I do not equivocate. So the question becomes, How will I feel when I meet you? Will all of the matters stated above cause me to commit my life to you? Will our meeting cause doubts to enter our minds? Questions? A need for more time to reflect and understand? What in us will decide? What voice will we listen to? Who indeed will make this decision? I simply cannot answer these questions. They are part of a mystery greater than I, and I just pray to God for the guidance to see clearly and act with wisdom.

My dear Vatsala, let us try to set aside our fears and worries and meet each other without trepidation, opening our hearts without expectations or fixed ideas, but letting the spirit move us and have what's true and appropriate realized.

I have read your letters over and over again and am quite moved, as well as delighted, by their content. I, too, am on a search—a search for meaning. Why bother with all this life activity, these interactions and relationships, building homes and businesses, traveling the world, discovering other cultures? All this incredible activity is only of value if it creates meaning in one's life.

I have been on a search for meaning since as far back as I can remember. Even as a young schoolboy, I would question my teachers as to the meaning of what they were saying. I excelled in mathematics, and would ask questions such as "What is the meaning of the square root of 2?" My teachers were incredulous—"What *is* he going on about?" It was only later that I discovered that in the square root of two, the golden mean, and other sacred measures were the keys to transcendence and an understanding of the deeper mysteries of creation. These things were not to be found in school, but rather in my own search for meaning.

Can there be a meaningful life without a wife and a family? For most of humanity, including myself, the answer must be no. In woman is the possibility of man's realization. In devotion to her and family are reflected the virtues of that greater devotion to God, which can only be realized through action—or in the Judaic tradition, *mitzvoth*, loosely translated as "good deeds." The deeper meaning is to be an instrument of truth and beauty in all your actions.

I'm in complete accord with your sentiments around marriage and what makes for a happy home. I trust in God that your "fears" would not be realized in a relationship with me (my horns only come out in defense of the family and those I love . . .). I do not, however, believe that a man and a woman can be "equal." This concept has gained a lot of popularity, but I've never in my experience seen it practiced. Equal, which is a mathematical term, means an equivalent sum on either side of the equation. It seems to me that relationships are dynamic; if they were truly equal, they would be at rest, hence, dead.

I see no equality between men and women. As the saying goes, "Women are born, men are created through culture." A woman, by her very physical nature, has within her the power to create life and the initiation of life and death, blood and pain. By the very act of giving birth, she is initiated into a new and different state of consciousness, that of a mother. She has to face the potential of death during childbirth, the great pain and suffering, which is mixed in blood and is the only portal through which humanity may enter this world. Men, on the other hand, have to be made. Through life and experience, through pain and suffering, they have to be formed into real men. Being born with the physical organ does not make a man. Men are known by their actions.

It has been my experience in life that women are the better part of humanity. I have met many more women of quality than I have men. This is not a statement about men per se, but rather about the culture and society in which we're currently living. It is not very successful in creating men. Thank God that women do not need these external sources to become women, that they are born women and consequently, the world has some possibility for a future. It is through women, acting as the first teachers to their children, that virtue and principles can be propagated in this world. It is through mothers whispering in the ears of their children that the world will change, not through the laws and armies of men. So I do not wish to treat you as an equal, but rather to honor you for what you are, a woman.

Your list of dos and don'ts should be included in our marriage contract. I would insist that everyone in my family live by them, and I would not change or alter any of the thoughts expressed in them. May I add a few of my own that are somewhat covered in yours, but bear expressing?

DO: Love, honor, and obey your husband and accord him his rightful place as head of household.

DON'T: Challenge, criticize, contradict, or ridicule him.

DO: Expect your husband to put you and family before his own interests.

DON'T: Be demanding.

I'm adding these because my life experience has been such that I've always been the ultimate and final authority on decisions and matters that surround me. Having recognized early on that my decisions and authority had significant and deep ramifications on other people, I decided that the only way for me to feel good about being in such a situation was to put the truth and others before my own interests and desires. Now, I find that there is no conflict between myself and what I need to do, that I most often operate from a sense of certitude, that the people around me are supportive and help me "tune in" to what is the best possible decision for everyone. This inner tuning is what guides me. I never allow myself to make an important decision or take action when I am unhappy or angry, sad, or in any other way off-center. I simply wait patiently to return to myself, and then act.

It's very important for me that my wife recognizes this, supports it, and is able to place her trust in me and my judgment. This is not to say or in any way imply that any decision that faced the family would not be explored in depth and in detail and with complete openness with my wife before I make a decision. Even in my work, I hardly ever make a decision that is not based on consensus. I go to great pains to explore the issues and garner support before making a final determination. However, I do make the final determination. The same thing needs to be true at home with wife and children.

I'll give you an example of how I work with Deborah, who, as I said, runs the company, particularly in my absence. We discuss all decisions of consequence to the company, from the sublime to the ridiculous. I've never made a decision that Deborah didn't agree with.

When an issue presented itself recently where we had differing points of view and we each saw a different approach as being appropriate, there was never any question about me making the final decision. However, seeing that Deborah didn't "feel good" about my decision, I did not make it. Rather, I continued to work through the feelings around the issues until Deborah felt good about it. When we both were feeling really good, I made the decision. At the same time this was happening, I told Deborah that I was fully prepared to follow her view on the matter and make a completely different decision if it would make her feel better. She, of course, didn't want me to do that, although I was absolutely prepared to do it, even though I thought it was the wrong decision. We both worked through it and finally reached a consensus, and I made a decision that we were both happy with.

Keep in mind that I'm a decision-making machine. Every day, I make endless decisions, all having financial, emotional, and psychological ramifications. Somehow life has handed me this role and I've taken it to heart. A saint in India once told me quite perceptively to give up on the idea of being an ascetic, that that idea was from a past life, that I had already done that trip. He said, "In this life, you must act." And acting I am. Any wife of mine needs to be prepared for that life of activity and action, and provide a fertile ground of love and support, nurturing and devotion, so that my actions may be graced with the spirit of the feminine, the *Shakti* that's in all of us.

I think your concepts of privacy and individuality around the subject of nudity are romantic and charming and I can fully support them. I see your view as similar to that of the hidden and covered nature of the central deity in the temple—only brought out for special occasions, for worship. So there's really no need to talk to me about it; I'm already with you on the matter.

Nevertheless, I have been in cultures, remote and far off, that don't wear clothing. I feel completely comfortable in these environments, just as I do when wearing a dinner jacket or tuxedo at a formal gathering. The problem nowadays is really, as you say, atmosphere. A few hundred years ago, women in the south of India were barebreasted. Today, nothing is exposed except the flesh from the upper arm to the fingertips. Why is this? What has happened?

Psychotropic plants are not addictive. This is from a scientific/ medical point of view. Narcotics are. They create biological addictions. Having grown up in the United States in the 1960s, I was exposed to all these things. So you're probably wondering, What happened? Well, I learned to have a healthy respect for the tradition of psychotropics. I have published *Plants of the Gods* by Dr. Schulte, the world's leading ethnobotanist and professor emeritus at Harvard University. This book is considered the definitive work on the subject.

I have received a lot in the way of understanding from these healing plants. Ganja came with Shiva and is taken in devotion to him. I have found it to be the most beneficial and helpful of these plants. The other psychotropics are too powerful and dramatic in their effects for any regular use. No one could become addicted to them; to the contrary, one could become frightened and avoid them. So you're probably asking yourself, What is he addicted to? Nothing. I simply don't have that kind of a mentality. I did smoke cigarettes many years back, decided that they weren't good for me, went out and bought a carton, put it on a shelf so that I would feel confident that the object of my addiction was present, and never smoked another cigarette. The biochemistry was such that I felt a craving. This craving would rise up in my mind and tell me to have a cigarette. I would acknowledge this voice, but never do what it said. Soon the physical craving, finding no comfort in me, left my body, never to return.

I don't drink alcohol, smoke cigarettes, or indulge in any excess of any kind, whatsoever. I may occasionally take a drink when offered it socially, even smoke a cigarette in India, where so many people do. However, I have no interest in these substances. I do drink coffee every day, but again, it is of no consequence to me and I can stop, as I do when I'm in India or in other places where coffee is not consumed. For me, the addiction is to meaning and truth—I'm hung up on these things, and I don't think I'll let go.

As I'm sure you're beginning to realize through my letters, I have an absolute commitment to the values, traditional verities, and ground upon which spirituality rests. Along with this, I have a free and open attitude toward life, which can manifest itself in very unconventional and wild experiences. A person seeing me in a suit and tie at the head of a publishing company might be quite shocked to find me in the longhouse of a shaman deep in the Amazon jungle. Or sitting with babas smoking a *chillum*. However, it's the same Ehud, the same commitments are there. So this package comes with a warning label: BE PREPARED FOR THE UNEXPECTED AND UNCONVENTIONAL. A GREAT SENSE OF FUN AND HUMOR NECESSARY.

With best wishes,
Sincerely . . . .
EHUD

Well, this letter of 11 September did not disappoint me, just as Ehud's previous letters had not. I did come across some new thoughts/ideas that were cruising his mind and that made me do some of my own thinking: 1) examining my own Hindu cultural heritage; 2) stock taking of my total situation, both past and present; 3) examining the social milieu in which I had lived and breathed so far; and 4) clarifying for myself, without any trace of doubt, what I needed and was looking for in a man.

The Hindu culture: Not that I am any kind of expert on Hindu culture, but, yes, since that is my heritage, I have at least a little understanding of its basic tenets and prescriptions for a happy, balanced life. Regarding the place of the woman in Hindu culture and society, the wise sages of the past composed a *shloka,* a verse in Sanskrit: "*Naarya yatra poojyante, ramante tatra devataa.*" Translated into English, this verse means "Gods reside in the place where women are worshipped."

I interpret this idea in my own way—wherever the feminine part of the creative energy (Shakti) is worshipped, the masculine part of the same creative energy is very happy to reside there, because in the cosmic energy field the feminine and masculine energies do not oppose, contrast, or negate each other. The whole cosmos could be created (by Nature or by God) only because the feminine and masculine energies supported, complemented, and enhanced each other, creating a unit that became greater than each single energy source. It is not the female body or anatomy that is being worshipped per se, but rather the creative feminine energy . . . I believe so from my heart.

My past and present situation: Although I was born after my dear parents already had four daughters and a son, they did not see me as . . . Oh! yet another mouth to feed, yet another dowry issue. They saw me as a little human being who gave them one more opportunity to express their love and sense of commitment. In my own home I never felt my parents extending any special favors to any particular child . . . male or female . . . We were all given the same love, caring, comfort, food, opportunities for self-expression, education, and growth. And those formative years grilled it deep and strong in me that the world belongs to me just as much as it belongs to a man. I don't have to draw any special attention to myself because I am a woman; I must always strive to become a better human being who also happens to be a woman. This is what I saw my parents do—my mother was never a slave and servant to my father. My father never behaved as the tyrannical lord and master of his flock. He treated my mother with utmost gentleness, respect, and courtesy, and extended all the love, reverence, and honor she so richly deserved. He always kept my mother and us above his own needs, whims, and fancies. In turn my mother treated him with consideration, care, love, concern, respect, and a pure sense of worship and devotion. There were never any ego battles. The two were complementary, supportive, nurturing, and worshipful of each other in public and in private. It is from such a home that I came out to taste the world on my own.

In my professional career I made an independent living, and over the years I developed a solid reputation for professional integrity and competence. My word carried some weight; when I spoke to my colleagues—be it men or women—about my views on any topic of my specialty, they listened to me carefully. Nobody took me lightly or brushed me aside and under the carpet just because I was a woman. And no one gave me any special favors or credits just because I was a woman.

My upbringing and my professional life made me strong enough not to feel the need to use a man as my walking stick or doormat. I was not afraid to challenge, criticize, and demand good response and behavior from a man if I felt it was necessary. I could not be ruled, dominated, ill-treated, enslaved, subjugated, or used as an object of entertainment and procreation by any man. And if I ever felt that any man was trying to toy with my femininity, I knew instinctively that he was inviting serious trouble.

The social milieu in which I grew up: Well, the picture is not all that rosy. In modern-day India, as press coverage attests, even though women have become equal to or smarter than their male counterparts in many, many areas of life, there are still ongoing incidents of female infanticide, dowry-related deaths (murders) of women, and other negative aspects that threaten a small percentage of women. Fortunately, I happened to belong to the greater majority of women who were treated well in the Indian society, and so there was no need in me to submit to a man only because he happened biologically to be a man.

What I needed and was looking for in a man: Well, obviously, it was not simply his sex organ. This was just one of the slightly interesting features in a man's anatomy. But for a man to command any respect and attention from me, he must be a refined, sensible, decent, and wise human being who would treat me well simply because I am a good human being (like him), and not because I have a better figure than his previous girlfriend.

So the whole thing was about two human beings treating each other well. In that equation, their individual sexuality did play a role, but not the predominant, decisive role.

When I got around to reading the "thoughts/ideas" part of Ehud's letter of 11 September, I smelled the presence of the concept "Gods reside where women are worshipped." His treatment of women (feminine energy) was about good deeds, appropriate gestures, truth and beauty. I did not find the slightest streak of male chauvinism, which I was very sensitive to and very capable of revolting against. He did not intend to treat me—the woman—as *a female,* he intended to treat me as *feminine energy* . . . and that was quite fine with me.

As I read on I could not but agree with his belief that "women are born, men are created through culture," and that "women are the better part of humanity." My own observations on Hindu culture, Indian history, and the present-day Indian society had strongly convinced me about the strength, integrity, and capabilities of feminine energy. Ehud held similar beliefs and observations, and was not just trying to please me, woo me, win me over, or curry favors with me.

After agreeing to and accepting my set of dos and don'ts pertaining to general human behavior, Ehud had come up with situations specifically applicable to married couples. Essentially, if my set of dos and don'ts were followed in a husband-and-wife relationship, I figured, there would never arise the need for the wife to challenge, criticize, contradict, or ridicule her husband. And she would never have to be demanding, because a husband who also religiously followed the set of dos and don'ts would command (as opposed to demand) love, honor, and obedience from his wife, and would win his rightful place in his family by always putting their needs before his.

I wondered what would have been my reaction to these lines had Ehud written them to me in his very first letter, saying this is what he expected from his Indian wife. What reaction did he expect from me now, when so fearlessly he had said something which was, at surface value, politically incorrect not only in his own country . . . USA . . . but also in mine . . . India . . . where, according to traditional roles, obedience is not seen as a negative trait? I am sure I would have been annoyed and angry, and most likely I would have gone off the handle. I would have never replied to him, asking myself, why did he expect me to *obey* him? Is he thinking that women from India are easy game— that they have no independence, that they have been raised in a servile, suppressive, male-dominated environment and will therefore willingly submit to a man just because he is a man?

Well, from Ehud's letters, I understood that he was by no means a male chauvinistic pig. He seemed to respect me as a human being and he expected that I would have a similar respect for him. Moreover from my letters so far, he had a more than clear perspective of what I was all about, and I had given him enough hints that he could not afford to treat me as a lesser being. So what about my list of "dos and don'ts" that I wrote to him in my letter of 7 August? I pulled out a copy of that letter and read it again. After scrutinizing it carefully, I found that in that list, not once had I mentioned the words *man* or *woman*. The entire list was about expected optimum, positive human behavior, and this behavior could be the foundation stone for any possible form of human relationship leading to goodwill and peace, acceptance and love.

After reading this letter of 11 September, my whole correspondence with Ehud took on a new meaning, purpose, and depth. And a sense of relief came over me: well, this man was as committed to sound and sensible human behavior as I was.

His decision-making process did sound democratic, but not 100 percent democratic. As I examined my reaction to his description of this process, I had to review his background in business. After all, he had started his company single-handedly, and twenty years later he had more than thirty-five employees and close to five hundred titles in print that sold in twenty-eight countries all over the world. He could not be hollow, stupid, or insane. And to manage his enterprise, he needed to have some practical insight into human strengths and weaknesses, some leadership qualities, some certitude about right and wrong, some sense of timing, and also some courage to put his ideas into action. From what I had learned so far about his views on feminine energy and family, if he applied his sense of certitude to the home front, making decisions concerning household issues, wife, and children, he would be careful not to make a fool of himself. He must have learned to take responsibility for the consequences of his decisions and to use all his intelligence, courage, and willpower to avoid bitter failures.

Well, I thought, *here is a man with a functional, upright, intact vertebral column. His cervical vertebrae hold his head in the right place and give it the angle of rotation for maximum vision.* And again a sense of relief flooded me. With this man, I could let my defenses down. I would not need to take up arms and raise my voice to defend myself and assert my femininity. I could trust his wise judgments, and I could count on him if and when the need arose.

Thank God, finally I had met a complete human being who happened to be a man (or, in my view, an expression of masculine energy), and all I needed was to merge with him and try to create a unit stronger, more powerful, and larger than each of us—something greater than the sum total of the two of us.

20.9.95

Dear Ehud,

Want to know what effect your letter of 11.9.95 had on me? It relaxed me and it had the most soothing effect. Before it came, I went through all phases of anxiety, and once it arrived, I just felt totally at ease, as if my anxiety had never existed. Next, do you want to know in what condition the packet arrived? The envelope was torn and so were the pages, across the width. The envelope with photos was also torn. (Your message, of course, retained its pristine beauty.) I cursed the person who did it. Would you like to try DHL or Blue Dart (the Indian counterpart of the American company Federal Express)? It will be more expensive, but your letters are precious to me and I do not want anyone else to lay their dirty hands on them. I think I will go through your letter many times, simply to make up for all the days I have been longing to hear from you and I did not get a word.

I am not worried about beautiful women, married or otherwise, and just so you need not worry about men I meet. I do trust you, I need to, and I hope you too will trust me when it comes to my inter- action with men.

Nice meeting Debby, Ima, and Aba in the pictures. Hope to meet them in person soon some day and I hope to strike a chord of friend- ship and closeness with them. The sunset in the background is beautiful, I never tire of admiring nature. I am very sorry about your colleague's husband passing away.

That was smart of Dada to transform you to guest and himself to host. I thank God for all his good predictions for our horoscopes. Romance with me around children? Better. You are most welcome. With the possibility of three or four kids I am happy, and won't mind a few more if our biological clocks permit us. I never knew horoscopes could predict even physical compatibility by way of our bodies liking each other. We had better be compatible in the room from where many domestic storms begin. For me, this entire drama of compatibility begins in the mind. If the top story is compatible, the rest, kids and all, follow naturally. (What is fait accompli? Please excuse my ignorance and tell me if it means "certain" or "almost certain.")

That is interesting, including the additions to the list of dos and don'ts in our marriage contract. Where shall we put the list up . . . in the kitchen or in the bedroom? About your additions, well, I agree, I do not intend to alter them. I am for both the dos. I will never challenge, contradict, or ridicule you, and will never be demanding. And this agreement between us is unconditional. In one of my previous letters, I told you that the children will be made to understand that their father is the center and axis around which the household revolves. There cannot be two power centers, two axes, two contradicting forces, and two opposing individuals in a single home. For the good of everyone, a willing merger is a wise step that I look forward to taking.

So far, I have understood about you that you are the boss. I understand also that you are a democratic boss. Getting along with a democratic boss at home will be my unique pleasure because democracy, which I respect and love, is based on a sound sense of justice, fairness, and priority to duties (not rights). Let these basic concepts go and see how the grand edifice of democracy comes crumbling down. I think it is because you are a democratic boss that you have such a wonderful friendship and working relationship with Deborah. You both are mutually lucky. From what you have written about her and her husband, I think I already like him. I wonder what prompted Deborah to tell you all along that I am the one for you. Incredible. Please tell her I thank her immensely for her support.

Your mathematical definition of equal impressed me. As man and woman, we are and we will remain unequal such that there is always some potential difference, and the current of compassion and love can run sometimes from me to you and sometimes from you to me.

What you have said about the popular concept of man and woman being equal may raise many a feminist brow. On the face of it, the statement is shocking and it stinks of a chauvinistic male attitude. (My eyebrows remained firmly in place and I did not smell any chauvinism; stay relaxed, Captain!) My response to your statement was just calm and normal because you have given me the privilege of sharing your logic about what goes into the making of a man and a woman. Yes, women are born and men need to be made and identified by their actions. Very correct indeed, but both have exceptions.

To a man of substance, or say to a man whose identity is his actions, a woman never hesitates to give herself, lose her identity in merging completely into him, with him. Such a man, with the merit of his action, commands (as opposed to demands) such a total merger of identities . . . And in doing that with such a man, a woman never feels loss of face, loss of her personality and identity. In fact, what she feels is what I have just told you . . . a part of her—stronger, more powerful, more assertive than her—being restored to her. This is the union for which she is made, and if this occurs, she will feel the fulfillment that she so richly deserves.

This is a very delicate equation where, according to you, equality of the two components means death; a=a is nil, of course, it makes sense. To keep an equation alive, potential difference must be maintained. How big a potential difference ensures healthy survival of the equation? The equation $a=a^\infty$ (to the power infinity) will cease to exist because there is a very big potential difference; they will bang, clash, crash, and nullify each other. Is this what is meant by the 1 to 30 score you mentioned? Scoring 1 on a scale of 30, like $a=a^\infty$, may not give a positive result. Scoring all 30 is like a=a. I think that according to Dada, what we have scored is good enough to avoid nullification and assure healthy maintenance of the equation in a live state.

By now, as much as you know me, you must have realized that here is a woman who can merge beautifully in seeking completion and fulfillment with a man of substance who commands such a merger by being what he is. His qualities as a human being matter to me most. Mine is however, not a blind, mindless, subjugated, dictated, and desperate submission to the physical mantle of man. To merge with a man, his maleness and the substance and character that define him, I must see some sense in the whole package. I wasn't blinded with passion even when I was younger and very vulnerable. I am not blinded with passion now either, when I am anything but vulnerable.

If you are that man and I am that woman that our ancient scriptures describe as two halves of a creative power, then I have no fear, Ehud, Captain—our merger will fill us with peace. It will restore us to ourselves. We will gain by losing ourselves to each other. It will be a different kind of equation and mathematics. Have you noticed I have been addressing you as Captain? Do you mind? Anyone dear to me gets some name from me. For example, Amma at home is called *Ammu kutty* (= "mommy baby"). If you don't mind, between the two of us I might call you Captain or Boss or whatever comes to mind. It implies that you are dear to me.

I have been so humored by your description of yourself as a decision-making machine that I feel quite comfortable letting you decide for me, take the lead, initiative, and responsibility. For once, I can just be carefree about myself because of the assurance that your decisions will be made with sense, wisdom, and practical consideration.

Remember, in one of my earlier letters I told you that I am fond of you and like being in touch, and will tell you exactly when I feel the first warm glow of love for you? Shall I make a confession and tell you it is now? Well, Ehud, do not be shocked. Please take it gracefully. I have not met you yet, and for sure I do not know how we would react to each other on meeting personally. But as far as the mind that you have put forth in the form of your thoughts and ideas, via the medium of printed words . . . I do love that mind (and I am hopeful the rest of the course will follow naturally). With hope and without unnatural expectations I am looking forward to meeting you. I do hope we will come to a positive decision without being clouded by fear, mistrust, or uncertainty.

With love and best regards,
Vatsala

Dear Ehud,

Well, coming to some news, the most sensational is that on 22.9.95, Ganesha, the elephant-headed god, drank milk in almost every temple all over India. This news was flashed by BBC on the TV. I took Amma along at about 9 P.M. to a nearby temple and we both saw the event. Immediately, rationalists and spiritualist groups have begun arguing about the impossibilities and possibilities of the event. I am on neither side. I took it as something uncommon and interesting . . . the darling Ganesha gulping away gallons of milk to the absolute amazement of the stunned onlookers. Amma was thrilled; she made milk from milk powder, added sugar to it, and tried feeding our Ganesha at home. But by now it was 11 P.M. and Ganesha must have been very tired of drinking milk, and sleepy too, so he refused to drink her offering, in turn disheartening his old fan. Our hospital Ganesha drank liters of milk all through 22 September.

Next, my next-door neighbor is keen that I help her with Tanjore art. I am starting that on Sunday. It is a creative medium and a very unique style of Indian art. It is traditional too, originating long back in the temple art of Tanjore, in South India. I have decided to learn, practice, and master it by way of helping my neighbor. I might try popularizing this art form in the future, and, Captain, if you decide about letting me be your wife, then what about letting me have an art studio at home where I can paint, draw, and study in the time I will get (if any) after being with you. Think about it, and relax, I am not demanding any of it, OK?

Ehud, writing to you or, say, speaking to you via the medium of written words gives me a healthy diversion. It takes my mind off the impending issues, for a while at least, and when I try getting back to work, it happens with increased zest and enthusiasm. Is this what communication does to people? People may talk less or be a chatterbox, be a dumb listener or active listener, or dominate the conversation with a me-me-me-me attitude . . . but communicate they must, or else the bridge that links people to people gets swayed away.

Ganesha, painted by Harish Johari.

At home when I have a choice between watching TV or going to a gathering where I alone am invited, I prefer putting the TV off, avoiding the invitation, and staying at home with Amma to talk to her, listen to her. And so we communicate. The trend was the same when all her kids were still at home and not yet married. We always got together as a group . . . during meal times, prayer times, study times, or simply anytime we could manage to be together. And we listened to each other, spoke to each other. Decisions, however small or big, were taken after several rounds of discussions, and if made by an individual in a hurry and alone, were always explained later in detail, with all points for or against it. This open, democratic environment which encouraged freedom of self-expression (with due respect to manners, courtesy, code of conduct, sentiments, and others' individuality) encouraged us to pour ourselves out to others and, in turn, to absorb them into ourselves, i.e., to interact with understanding and without barriers. And friends as well as guests were never for just one of us. It could be a classmate of mine from my fifth-grade class dropping in to check about the homework, and that little person would be attended to by my father right down the line . . . me and all others in between. The little

One of our many family gatherings. Four generations are present.

guest would leave the house very reluctantly, feeling like a queen with all the attention showered on him/her by our entire household.

Having grown up in such a friendly, warm atmosphere, I wonder what my future household is going to be like. If that household is to be with you as its center and leader, will it echo with the fun and humor of a pleasantly shared moment? Will we let ourselves reach out and communicate (not just talking and listening mechanically)? Will we spend time doing things together, just being in each other's company, sharing the ups and downs of life? This is how I have grown up, and this is how I like to be, now and in the future, and I would pray to God to help me create a similar, positive environment in my household. I simply can't imagine my future family living with walls instead of bridges between its members.

Then Ehud, tell me how you feel about the role of communication in a family, and how you feel about the revival of my old passion, i.e., art? Have you ever wondered why I am so open in my communication with you? Now you have the answer . . . that is the way I am built . . . reach out, draw people out, interact with them, share a moment, share life. I have not known what living inside an isolated hole feels like, and I don't want to know this. I have always known that the environment that helps people be their true selves is the best one to perpetuate the culture of mankind, of love and human values. Ehud, if you are in the process of deciding about committing your life to me and helping me commit my life to you, then be prepared to meet a person who is communicative and will try to see that you too remain communicative. The biggest question right now is, Are we going to commit ourselves to each other's care, or will the hands of fate, having given us the privileged moments of sharing each other's life via the medium of letters, escort us back to our separate orbits and push us away and ahead in our own separate spiral of life? God-only-knows . . . I do not know . . . No matter what is the outcome of this entire exercise, I will be happy if you find peace and satisfaction in the way and in the direction in which events are moving.
May God bless you.

Sincerely,
Vatsala

27.9.95

Ehud,

First, may I say something about Amma? Presently she has completed making three rabbits—one mom and two baby rabbits. They are snow white, have sparkling red eyes, and are quite fluffy. Though on the face of it they are just lifeless imitations of rabbits, for me they are yet another example of thoughtfulness, originality, inquisitiveness, inventive pursuits, problem-solving capabilities, organization, concentration, consistency, hard work, ingenuity, fertile imagination, and enthusiasm present abundantly in my mother. Never mind if her bones are 75 years old, all but four of her teeth have fallen away, all but a few hairs are white, muscles have sagged, and she walks with effort—she is youthful, zestful, and perpetually creative at heart and in her mind. I am sure if she had any formal university education, she would have had several patents to her credit for her original inventions. I wish I had inherited at least a few of the talents that she is so richly blessed with. I simply admire her. It is not a mother fixation. It is a recognition of her capabilities. And think of it, after all the wonders she is capable of creating, she is polite, humble, soft-spoken, and undemonstrative. This is an unbelievable package of positive facts.

Well, rabbits are done. I am on my way to the shop to get them framed. To my kids (shall I take the liberty and say "our kids," if, God willing, we get around to marrying and producing a few) I will pass on these legacies and stories about Grandmother. I will never tire of telling them how she moved about creating small wonders and small packages of joy in her simple domestic world.

With the days of your visit approaching nearer, I am getting rest-less. I wasn't restless in April this year, when our correspondence began, or subsequently. When I first wrote to you and received your reply, I liked something in it. On my end, liking has obviously matured into better and more passionate feelings. But this last-minute impatience . . . I simply don't know what to do about it. I can't deny the presence of that one unmistakable feeling . . . . . . this is the man . . . . I have been looking for all along, through the long and cir-cuitous route of my years so far. It comes back to me over and over again and it stays on . . . Then I ask myself, *What else am I waiting for?* The very supposition that we must meet first personally, evaluate and examine each other (and our responses to each other), and then *think, think, think,* and *then* decide we shall (or not) marry seems an utter waste of time. I do believe in fait accompli. I do feel like believing Dada's prediction and letting myself flow with time and tide. Then what I feel with intuitive certainty is marry we will. We are just buying time to come to terms with what life has in store for us.

You may differ from me and look at the whole issue with an analytical rather than an intuitive outlook. And in analyzing the facts, you may choose to make a decision contradicting the intuitive outlook. If God wishes so, you will be free to do that, and will find peace in that process. But I feel it will all be better than we ever thought it likely to be. This is not expectation, not hope either; it is rather an intuitive premonition of events yet to occur. Only time will testify its truth.

Ehud, I am trying to imagine what it is going to be like to be engaged to you, to be your wife. I recall you saying that any wife of yours must be prepared to be action-oriented. She had better be. Indeed, you are taking a strong deviation from the regular trend in the West, where only after elaborate mating experiments are any decisions for or against marriage made. Does it occur to you that just like you, I have taken a route very opposite to the one that is usually taken by an Indian woman of my background?

I am in a strange position. I was born and raised in a traditional family with deep roots in the Indian culture. My family, however, was progressive: open to new ideas, to concepts like education, career, and identity of women. This progressiveness made it possible for me to travel, study, have a career, and be on my own. It left me free to pursue my dreams for over a decade during my prime years as a youth. During my sojourn through the universities, I saw what happens to youngsters who lose track, forget their roots, and try aping a lifestyle that has no approval from the unwritten rulebook of our culture. I had the opportunity and the freedom to choose that lifestyle. However, the whole package never made any sense to me. I would not like being a mindless doll in the hands of the elders in the family, dictated to about what to do, all in the name of my culture. I also would not like fooling around and experimenting with condoms, spermicide jellies, hormone pills, abortion clinics, and a long list of boyfriends, all in the name of "love."

For myself, I thought, I must make my own path. Within the norms of my Oriental roots and culture, without becoming a copy-cat, I must try to find a man, explore his mind and thoughts first and other departments later, and that man, too, must be open to such a concept and exploration. He must not be blinded and numbed by the intensity of my culture, he must search for meaning and sense in what is being offered as Indian culture. Also, he must not demand to consume before he takes me as his wife . . . How do I find such a man? Those chosen by the family might not care to exchange two hellos before deals are sealed, and I might discover later that he and I did not have any compatibility other than horoscope compatibility, which can be manipulated with a few wads of currency notes. On the other hand, my open and progressive views might be considered a signal for a physical relationship by those who see that as the main characteristic of a liberated woman. In the middle of this dilemma, Ehud, you walked in. The relationship and the understanding that we have developed through correspondence might not have been possible with an Indian man. He might mistake me totally—how dare a woman take rational decision about her own marriage? You, on the contrary, have taken me for just what I am, without misreading my efforts at seeking a middle path that combines the sanctity of my culture with the open and free air of present times. My search for you and my finding of you have not violated my person as a woman; instead they have fortified my image of myself as a woman, one who can't be taken for a ride by the fundamentalist or revolutionary groups, who has her own mind and ideas.

You have been taken on a detailed and guided tour of my mind, its thoughts, its responses and reactions to various issues that affect day-to-day life, its hopes, dreams, and fears, its aspirations as a wife and a mother. You still don't know my bank balance, and might only be able to make a mild guess at my vital statistics (first is nil, second is . . . breathe easy, Boss, just near normal). I still don't know how many credit cards you own and use or what your possibilities are as Homo sapiens, subspecies man. Well, I know what you are searching for in your life, profession, family, and wife. And what you have taught me about your mind is fine by me. I like what I have found.

And I am absolutely glad and jubilant that I could adopt a rational, sensible, practical, and clean route to marriage with a man I like. I was not throttled by the weight of my culture, not fooled by the glamour of imported value systems. I could be "me" and God helped me in finding a man (that is you, Ehud) who will take pride in the way I am made and maintained. In taking this strong deviation and detour, God has helped me so far, and it seems like his promise of peace and goodwill will be fulfilled. Captain, have no fear. You too have taken a detour and I am sure God will be with you in every step you take. Have no fear, no doubts. I can foresee that this common journey of two people who have deviated from the much-trodden path is going to be just super-fine, believe me, and God willing, if Dada is correct, this common journey will be studded with kids . . . have faith . . .

Sincerely,
Vatsala

29.9.95

Dear Ehud,

It is 10 A.M. In the department, and the initial rush is over. A student has just left after a long discussion, extended over several cups of tea. I am guiding him in presenting a part of our research findings in the forthcoming microbiology meet. He has left with a look of satisfaction and I hear he goes around saying that he enjoys these intellectual discussions with me. That, I think, is a compliment.

For my Ph.D. supervisor, I could not think of any such compliment. My relationship with him was on the verge of collapse all through our six years of association. Somehow our personalities were grossly mismatched, and there always was that nagging fear of explosion, rejection, breakdown, collapse . . . Those six years broke me in several ways. They also made me in several ways. Now when I am out and away from the professor's path and have my own identity, place, and weight in the microbiology circles, I do sometimes take stock of the years spent in his lab. I recall that while I was breaking down every day, experiencing a very painful, slow, and torturous death of "me," the human being, a part of me was busy learning lessons for a lifetime.

I learned that as human beings we play several roles in the relationships that bind us to people. Fine. The decay starts when we take ourselves, our roles, and our relationships too seriously to the total exclusion of the fact that we are human beings first and anything else later. In being a professor, my guide took himself so seriously that he forgot this. That was the death of the human being in him. Only the stern, ambitious, fierce professor remained alive, minus any trace of humanness. This lack of humanness in him hurt me very deeply, and I resolved to preserve my own humanness at any cost. To my colleagues, students, friends, and even to strangers, my instinctive response is to be courteous, polite, unselfish, soft-spoken, sensitive, and responsive to their needs. I try to be kindhearted, helpful, and warm. I interact with them closely, know their families, personal histories, and needs . . . we share fun, work, studies, and life. Regarding work they understand that they cannot mess with me, fool around, and give me the slip. I treat them with concern, sensitivity, and awareness that they are just as much a human being as I am. In turn, they work hard, and never compromise on quality or consistency . . . that is my only expectation from them. And as a team we have a whale of a time . . . there is trust (not mistrust), honesty (not deceit), love (not hatred), acceptance (not rejection), and warmth (not cold aloofness). In this microenvironment, with people with whom I interact closely, by God's grace I have been able to create what I missed in my years with my professor. This I consider more important than being a microbiologist and chief of the service. This is a label that I happened to acquire subsequently.

My first encounter with life was in the form of a male and a female gametocyte from my father and mother that developed into a healthy neonate. Why forget that before I took on any roles, I was just a simple, pure, delicate, soft, innocent human being unaware of the dirt and muck of the world and the meanness of people that live here? Returning in my mind to that just-born status helps me in retaining happy, warm, friendly, nice relationships.

With you what is it going to be like? Meeting you as a stranger, becoming a friend, hoping to become your wife and bear your kids . . . well, Ehud, I am not likely to forget the lessons that I have learned about being myself, being in a state of just-bornness. So you can expect a simple, straight relationship between us that will pay more attention to our humanness than to our acquired roles. Does this logic make any sense, Boss?

Vatsala

2.10.95

Dear Ehud,

The best way to live is to live in the present moment, consider bygones as bygones and the future as something yet to come. It is *now* that matters. Quite practical, quite philosophical, yes. It will cut down time spent in crying over spilt milk, brooding over the past, thinking, worrying, or even feeling happy about what one is expecting to have in the future. Makes sense, right? And time thus saved can be invested in living in the present, living it well. Sounds good, and it can even be prescribed as a key to relaxed living.

At this moment, it is rather difficult for me not to think about the future. Just a couple of minutes ago, I was intensely concentrating at the microscope and going through the slides awaiting my opinion. When finished with this job, I continued to sit where I was, and caught myself unaware, simply staring out through the window. I was watching a man lifting his giggling child high in the air, and his wife admiring her child and her strong husband. The child (8 to 10 months old) had slings attached to both his arms for intravenous lines, and the left side of his scalp was shaven—a telltale sign that a neurosurgeon had been scavenging around his brain. The positive side of this picture was that the kid was in the very last phase of his hospital stay, and looked well and ready to go home. Well Ehud, excuse me for sidetracking into the medical history of this kid, which I could not help noticing. The main thing that caught my attention and held it for quite some time was the togetherness and fun this family was sharing despite the gloomy hospital environment. I could not, in my mind, help replacing the man and the woman with you and me, but for the kid I could not imagine a face. Well, it is togetherness that touched me deeply, and I could not help myself saying *Yes* when my mind asked me, *Is this what you are looking forward to in trying to work out a relationship with the man whom you are likely to meet shortly?*

I have also been thinking about what a man's close presence can do. It is easy to understand that waking up alone in the morning is different than waking up and finding a man next to me—one is now, the other one is an intangible future. I think, rather I am sure, I am going to enjoy togetherness as religiously as I have been enjoying my celibacy and single status. I could meditate, pray, and do breathing exercises in the bed, only to wake up in the morning and find it so clean and unruffled (I don't like making a mess). I don't think any of this is possible with you around commanding attention. And the beauty is, I just can't wait anymore to shower all my attention on you, be with you, wake up with you.

Well, this piece of imagination or looking into the future with expectant, hopeful eyes will have life to it only if we decide we want to marry each other, commit ourselves to each other, and give ourselves to each other. Or else the unruffled bed, meditation, prayers, breathing exercises will continue for God only knows how long. And I will continue dreaming about the elusive togetherness, watching the playful fathers, proud mothers, and giggling kids outside my lab window.

It is water that flows underneath the bridge. The bridge stays (rather, should stay) where it is. And only an avalanche, a flood of love and needing by a man, can move the eternal bridge that a woman is. Nothing else can (should) move her except that. How fortunate I will be if I can find that love and needing in you. Only the future can say if it is possible. Tell me, Ehud, is there a way not to think about that future?

Vatsala . . .

October 2, 1995

Dear Vatsala,

I'm very happy that my letter has had a felicitous effect. I sent it via Express Mail in the hopes that you would get it more quickly, as I was also feeling anxious, having through circumstances taken so long to respond. The nerve of those small-minded fellows, shuffling through our papers and photographs! What an incredible waste of time and what an affront to privacy. What possibly could be in an envelope that would merit the scrutiny of some petty bureaucrat from the postal service?

Fait accompli is a French term that's entered English and means literally "it's already happened." It is used to mean that a situation is certain to occur, as it is already certain in the mind. Dada has a living knowledge of astrology, although he rarely uses it, and you would never know he had this knowledge. The traditional sciences of India as practiced today are in most cases simply the form without the substance. Astrology is reduced to sun-sign compatibility and newspaper nonsense. Ayurveda is bought in a bottle and sadhus roam around in an effort to avoid life and work. However, there still exist some true practitioners of the traditional arts, and Dada is certainly one of those.

He only explored a little bit of what he was able to see in our horoscopes, and much more would be possible. But he knows that I don't care much for these matters, preferring to carry the stars within me, and looking for them to shine in my day-to-day actions. What purpose in knowing the future if all we truly have is the present moment? True actions in this moment are, in my belief, certain, with God's grace, to yield a future in harmony with our true selves.

Absolutely, the list of dos and don'ts should be posted in the bedroom, where it will find expression in actions rather than words. The kitchen requires no list, as certainly it is a domain in which you will rule.

Did you know that in the lexicon of the '60s black ghetto, in which I had experience, *boss* meant "good"? So if someone said, "That's a boss-looking outfit," it meant a good-looking outfit. So definitely, boss can only work where a sense of justice, fairness, and a priority to others is the hallmark. What is potentially exciting about your reaction to these statements is that for a man to truly achieve the status of "boss," he absolutely requires the touchstone of the feminine. Without the feminine to guide, support, and nurture the higher ideals, men fall into barbarism and egotism. This is a secret that has been lost in the relations between men and women in the West. Consequently, there is endless strife and bickering between men and women in this culture.

I, too, very much look forward to our meeting in October. Don't worry about Ramakrishnan's managed or monitored event. Things will happen naturally and spontaneously, and of course we will have time to get to know each other without anyone listening in. My first priority is to make myself available to you and to your family.

I will take care of all travel arrangements and accommodations—Captain Ehud at your service. By the time this letter reaches you, I will already be en route to Germany, so if you wish to be in touch, drop me a letter at the Oberoi Hotel.

Until we meet, I send you my love and affection.

Ehud

13.10.95

Hold for Guest, Ehud Sperling, Oberoi Hotel, Delhi
Dear Ehud,
Welcome home.

I have been looking forward to meeting you and, accordingly, I have arranged duties in such a way that my assistants will be able to run the show jolly well. The only condition is that I will call them at least once every day to find out how they are doing, and whether I am needed for any decisions regarding reports. And just like you, I have a list of priorities, and my topmost priority is being able to spend time with you.

I am touched by your offer to take care of our travel and accommodations arrangements. My thanks to Captain Ehud. I had been wanting to be in touch with you and you have given a good idea regarding writing to you at the Delhi address. This is the first letter from me being addressed to you within the geographical limits of my country, and this very thought makes me a little sentimental. All along you were in another world, and now you are here, breathing the same air that I breathe.

Anna, my big brother, is coming to Madras on the 18th. He will meet you on the 19th and leave the same day. When I discussed with him the contents and purpose of our correspondence, he showed keenness in coming along and meeting you. Appa can't come, as he can't travel yet. Manni and the kid are staying back to be with Appa.

At my home, I have been restless, trying to figure out the possibilities of our meeting. If you find the home a little out of shape and in disharmony, I give apologies in advance. If my juggleries in the kitchen don't amuse you or tickle your taste buds, I again apologize. You can understand that you are making me nervous. If I don't look as composed and confident as I appeared in my letters, Captain, the reason is your effect on me. This is also called nervousness. Hope you can understand this state of a woman's mind.

You have sent me your love and affection until we meet. Ehud, I could use more of that always, and from me you have the same always and in abundance.

Love,
Vatsala

14.10.95

Ehud,

Dr. Ramakrishnan and his brother's two kids called on me today. We had a friendly chat and he got around to making a list of possibilities of what might happen when you and I meet. The first possibility he put down was 1) nothing happens, 2) something happens, 3) I like you and you don't like me, 4) you like me and I don't like you . . . This list looked totally outrageous to me and I mentally ruled out the possibility of nothing happening or one-sided liking.

It hit me hard and again that through our letters we know each other more deeply than some people who live together for over half a century, and that is why what is likely to happen is positive, affirmative, good . . . It is not expectation, it is hope that, God willing, we will be able to give peace and happiness to each other.

Then Dr. Ramakrishnan wanted to know if anything romantic is cooking between us, and he wanted to read our letters. This seemed utterly, utterly outrageous, as I just can't imagine a third person getting hold of our correspondence and helping himself. What I write for you is just for you. If it is for the public, I might just publish it in the newspapers. Well, try as he might, he is not likely to get a glimpse of our letters.

This made me wonder, are we romantically oriented too? Talking about kids, where to put up our list of dos and don'ts, mentioning on the basis of Dada's horoscope readings that our bodies will like each other, telling you I miss you and I love your mind, your thoughts . . . is this the making of a romantic relationship? To me, no way. Mindful of the way in which romance or the lack of it is overemphasized in a man-woman relationship, I consider our opening up to each other as the only and the right way in which we can hope to educate ourselves about each other across the continents without having met in person. If I don't write to you about kids, how do I learn how you react to them? I love them and if you just don't want any, that might crack the very foundation on which we stand. Since oneness and solidarity is the strength in any marriage, I must learn that on the issues that affect the day-to-day life, our views are compatible, such that our oneness can remain intact. If our correspondence around these important issues stinks of romance to someone's oversensitive nostrils, we just don't care. It is a problem with their nostrils—let us refer them to ENT surgeons, and we can continue to carry on with our business.

I might ask you this in person, Boss: if we decide to marry, just how soon can we do that? Having made a positive decision, I am in a mind-set to finish the task with minimum formalities and hassles in as brief a time as is humanly possible. Of the two favorable years predicted by Dada, I do not want to waste a single moment.

Now with the days of your visit coming close, I am literally on my knees asking God to help us know what is good, what is bad, and the difference between the two. Please, God, please help us and please do not leave us alone with our limited wisdom to deal with a decision of such a great magnitude as committing ourselves to each other. Please be with us, dear God.

Vatsala

Ehud,

Spoke to you just now. Looks like we will be able to chat for hours on end, nonstop. It may not be just gossip and idle talk. I see it as something like we will feel absolutely free with each other to simply put forth our thoughts in words and speak with each other without the fear of being misunderstood, and always enjoy doing that. You are here already, my goodness! And you also have my latest letter. I was just hoping you would receive it before you leave Delhi for Madras. Ehud, for once I don't know what to write or why I began writing this letter. It is, I suppose, meant to neutralize the palpitation that I felt on suddenly hearing your voice on the phone. The talk ended as abruptly as it started, and I had nothing to hang on to. This is what I dislike about telephones, and thank God we did not depend on the phones to get to know each other. In trying to address you in these pages, I feel a continuity, as if my contact with you did not end abruptly. It is going on . . . via the medium of written words. Well, hope to see you on 19.10.95. And shall I tell you I am looking forward to our meeting like crazy?

Love,
Vatsala

Anna came home on 18 October to meet Ehud. He took hardly any time to unwind from the intense overnight train trip from Madurai. Soon after he finished his tea, he settled down to reading some letters, looking at Ehud's catalog, and discussing my decision. As well as Anna knew me, he figured that in pursuing a relationship with Ehud I was not making an emotional decision based on insecurities, fears, escapist tendencies, boredom with the current trend in life, or greed about a foreign connection. He also knew that I had not fallen prey to physical urges and attraction for Ehud. At the end, he said, "You will be fine. He seems like a nice person. I hope you are clear in your head as to what you are reaching for."

I read a sign of relief on Anna's face. Since I had chosen to be my own spokeswoman, and had taken charge of shaping my future with my own hands, Anna would not be held responsible. Anna served as a sort of father figure for me, and always offered his ideas, suggestions, and opinions. I, being his obedient little sister, always respected and honored him for his role in my life, but I had made it clear to him that I would use my own judgment and intelligence when it came to making decisions as serious as marriage. My future was going to be my own doing or undoing.

This idea suited me quite well. One drawback of most overly protective, close-knit, family-oriented relationships in India is that the commitments, responsibilities, authority, and discretion are concentrated in the hands of the head of the family. He is bestowed with this unwritten power to make all decisions—small and big—concerning each and every family member. While the decision maker's back crumbles under this heavy responsibility, the other members of the family may lose the art of being responsible for their own lives. Since gratitude is a trait that is disappearing fast from the pool of human expressions, the senior decision maker is hardly ever thanked, but is always held solely responsible for everything that fails. I was tired of this game in my society, and was glad that my family was more democratic than most.

Anna became a father figure for me quite naturally. He is eleven years older than I am, and right from my childhood, he participated with my parents in making all major and minor decisions. Always he exhibited a calm, focused, and friendly nature. He acted with courage and spoke with wisdom, and was very nurturing and kind. Deeply spiritual and very tolerant, he never indulged in bad company or picked up wayward habits. With him as my older brother, I felt like a little queen . . . sheltered, protected, nurtured, and loved. Anna exhibited such strong paternal instincts that soon my father turned the responsibility of many of the household affairs over to him, which he handled excellently. As my father grew older (when I was born, he was already forty-six years old!) he devoted more and more of his time to prayers, studying religious texts, helping the needy, and indulging in meditation and other spiritual pursuits. So in my eyes, the eyes of a young child, my biological father became a very loving but very distant and remote figure, but my brother was always there to guide me.

His approval meant a lot to me, and I was happy to have him by my side for my first meeting with Ehud.

Haridwar Rishikesh
Bareilly
New Delhi Lucknow
Varanasi
Jaipur Chitrakoot Bihar
Ganga River
Jamshedpur

Nagpur

Mumbai
(Bombay)

Bay of Bengal

Arabian Sea

Madras
(Chennai)

Tamil
Nadu
Thanjavur (Tanjore)
Kerala
Kochin Madurai
Tenkashi
Trivandrum

Sri
Lanka

0   400 km
0   300 mi

Indian Ocean

chapter 7

SAILING THE BACKWATERS

O n the morning of 19 October, Anna, Ramakrishnan, and I drove for two hours to Fisherman's Cove, the hotel where Ehud was staying. As we negotiated our way through the traffic and reached a sparsely traveled highway by the seacoast, I noticed a "what-if" ghost stirring lazily in my head.

What if . . . this person I am about to meet—Ehud—to whom I have poured out my heart with all honesty for these past months—is not the real writer of his letters?

What if he has hired some writer to do this job . . . after all, he meets hundreds of authors all over the world . . .

What if I find Ehud—in person—very different from his letters and the photos?

My panic on encountering these what-if ghosts brought tears to my eyes, and my palms grew sweaty, even in a car air-conditioned to 66 degrees Fahrenheit. I secretly wiped my eyes, and tried to look out the window into the sea. *If there is God . . . truth and goodness shall prevail . . .* I heard these words in my mind, as if the sea were trying to reassure me and chase off the ghosts with his mighty roaring waves.

When we reached the hotel, Ramakrishnan suggested that we relax for a few moments before seeing Ehud. We sat on the porch overlooking the sea. The salty, humid breeze passed through the coconut groves and gardens bursting with all sorts of brightly colored oriental flowers.

I took deep breaths, wiped the moisture off my glasses, and looked over at Anna and Ramakrishnan. These two men seemed unusually nervous.

Soon, Ramakrishnan knocked at Ehud's door. Within seconds, the door opened and Ehud stood in front of us, his hands folded in a customary namaste and a bright smile on his lips. He wore a red T-shirt and black trousers, and was as handsome as he had looked in his photographs.

I returned his namaste. Anna and Ramakrishnan hugged him, and we all stepped into his room. As I settled comfortably into a chair cushioned with beautiful leather upholstery, Anna found a seat close to Ehud. Ramakrishnan wandered around the room between the fridge, phone, bathroom, bed, counter, Ehud, Anna, and me as if with his steps he was trying to connect people with people, people with place, and place with place.

Ehud asked me some polite questions like "How are you, how is your work at the hospital, how is Amma," and on receiving short, polite replies from me, he got busy with Anna and Ramakrishnan chatting about weather, travel, job, politics, business, dollar versus rupee, his company and books . . .

Anna took out a small album he always carries and showed Ehud some pictures of our family. And then Anna told Ehud how precious I was to him . . . his darling little baby sister . . . and how he wished me to be happy.

Throughout this conversation, Ramakrishnan continued rolling his curious eyes from Ehud to me and back to Ehud, trying to detect the presence of any romantic flame, and to determine whether we were stealing any glances at each other. Ehud was very focused on his conversation with Anna, and his eyes did not wander restlessly. I liked his focus. I also liked his calm, humorous, friendly mode of conversation. I could easily follow his English—I did not have any problems with his accent—and he had a very gentle, assertive, confident way of carrying himself. Even though I was not being addressed directly or often, I liked being an audience in this room.

Ehud ordered some coffee over the phone, and the room service boy brought it in within minutes. In between sips, Anna asked Ehud what his plans were for marriage with me. I did not see Ehud swallowing hard at this question, or showing any other nervous clues of a sudden confrontation with such a serious question. He remained calm and answered, "I will have to think about it and tell you tomorrow."

I heard this answer, looked intently at Ehud, and laughed in my heart. It amused me that Ehud still needed to "think" about the decision he and I had made even before we met.

A little while later, Anna and I took leave and rushed home to tell Amma about our meeting. I confessed to Amma that after my first-ever eye contact with Ehud, my pulse remained normal, I did not skip any heartbeats, I did not hear any bells ringing in my ears, and my body temperature and blood pressure remained normal too. On meeting him, I was not gripped by any new fears, questions, or uncertainties, and I did not get any confusing, mixed signals from him. My first-ever sighting of Ehud was a plain, nonromantic, normal, and calm event. I felt at ease. Aware of Ramakrishnan's probing eyes, and of Anna's and Ehud's solid and positive presence, I felt good. Ehud did appear to be exactly the one who wrote me all the letters. He was indeed the person who had appeared in the photos, and it filled me with delight to see the author of the letters alive, vibrant, and full of such positive energy.

I also told Amma how I had laughed silently when Ehud requested overnight time to think and make up his mind about marrying me. *Intuitively,* we had known before we met that he and I were meant to be partners for seven lives to come, not just this one. And our decision was made solely on the basis of our letters. I could detect very well that Ehud was writing to me from the depth of his soul, and not from the shallow and murky surface of transient thoughts.

The power of our honest, straightforward, and trusting communication amazed me. And these thousands of words were written in as lonely an environment as we could manage to get and work in, and were sent to each other by mail. The very fact that nothing ever went wrong or missing in this chain of events filled me with renewed faith and confidence in my intuitive feeling and decision . . . this is the man for me. I had made up my mind to get married to Ehud, and that decision would not change by thinking overnight, but if Ehud needed this extra eighteen hours of time, he could have it. I had lots of patience.

The next day, I took Amma's blessing before leaving home with Ramakrishnan and Anna to meet Ehud again. She hugged me and said, "Be brave. Conduct yourself with truth and fairness. Trust in God and always seek His help. He will not let you down because He alone knows what your needs are . . ." I looked at Amma with a thin film of tears in my eyes, and for a moment, she looked to me like a wise sage from the time the Vedas were uttered and created. I felt in my heart that with this saintly and divine mother as my anchor and compass, I could never get lost in the chaos and confusion of the world.

During that morning's two-hour ride to Ehud's sea-resort hotel, I was as relaxed and calm as I could be, and the sea appeared like a quiet and still lake. When we knocked at Ehud's door, there he was in a beige shirt and jeans, all smiles, bubbly, very cheerful. The twinkle in his brown eyes gave away his decision even before he said, "Anna, I have made up my mind to get married to Vatsala."

On hearing this, a very small smile came over my face. In my mind I saw the smiling and happy face of my mother floating in front of me. She was glowing.

Ramakrishnan let out a low whistle and jumped from his seat, reached Ehud in one long stride, and gave him such a hug I almost heard Ehud's ribs crackle. Anna turned to me, took my hand in his, and asked, "So, Mukta, are you willing to marry Ehud?"

I looked Anna straight in the eyes and said in a loud and clear voice, "Yes, most certainly."

❋❋❋

Reflecting on life: Amma at Marina Beach, Madras.

Two days later, amidst the loud noise of crackers (22 October happened to be Deepavali festival when, all over India, firecrackers are exploded and lamps are lit to celebrate the arrival of Lakshmi, the goddess of wealth), and in the presence of Amma and Ramakrishnan's family, Ehud and I were engaged.

At the auspicious time, a magnificent oil lamp was lit in the *pooja* room. Vijaya, Ramakrishnan's wife, arranged on steel trays the offerings that Ehud and I were to exchange as engagement mementos. She then placed them at the pooja altar. My mother and Ramakrishnan officiated the ceremony by chanting prayers. After that, Ramakrishnan and Vijaya, representing Ehud's family, presented me with a silk *saree* and flowers. My mother presented Ehud with *dhoti, angavastram* (traditional outfits for Indian men), and flowers.

I changed into the saree and went back to the pooja room. Ramakrishnan and Vijaya asked my mother for the hand of her daughter in marriage to Ehud. My mother gave her formal consent, and expressed her joy at having Ehud join her family as a son-in-law. Upon receiving her consent, Ramakrishnan announced that with the approval and blessings of all the elders in Ehud's and my family, and with all the people present in the pooja room as witnesses, and with the witness of God, Ehud and Vatsala were being formally engaged to be married on 22 February 1996. This auspicious date was determined in consultation with Dada Harish Johari, who had done the necessary astrological workup on our horoscopes.

After this engagement announcement, Ehud and I prayed together at the pooja altar, and took the blessings of my mother and all those present. The ceremony was followed by a simple dinner that I had cooked that evening. I was glad to note that all the guests and Ehud were gleefully devouring the fresh *chapatis* smeared with *ghee, pulao, palak-paneer, alu-matar, chole, halwa, kheer*, and *nariyal burfi*. The dinner was a hit.

The next day, Ehud and I were invited to Ramakrishnan's brother's home for a lunch party. On the way, I asked Ehud why he had needed overnight time to think about marrying me. To this, he said that he was feeling so much love for me over the months during which we wrote to each other that he wanted to check with himself that he was not being blinded by his love for a woman, but was in fact making a conscious, real decision to commit himself to me for the rest of this life and beyond. He wanted to make sure that he was not being led, and not jumping to a conclusion. He also added that once he met me, even though we did not say anything more than "How are you, I'm fine, thank you," he felt totally at peace and relaxed, and after we left, he found that he was in such a state of deep calm, relaxation, and certitude that the very act of thinking and analyzing seemed futile and unnecessary. He felt that he did not need to go over and think again about the truest thing he felt . . . that he had at last found his true wife. And he just drifted into a peaceful, deep sleep, imagining my face.

At Ramakrishnan's brother's home, Ehud was taken into a gathering where all the men sat around chatting and swapping their Diwali stories. I was whisked away to a women's gathering. We sang songs to celebrate the occasion, and everyone seemed utterly delighted with my engagement.

Ehud noted with pleasure that even though I had gotten engaged to a rich American man, I did not give up my place in my own society. I maintained my connection with the women (as it is done in traditional India—men and women assemble separately for public celebrations). Also, he was relieved to note that I was so self-assured that I did not feel the social or personal need to cling to my new fiancé and demand that he focus himself 100 percent on me. Ehud was developing renewed appreciation for my self-contained, calm, peaceful nature, and felt over and again that I would be perfect for him in every way. My feeling of admiration for Ehud grew sharply, as he treated me with total courtesy, respect, decency, and ease, and I never felt he was trying to create a good impression or was not being himself.

During the seven months of our correspondence, I had asked him many questions and received believable answers. One question that often came to my mind and for some reason I had never got around to asking him, came back to me again. I just had to know how Ehud could possibly have come up with the idea of placing the ad and looking for an Indian wife. Certainly, he had all the qualifications to attract and marry someone of his own cultural background. After all, he was successful, handsome, and still young enough to be a good catch. So one day when I went to meet him for lunch at Fisherman's Cove, I asked, "Ehud, out of all the countries in the world, why did you choose India to find a wife?"

He responded with the following tale:

"I was in New Delhi, working on developing the Inner Traditions India program for a launch the following year. One of our authors, Bhaskar Bhattacharya, who was at the time working for Business India as program manager for their new satellite TV station, threw a party for me. During the evening's get-together, I mentioned that I'd never been to the South of India, that I was planning on taking the next couple weeks off, and would like to find a place where I could unwind. I didn't want to go any place built up or commercial, but a simple place by the beach where I could be by myself and reflect.

"This was the first chance I'd had to be alone since my marriage had ended six months earlier. When my wife left, I had made a vow to keep to myself for one year to get over the experience, and to really hone in on what was important to me in a marriage. I was determined to remarry, as I was convinced that marriage was the right and appropriate vehicle through which I would find happiness and fulfillment. However, I was disturbed and confused by my lack of success. I had been married previously and also had been actively engaged in a relationship without interruption for years. You know, like most people in the West, I have been through it."

I was intrigued by this answer, which seemed like a brief prelude to an elaborate answer that was waiting to find its way out. "You have been through what?" I asked.

"The game of searching and not finding. Look what happened in my previous relationship . . . In June of the previous year my wife, who was still, after eight years of marriage, searching for herself, the meaning of her life, and whether I was the right man for her, decided to travel to Peru and stay with a shaman there who was known to her. We were both unhappy in our marriage but for different reasons. She wanted to be 'free,' a woman of power, and didn't want to stand in my shadow. She did not see herself as my partner and wife but as my competitor, and wanted an identity independent of me and my work. She had a need to be recognized for herself alone. We had gone through almost two years of therapy together. The therapist had told me that I had worked through my problems and grown. I had decided to let go, love my wife unconditionally and no longer fight with her no matter what she said or did. The only caveat was that I would not allow her to take advantage of me and cause me to act in any way I thought inappropriate. In fact, when I had asked Harish Johari the year before what to do in my marriage to improve it, he had said, 'Nothing.'"

That surprised me. I stopped nibbling at my salad greens and tried to understand why Harish Johari had said that. My mind quickly raced for possibilities, but I could not decipher the meaning of "Nothing." What did he mean by saying to do nothing when his friend was going through a serious crisis in his marriage?

"This is in fact what I did: I remained myself without trying to influence or guide my wife in her decisions or actions. I remained nonjudgmental and waited to see how things would unfold. I was very clear myself as to what I needed and wanted in a relationship with my wife, and the atmosphere in my home. I needed commitment and devotion from my wife. My home needed to be a safe haven and a refuge, not a battleground. I had no interest in playing out the contemporary battle of the sexes for dominance and authority. It was very clear to me that I was an alpha male just like my alpha dog Ngurra. I was very unhappy with the conflict-filled and argumentative home environment full of acidic and hurtful verbal assaults. I was in great need of a spiritually uplifting, peaceful home environment. Well, my wife left for Peru and I settled into a happy routine of work, playing with my dog, enjoying the peaceful and reflective environment of my home. I spent much time gardening, landscaping around my home, hiking, biking, swimming, and horseback riding. Joy returned to my heart and I felt at peace with myself. The two months passed quickly and one day I received a phone call from a stranger in Peru, informing me that my wife would be delayed and was not reachable by phone. I later was to learn that she was actually in New York planning her escape. A few days later, my parents arrived in Vermont to celebrate my mother's seventy-fifth birthday. My wife was supposed to be present, but instead she called from New York: 'Ehud, I've decided not to come back home.'

"My spontaneous and immediate reaction was, 'Well, don't. You've made your decision, so let's work together to part amicably without creating further bad feelings or negativity.' To her credit, that is what actually happened. We settled all our property and logistical issues amicably, and she went on to continue her goal of being a free and independent woman."

I had read the statistics that in the USA one in every two marriages ends in divorce. But listening to one man's true story was more shocking than the statistics. The fact that a message of such magnitude was conveyed over the telephone stunned me. Was the bond and relationship called marriage so fragile that it could be broken by just a phone call? This marriage was certainly very different from the traditional marriages in Hindu culture—marriage for the next seven lives—and certainly marriage the way I looked at it and believed it to be could not be broken by a simple phone call. I was saddened to hear of Ehud's experience as he continued his story.

"I went through a period of deep grieving and recalled how eight years prior, while Dada was in Vermont, I had announced to him, 'I am going to get married,' to which he responded, 'Don't.' I in turn said, 'But I have given my word,' to which he said, 'Well, then you must.' Dada was now in Germany. I thought to myself, *Well, why not give him a call?* 'Hi, Dada,' I said in a deeply troubled and sad voice. 'I have some disturbing news. She has left.' He responded joyfully and enthusiastically in just one word: 'Fantastic.' Instantly the cloud of grief lifted from my mind, my heart jumped, and all feelings of loss and sadness vanished. I realized that Dada had known from the beginning that this was an inappropriate liaison, and was only patiently marking time until it was over. I also found out later that in the horoscopes that he had cast for me and my wife years after our marriage, he had seen quite clearly that this was not a suitable match for me, and also that I was to have a make-believe marriage prior to the 'real wife' appearing. However, he never confided this to me, and tried to the best of his ability to help me cope and see my commitments through in an appropriate manner."

I noticed a joy in Ehud's voice when he described Dada Harish Johari's reaction to the annulment of his marriage, as if for Dada and for Ehud, this annulment was a big relief in life, as if a ghost were being exorcised from their midst. I could not help but wonder about the woman who created much grief while she was around and whose exit created such a sense of relief, freedom, and joy. "Must be a remarkable woman . . . ," I mused, and what Ehud said further confirmed that she indeed was remarkable. After all, she made one man sit up, take stock of his life and priorities, evaluate all his perspectives, examine himself and his needs in detail, and meditate over the direction he needed to take in his life.

"Now that the grieving period was over, I thought to myself that I needed to find the right home environment and the appropriate role for myself in the environment. I thought of myself as a captain of a ship—that is the role I had been cast into in my work. For my entire professional life, I had acted like the captain of a vessel. I thought, *Could I be any different at home?* The captain apparently makes all the decisions about the ship and the crew for the welfare of everyone on board. He may give the impression of being a dominant alpha dog, but a captain can only be as good as his crew, and to lead the ship successfully he needs total cooperation, trust, and obedience from his crew. In the absence of these traits, an errant, unruly crew can create obstacles in the functioning of the captain, resulting in the ship's straying dangerously off course. Well, it is only a role, but in a family setting, it is no better than or wiser than a wife's. It is only reasonable that someone needs to bear the decision-making responsibility in order for a family to function effectively as a team. If everyone chooses to be autonomous and go their separate ways, how can the unit be called a family?

"Obedience and willingness to allow the husband to have the authority for decision making is not a blind and dumb tendency. An intelligent, rightly centered person (wife) could be my most severe critic if and whenever I deviated off course and chose a wrong direction for the family, and that criticism is most welcome. But nagging, ridicule, chronic dissatisfaction, and habitual indulgence in criticism just for the sake of putting the husband down and devaluating his contributions to the family are very dangerous elements that

*Ehud's travels through Planet India
made him feel as if he'd returned home.*

I would like to avoid. I have always believed and conducted myself on the basis that the feminine is the light and the truth by which to measure one's course—not just the outside feminine, but the internal and eternal feminine that resides within all of us. That feminine quality is life-affirming, and is a divine influence totally committed to the welfare and nurturing of the human family. In fact, it is she who gives birth to the whole game. The big lie in the contemporary dialogue about gender roles is that nobody wants to admit any difference exists between males and females, and yet in nature we see distinct differences. These differences play themselves out in the worldly game, but not in the inner core of humanity. All our bones are white and our blood is red. However, when we have to play the roles in the worldly game, then one question that comes around is how to play these roles well without losing ourselves in them or associating ourselves exclusively with the role to the extent that we forget in our core we all are simply human beings first."

Ehud paused to catch his breath, sip his lemonade, bite into his bread, and wash it down with another sip of lemonade. He also scanned my face carefully to see if his story was sinking in. Finding assurance that I was ingesting and digesting every word, he continued earnestly.

"In the world's view, I was a highly eligible bachelor. Friends wanted to introduce me to women and hold dinner parties for me, and they generally tried fixing me up with suitable women. However, I was saturated. I lived like a hermit, keeping to myself, and did not participate in even one social engagement till I returned to India in January 1995. I was no Indophile to begin with, but had years of publishing contact with India, bringing out books on Indian culture, philosophy, traditions, food, history, religion, and lifestyle. I was never brainwashed or impressed beyond redemption by any Indian guru offering instant nirvana (for a fee); however, my years of travel in India made me feel that in India there existed a possibility of finding a wife who would perfectly fit into my life.

"Well, back to the party that Bhaskar Bhattacharya threw for me in India. Bhaskar had invited the foreign correspondent, Asia desk, of the *London*

Independent. Having a vast experience of Asia, he suggested that the very best place for me to go for some time alone would be the Surya Samudra, a small resort with thirty bungalows, all traditional Kerala hand-carved wood houses that had been collected and rebuilt on a private beach south of Trivandrum, practically at the tip of India. I thought that this would be just perfect for me. I made arrangements, and two days later I was on a plane to Trivandrum.

"Oddly, after coming regularly to India for almost ten years, this was the very first time I'd been on my own. I had always been accompanied by Indian friends and/or colleagues, and always had an agenda, a direction, a goal, and an activity. This time, it was just me, and no idea other than to rest and contemplate.

"I was picked up at the airport and driven to the Surya Samudra, and collapsed in my room, exhausted. I had dinner early that evening, kept to myself, and went to sleep. When I woke up and walked out of the room the next day, I encountered a tall, elderly gentleman of British descent who was staying in the room opposite. He said to me, quite unceremoniously, 'Who are you?' I was taken aback, but at the same time, amused and charmed by his directness. He turned out to be Sir Lance Dane, one of India's leading experts on temple sculpture and numismatics, as well as a photographer who had traveled the country for more than fifty years, photographing its monuments.

"It turned out that Lance's photographs had appeared in many ITI books, and that we had several publishing friends in common. We became fast friends, commenting that India produces these kinds of serendipitous encounters. Lance decided that he was going to take me around to the temples and palaces of Kerala. Well, that was the end of my time alone—it lasted less than twenty-four hours—but no regrets. Lance was amazing. He was known at all the monuments, and we got private access to many of the rooms no longer on display to the general public, including a viewing of the famous eighteenth-century frescoes in the pooja room of the palace of Padmanabhapuram, which are unbelievably beautiful and well preserved."

Hand-carved wooden house at Surya Samudra.

His use of the word *serendipitous* to describe the way encounters occur in India caught my attention. Yes, in this land, somehow, inexplicable events happen that nobody could have predicted, expected. But not for such possibilities, I could not explain how and why I had crossed Ehud's orbit, and today we were sitting face-to-face.

"Four days into our travels together, I learned that there was a once-a-year festival taking place in Trivandrum in honor of the goddess Durga. Over half a million women were to attend, and the whole city was closed off for this, the largest women's festival on earth. I asked Lance to accompany me, and he said, 'You're crazy, no way in the world I'm going. It will be a madhouse!' Nevertheless, I determined to go on my own. I had Hi-8 video equipment with me and wanted to film the festival. I grabbed a cab and made for Trivandrum. On the outskirts of the town, we were stopped by the police. With the little bit of English the cab driver had, he was able to tell me what the police officer, speaking Malayalam, had to say. 'Women. No men. Women only.'

"I tried to persuade him that I needed to go into the city, but he didn't understand a word I said, and neither did the cab driver. I was getting quite agitated, when, from out of nowhere, a voice in impeccable British-style English said, 'May I be of assistance?' I turned around and saw a rather tall Indian in his late forties, dressed in western trousers and shirt, standing next to a white-haired, saffron-robed *shaivait* sadhu—quite old, with white hair and a white beard, holding a massive trident in his right hand.

"I said, 'Yes, you may. And let me introduce myself.' He in turn told me that he was Dr. Ramakrishnan, he had just returned from the Himalayas with this sadhu in tow, he spoke Malayalam as well as Hindi, Tamil, and a number of other languages, and he'd be happy to help. Ramakrishnan is a Tamil Brahmin, and in the South and with certain groups, that high-caste birth still carries some weight. In a very authoritative tone, he told the policeman to simply disappear, and, lo and behold, that's what he did. I was in.

"Ramakrishnan then took me to the VIP viewing stand opposite the main temple, where the government officials and dignitaries viewed the festival, and I was able to film this extraordinary event. As I moved through the festival, surrounded by hundreds of thousands of women, beautifully decorated for this festival, I thought to myself, *What an unbelievable expression of devotion, and how beautifully these women carry themselves, full of this ancient culture and tradition.*

"I also was aware of the dichotomy and extremes in this encounter. I'd lived like a hermit since my wife left, refusing to socialize, to be introduced to 'appropriate' women; in short, I had kept to myself. And here I was, surrounded by the feminine in an expression of deep devotion and joy. Ramakrishnan, of course, was very curious as to who I was and what I was doing there, and we began to tell each other our stories. He had spent the last two years in the Himalayas, searching for himself, studying with the saints and sadhus he encountered, and just now, this very day, he was returning to the 'world.'

"We decided to spend some time together, and traveled to Tenkashi, his ancestral village, and collected his wife and two sons. I then rented a rice boat, and Ramakrishnan and his family and I traveled up the backwaters of Kerala, much as Indians have done for thousands of years. During this trip together, I told Ramakrishnan about my desire to remarry, and my disaffection with what I saw as the traumatization of western women. In my own marriages and in twenty years of employing women and working with them closely, I had seen the damage done by abusive families, unresolved conflicts with the mother, and exploitation by men prior to and during marriage. In short, there was a huge self-esteem problem affecting western women, and a great disenfranchisement between their traditional roles and what society expected of them now.

"Further, I explained to him that I had been thinking quite seriously about looking for a wife in India, hoping that I could find someone who was ready to enter a relationship without bringing a lot of baggage. I had discussed this desire with Harish Johari, who had offered to help me this last summer, after my wife left. In fact, I had just left him at the wedding preparations for his daughter Swapna, and he had suggested that I do what he had done in arranging his daughter's wedding, namely, place an ad in one of the national Indian newspapers. I was really quite hesitant to take this approach, as it was such a departure from what I was comfortable with, having grown up in the West. For me, it was meet the girl, get attracted, get involved, go to bed, live together, and get married.

"Harish had promised to do something, but he was not introducing me to anyone, and I could see no apparent activity. It also became evident to me that in India, you do not get introduced except in the more westernized and cosmopolitan parts of the country, and then only to westernized Indians. What Dada had in mind, and what in fact appealed to me, was a traditional Hindu woman with a traditional upbringing and point of view.

"I looked out over the rice paddies, coconut palms, and bucolic setting of the backwaters. Traveling on the rice boat, watching the fishing and agriculture, one could easily imagine oneself a thousand years in the past. There was nothing in the visuals that gave even the slightest indication of the modern world. It was in this atmosphere that Ramakrishnan turned to me and said, 'Let me help you with this. Let's write an ad right now that reflects your interests and intentions. We'll place it in the *Hindu*. I'll receive all the mail, and with my nephew, sort through it and come up with a short list. I'll then travel the country, meeting the candidates, and will make my recommendations.'

"I thought this quite an extraordinary offer, and was moved at the moment to accept. Ramakrishnan had a doctorate in linguistics and was well acquainted with traditional India, but at the same time was well read in the Western classics. He also understood quite well the matrimonial system of India, and what would and would not make sense in an ad. We decided on the straightforward approach: I would simply say who I was and what I was looking for.

"It occurred to me that over the years I had been quite successful in gathering around me a staff of devoted and committed and highly talented individuals. I was supported and finally superseded in this hiring task by Deborah Kimbell, whom you'll meet at our wedding, and who has already played a very significant role in our courtship—but more of that later. And now it has become evident to me that being attracted to a woman, falling in love with her, and then marrying was not a good formula for happiness. In the West, the romantic ideal had, since the Middle Ages, come to dominated the courtship dance. For us, romance is all that matters. If it is not present, the dance will not even begin. But what of the qualities and virtues necessary for a successful marriage? What were the qualities I was seeking in a wife? In looking for a wife, was it in fact necessary to apply the same level of diligence that I would in assessing the qualities, attributes, and suitability of a potential employee? Was, in fact, 'wife' a *position* in my life, one that would require very specific skills and attributes?

"Well, it occurred to me that yes, this was the case, and in fact, in traditional cultures throughout the world, including my own Jewish culture, making a match was a job that entailed matching qualities and attributes ranging from the biological, social, cultural, and intellectual to the spiritual. I determined at that moment to follow the traditional approach with a twist, namely, that I, rather than my parents, would be making the choice, and that if I were to marry, I would do so according to the classical Hindu traditions of arranging a marriage and sanctifying it according to the Vedas.

"So we wrote the ad there on the backwaters, where the first non-Hindu community in the history of India—the Jews of Cochin—settled some two thousand years ago. That community lived in harmony with the Hindus, each community enhancing the other, all the way up until the twentieth century.

"When the boat got to Cochin, I flew back to Delhi to attend Swapna's wedding. Dada and his family were gathered in the housing complex of the temple in which the ceremony was to take place. About forty members of the family were now in residence, living there for the week, while prenuptial ceremonies and parties were taking place around Delhi. I was a member of the bride's wedding party, and attended all these very traditional activities. One day while I was sitting with Dada in his room at the temple compound, Om Narayan Rishi walked in. He was now ninety-nine years old, and no one expected him to make the eight-hour journey from his home outside of Haridwar to Delhi. I was particularly taken aback, as I had wanted to meet him for years, and had been encouraging Dada to take me to his house. Om Narayan had taught Dada the occult sciences and was an accomplished yogi, having been buried alive many times and committing many other yogic feats which Dada had filmed over the years.

"He was remarkably youthful for ninety-nine—I would have placed him in his late sixties. He sat down on and got up from the floor with ease, chain-smoked, wore dark sunglasses and a hat, and had outlived two wives and all his children. Dada immediately asked him to cast my horoscope and look into my marriage prospects. He calculated my horoscope mentally, without recourse to an ephemeris or calculations, an amazing feat unto itself. He went on to say that nothing would happen until later this year, and that I would marry and should marry a 'high-born' Indian. He predicted that this would be a successful marriage and would increase my wealth, produce progeny, and bring me peace. He laughed and said I was a good boy, patting me on the head. I really felt like a child in this context, and certainly, being fifty years my senior, he had the right to treat me as such.

"The wedding was an extraordinary experience. It had been arranged according to the ancient Hindu tradition. Swapna only met her husband for five minutes prior to their wedding, and they did not even speak. I was full of questions and doubts about arranged marriages, but Dada explained to me how he had placed an ad for Swapna in the newspaper, how he had met the boy and his full family, and how he had arranged the entire marriage. Swapna's trust of her parents' choice of a husband without having ever sampled any other possible mate, or having even gone out on an exciting, romantic date with her parents' choice—was it blind, stupid, illogical, childish faith in her parents (as we westerners might tend to view it), or was it her total trust in her parents, her belief that their topmost priority was her happiness and that they would never get her married to the wrong person? I began to see some sense in this age-old tradition of arranged marriages and in how children trust their parents, wife trusts her husband, husband trusts his wife. Each member of the family adheres to the time-tested code of roles, conduct, behavior; each person is considerate of the other and puts the other above himself/herself, and as a result, the family functions as a happy, secure, stable unit. It survives, thrives, till death parts them, and not the signed decree of separation and divorce issued by a manmade court of law.

"Still, I was quite skeptical of this alliance, as I knew Swapna to be an accomplished sitar player and highly educated, with a master's degree in English literature. She had been exposed to westerners since childhood, having lived in Berkeley, California, as a child for two years, and having a constant stream of Dada's western friends in their home in Bareilly, fifty miles from the Nepalese border. I could not understand how matching her with an Indian man who had never left the country or had any exposure to the West, let alone a background in English literature, would satisfy her. However, upon visiting her and her husband a week after their marriage at the home of his parents where they were living and continue to live, I was amazed to see how contented and happy and at ease they were with each other. It gave me a great deal to think about.

"I reflected on my many visits to Dada's home over the years. I had this need in me to search for positive feminine energy, and observed what role Pratibha, his wife, played in the home, what she got in return, how Dada felt secure, and how she conducted herself in relationship to her husband/in-laws/children/neighbors/guests/friends and to the six months per year absence of Dada from home. She didn't need him hovering around her all the time whispering 'honey' and 'sweetheart.' She didn't say, 'I don't see you for six months every year . . . maybe you are running a parallel family abroad, having an affair. Here, take this. I divorce you on the phone.' She was rooted to where she belonged. She did not seem to have ever-changing and ever-expanding needs for material glamour and possessions that could only be satisfied in the deluge of the mail-order catalogs that invade every American home every day, violating the sanctity of the home and turning it into a marketplace, tempting people to think that buying is a road to self-fulfillment. 'I shop, therefore I am.' Even though she had a degree in philosophy, had also lived in Berkeley for a few years, and had seen the glitterati of the outside world, she was a contented person who had created her own world within her own home. She derived much joy out of having raised three daughters and four sons, and having instilled her values in them. All these children, whom I had been watching from their childhood years, had turned into secure, self-assured, well-adjusted, confident adults adjusting very well to their lives and marriages.

"This quiet, contented woman was the foundation of Dada's life, and the life of every member of that huge family. With apparent material discomfort, very ordinary middle-class living conditions, nonstop and endless demands on her by the huge family, the absence of her husband for a long time every year, and an absence of physical and verbal display of affection by him, how and why did that marriage not break down? How and why were there no ongoing power struggles and ego battles? Were these elements that I just mentioned the foundation of a successful marriage, or was there more to it than the apparent, visible, tangible, and measurable? I often wondered."

Ehud's description of Pratibha did not take me by surprise. To me she appeared to be a very typical, traditional, conventional Hindu wife and mother—and in my country, the majority of households, including my parental home, were built on the strong foundation created by a woman for whom fulfilling her commitments to her husband and children was like fulfilling her commitment to God. These women had no hidden agendas, and did not expect to be canonized for having been a good wife and a good mother. And because—even in this day and age of blatant and selfish individualism—my country can boast of many wives and mothers like Pratibha, the social unit called family continues to be viable, powerful, and functional. What I heard further about Pratibha confirmed my views.

"Watching Pratibha over the years and trying to understand how that family functioned, I understood that her life was based on gratitude, thankfulness, love, giving, nurturing, devotion, human values, and the selfless attitude of keeping her husband and family above her personal needs. She expressed these traits without ever talking about them, demanding attention, claiming to have made a big sacrifice for the sake of husband and family, or demanding reward and recognition. This is a woman of strength and character. Maybe such a woman as I was in need of and looking for might exist in India.

"I was also aware of the plight of women in India: female infanticide, child marriages, brideburning for lack of dowry, giving less food and less education to the female child, and abuse of women in the present-day Indian society. But is it much different than the abusive treatment of females in the homes and society of America? My experience is that good people treat others well, and miserable people treat others miserably; this trend is definitely cross-cultural. Having seen so many marriages in the West end in divorce, was the formula of attraction and romantic love, followed by a test drive and a marriage in the chapel of love, the formula for success? I thought not. Well, would an arranged marriage prove to be superior? I'd have to wait and see what would unfold.

"Ramakrishnan placed the ad in the March 5th issue of the *Hindu,* and you responded, along with hundreds of others. I, of course, had no way of assessing, based on the initial responses, who would be appropriate and who wouldn't. Fortunately for us both, Ramakrishnan had this good sense and selected you and five others for me to enter into a correspondence with. Your letter arrived, along with those of the other candidates.

"I had determined that I wanted to have Deborah Kimbell oversee the selection process, as I had found her to be a superb judge of human character, a true friend who valued my happiness, and someone who would not be fooled or deluded in this very important task. She had proved herself to me over and over again in our interactions with the staff, and was a support for me during the difficult time of my divorce. Having deluded myself in relationships in the past, I wanted an outside, objective friend whom I could trust completely to help me in this very important, delicate, and confidential matter.

"As the letters came in, we'd sit together and read them. An attractive twenty-seven-year-old from an affluent family of printers in Madras? Maybe. A young Bharat Natyam dancer from a good family with an interest in Indian arts and traditions? Interesting and beautiful, I'll write back. Then your letter arrived. I read it and passed it to Deborah, who turned to me and said, 'This is the one!'

"I asked, 'How on earth can you know that?'

"'I feel that she's definitely the one—this woman has substance, she's a match for you intellectually and in terms of life experience. She won't be cowed or, for that matter, overly impressed by you. She'll be your equal.'

"Though meeting Ramakrishnan was purely coincidental, it did happen anyway, and it facilitated the first step in my search for a wife in India. Apparently this vague concept called providence seemed to be stepping in to make events happen for me and you, or how else could I understand, explain, or accept the fact that out of the millions of marriageable women in India, *you* saw the ad, you decided it was good enough to merit your response, things have developed as they did, and presently we are engaged to be married?"

Quite content with Ehud's elaborate answer, I chimed in, "To say as we Indians say, you were destined to marry me. I happen to be an Indian living in India, and so unconsciously your search was directed toward and focused on India." We both burst out laughing.

Ehud turned to me and whispered, "The only thing left to say is that you quite literally wrote yourself into my life."

PART II

Kalyanam

The River Ganga is believed to connect heaven and earth. Offerings made to her will reach our ancestors and complete the circle of love.

chapter 8

THE CIRCLE
OF LOVE

27.10.95

Dear Ehud, or, rather, My dear fiancé,

World looks different and I feel a bounce in my step. Is it because of you? Is it because of the turn our relationship has taken? Whatever it is, I am absolutely at peace with myself, contented and relaxed about the entire stretch of events. There was not a moment that looked unnatural, preplanned, or out of context and hence unwelcome. Everything, every event, every gesture, and every single touch merged beautifully and totally with the next, making the whole experience a soothing, healing tonic for my tense and anxious nerves. I just let myself flow along the current of events, be myself, and keep my trust in God intact, believing that only that happens that has to happen as per God's wish. If our wishes were as powerful, Ehud, I would have strapped myself alongside the baggage and come over to your (or, as you say, *our*) home and try being on my way to bringing forth a Junior Ehud . . .

Returning from the airport I wasn't myself at all. Your image of saying goodbye so gracefully with a gesture of namaste just did not go away. I kept closing my eyes and going over each and every line of that form. This image will ever and always remain with me. There are other images too, and the memory of your voice, your touch, that will remain with me. I cherish them deeply and can happily recall them and relive them whenever I feel the need to reach out and be with you. And from what you have found out about me, Ehud, you know that such moments will be many, many.

I was watching with awe and admiration the process by which a relationship comes of age and, from pen friends, matures into a level in which the two selves lose all fear and feel the preparedness in their minds for merging into each other. The whole process is simply beautiful. We were engaged on 22.10.95. For the onlookers it was simply an engagement, but Ehud, that very day, while praying to God in the lovely saree you presented me, I vowed to commit myself totally to you and take the first step in belonging to you as your wife. I vowed to be graceful, truthful, humble, loyal, faithful, gentle, and loving, and in doing that, I learned that I could pray with total detachment from the physical surroundings, with total concentration on God, at the oddest of odd moments, to help us, guide us, and lead us to discovering peace in belonging to each other. With this prayerful attitude, with total trust in God, I'm sure that our physical coming together, which both of us are anxiously looking forward to, will not be just an act of sex, postures, fun, and copulation. With serenity of prayer instilled into it, it will become an act of humbly offering ourselves to the spark of divinity that lives in us. It won't be my body at your mercy and disposal; it won't be your body causing me pleasure and pain; it will be a merging of selves in a prayerful, sublime state for restoration of peace, happiness, contentment, and goodwill. By the very same act of coming together, children are created too.

If marriage means this (to me at least), it is no longer a marriage of bodies (as the world sees it), but is a complete coming together of the two selves for fulfilling God's wish. And how earnestly I am looking forward to it. I am sure about you too. Ehud, my fear of you—the unknown—has been replaced by trust; my liking and appreciation have been replaced by splendid love. I think I am absolutely fortunate and lucky to be blessed with the chance to offer myself to you for attaining peace for the lifetime.

I do see a sacredness in our relationship. Is it my cultural hang-up that makes me see divinity even in a piece of stone? As far as I know myself, I am sure that I cannot be dictated by my culture to see sacredness in a physical relationship just because Rishi Vatsyayan wrote a treatise on the subject. I am rational enough to search for sacredness in the package and not be dictated to do so, and if I admit that I find the way we are interacting with each other as something sacred, then it is exactly what I have discovered, in a rational, non-biased, nonemotional state of alert mind.

Ehud, you have made it more than clear that Deborah reads all of my letters and helps you with typing the replies. How do I react to this, especially the post-engagement letters being read by her? Well, I don't mind, considering the very deep, healthy relationship of trust and friendship that the two of you have shared over many years. I look at her as a mutual, well-meaning friend who is a witness to the grand moment of the birth of love between two people. I do appreciate her magnanimity for reading and digesting my letters, seeing some sense in them, recognizing and understanding me in the right spirit, and recommending me to you. She has done for me what very few people would care to do. She has, in a very direct way, helped us in reinventing each other. I am thoroughly grateful to her for the wonderful role she has played in my life and in our relationship.

In Sanskrit, there is a word *kalyanam*. Translated into English, it means a state of mind in which a person no longer remains self-centered. His consciousness and his world expand to include the spouse and, later, kids. The general welfare of this new world, the family, becomes his/her prime concern. For this welfare, a woman learns to or feels the urge to pray for her husband and kids, and a man learns to pray for his wife and kids. In asking God to be with the spouse and the kids, the one who prays is rising above self and elevating to a higher plane that seeks the welfare of those closely related. Since marriage opens a new consciousness in a person's mind and attunes him/her to seeking and striving for the welfare of others, it is considered in Indian culture just as holy and sacred as taking *sanyasa* and renouncing the world to meditate for the welfare of mankind. What a *rishi*, the true one, can do by his yogic power in the caves of the Himalayas, a man or a woman who is married can do at home by concerning himself/herself totally and unselfishly with the welfare of the tiny speck of humanity that lives in the household. This is why Hindus consider marriage holy and sacred, a form of prayer in action. And that is why it is called kalyanam. As far as I know, there is no one-word English translation for this very sublime state of mind.

Although you have yet to take me as your wife, and we still have to wait till 22 February to complete the religious ceremonies of a wedding, since my prayers on the eve of our engagement, I have solely committed myself to your welfare. From that time on, your happiness, peace, and welfare have been my topmost, rather *only*, priority. To this effect, I will always pray to God—no matter where or in what state of body and mind I am, no matter where you are—a prayer for you will always be there.

About myself, I have known all along that I am capable of genuine affection, warmth, love, devotion, and loyalty to the right man. I am also capable of just the reverse to a phony impersonator. Both the possibilities exist in me. By God's grace, in you I have found the right man, one who deserves only the very best from me. I am not one for making promises, but yes, as my husband you can be sure of a nurturing stream of love, devotion, warmth, and loyalty from me. *Nurturing* is the word I closely associate with love and warmth. Depending on our attitude, love—the feeling and the expression of it—can heal, satisfy, comfort, and fulfill a person, or it can create endless hassles, agony, complications, illnesses, and problems. Our individual attitudes make all the difference.

I have a few more things to tell you. Shall I get back to basics now? Amma is feeling fine and happy because somehow she can sense that we will be happy with each other. Back at work today, I found myself staring at an amazingly long list of problems that needed my attention and intervention, but felt that I am on my way to somewhere, spending a little time in a transit camp (this hospital). I have kept the greatest news of my life to myself and haven't shared it with anyone, simply to avoid undue publicity and a mind-boggling array of questions, criticism, comments, envy, and—not the least— endless advice, ideas, and opinions.

Recall that you took me to Krishnamacharya Yoga Mandiram and introduced me to Desikachar, the author of *The Heart of Yoga?* Well, he assigned a yoga instructor for me, and I have to rush to get to the first class. Bye for now!

I am with you . . .

Vatsala

October 26 & 27, 1995
New Delhi

My dearest Vatsala,

I have arrived with only one thought in my mind—you. I am one day closer to returning and counting the days till we are united forever. Dada arrived Friday A.M., and is returning Saturday P.M. . . . He drove all this way just to see me and talk about the wedding. I've enclosed a note from him. He and his whole family are very, very, very happy. He is planning to come to our wedding, which will be his first time in South India. I'm about to start the long journey back to our home and Noogie.

All of my love for you,
Ehud

October 26, 1995

Dear Vatsala,

Ram Ram and blessings.

Meeting Ehud and speaking about you made me very happy. Ehud is very highly impressed with you and your family. After meeting you, his life has been filled with a renewed energy and enthusiasm. He is immensely pleased to have found you.

We shall meet soon.

Till then, best wishes and blessings,

Your Dada
Harish Johari

Dear Ehud,

Hope you are fine. I'm fine too, if getting soaked in torrential rains, wading through knee-deep pools of shit solution, and almost swimming (without knowing how to swim) to reach my work place—all of these contribute to a state of being fine. Today only one of my lab staff is posted in the morning, and I have about five appointments. It would be discourteous to just skip an appointment and not show up. Therefore, come I must to the department. When it rains so badly, the cabdrivers just refuse to commute, or rudely demand four times the regular fare. (Make money while it rains . . . make hay while the sun shines.) In this scene, the old and gold buses are the only modes of transport available, and they leak like hell from everywhere. Well, when I finally reached the hospital, I wished that nobody would see me while I was entering the building, and nobody did. Courtesy the heavy rains, the usually crowded reception and cash counter was practically empty at 8:05 A.M. Thanks to the spare set of shoes and dress I keep here, I could clean up and groom myself, be presentable again, and start work.

For keeping work as my top priority above my personal likes, dis-likes, and comforts, I have been given a hike of five hundred rupees. With a gross salary of 4000 rupees, I have been placed at a par with a junior consultant in the hospital. However, I don't believe "money" is a mode of giving me back what I give to the institution. An individ-ual's genuine contribution to a cause and monetary reward can (should) not be equated.

Now, Boss, I have certain questions for you. Take them seriously and answer me, OK? Do I take an extended leave without pay? Do I resign from my job? For taking an extended leave (something like a study leave), I need not give specific reasons. On completion of my leave, I can extend it further or send in my resignation by post. To resign while attending the service here, I need to give one month's advance notice. This will be, in the Childs Trust Hospital, equivalent to calling a crowded press conference and announcing my plans. And from then on, I can simply imagine the controversies, gossip, unrest, storms, and speculations this "news" will create. I would prefer going on leave, and later sending in my resignation. For the routine hospital work, I have given superb training to six of my assistants, and they will bravely hold the fort till a new clinical microbiologist is appointed. I will be able to make a quiet exit and hospital work will go on smoothly, too; thus no one gets hurt. It is a win-win situation.

Yesterday, I got your letter of 26 and 27 October posted from Delhi, enclosing three rose petals and a brief message from Dada. It was a natural reflex for me to kiss the petals and your letter. They made me very nostalgic and also made me acutely aware that you had touched them with your hands just a while ago. Deeply sensual person that I am, taste, smell, touch, sight, and sound mean a lot to me. At times I can recall them with vivid clarity and feel that you have not gone away anywhere, you are with me.

I have been thinking about how, without any convincing, argument, or cajoling, we agreed to take two weeks' vacation at our home. As far as I'm concerned, I haven't taken a vacation day in four years, so it is enough for me to be able to spend two weeks at home, not working, not thinking about sick kids and dying neonates, not worrying about the accuracy of microbiological culture reports. For me, Rochester, Vermont, USA, is as much an exotic honeymoon location as any other destination haunted by the newlyweds. For you, having traveled extensively and stayed at exotic/ordinary places, the only thing new is having me by your side. So you can have me with you in the quiet ambiance of our home. Logic is simple. Outcome is suitable to us both. Arrangement is cost-effective. Reward is there too—of being able to spend a quiet, undisturbed, relaxed time at our own home, which probably we both deserve. What better could we ask for?

About Dada's note, I am touched deeply. He obviously loves you a great deal and is happy because you are happy. In his brief message, he has conveyed his blessings and best wishes. I do thank him so much for his care and concern. Please convey my *namaskar* to him when you talk/write to him, OK?

Ehud, I have to invent some new method of reaching home. It is only 5 P.M., and looks like night already. God, is it possible to have a helicopter commuting between CTH and the rooftops of my residence?
Bye,
Vatsala

November 3, 1995

Dear Vatsala (I hope it's okay that I address you this way?),

May I first say how absolutely thrilled and delighted I am at the news of your engagement to Ehud? I have felt such joy and contentment since hearing this news. Although I have not met you, I feel I know you very well through your letters, and I have not a single doubt that you are absolutely right for Ehud.

You must know by now that Ehud and I don't have a very conventional boss-employee relationship! In addition to being colleagues, we have developed a very close friendship over the almost seven years we have worked together. He is my friend, my adviser, and my confidant, and I think that I play the same role for him. You probably know this yourself by now, but the man you are marrying is a person of tremendous generosity, warmth, and kindness for those people he truly takes into his life. I have a great deal of love for him.

The only lack in Ehud's life for years has been the presence of a person who was truly his equal in terms of giving love, concern, and caring to him. I have been blessed in my own life with my husband, Stephen, who has become my dearest friend and partner. So at home, I'm embraced by the love and warmth of my husband, and at work, I'm in the presence of Ehud's love and understanding. It has been painful to me to know that Ehud did not have the same situation at home, and I have often wished for that special person who would fill that role in his life.

I'm so looking forward to knowing you and welcoming you to this very different world. By this, I don't mean that I will hover over you at every minute, as I prize my privacy and quiet time, and I want to give you and Ehud the privacy and time alone that you need and deserve. (I have a feeling that you and Ehud will need little else when you are alone together . . .) But I do want you to know that I would welcome the opportunity to be your friend and to help you in any way I can as you make the adjustment to a life very far away from home.

There! Don't I sound like a sentimental mushball? In some areas, I am, I'm afraid, but it's a secret not many people know!

I send you a great deal of warmth and affection and love.
Deborah G. Kimbell

My Dear Ehud,

This morning, Amma suddenly asked me, in the middle of her prayers, when I joined in to say good morning to her and to the gods, "Once you go away in February, when will I see you again?" Her voice had a painful slowness to it. The thought of my going away is hurting her somewhere, though she understands that a daughter is always given away in marriage. She has done that before.

Now, probably the reversal of roles has occurred. Earlier, it was a young/middle-aged mother giving away her daughter. Now it is an old mom (better said, a "child" who practically considers her biological daughter as her mother) and the child in her is pained by the thought of letting the "mother," i.e., me, go away. Look, Ehud, what age does to a person, to a relationship. Once, as a neonate, I derived my life force from her. Now, as an old person, she derives her support, sustenance, and life force from me.

And I no longer look at her as my mother from whom I can "take" anything. The level of protectiveness, compassion, concern, care, and love that I feel for her is just what I would feel for a child, any child, our child. At this stage of my relationship with her, I can only give everything to her the best I can, with *love*.

In sharing my life with you, creating a relationship with you, I will be blessed if, by God's grace, I am able to *expand* and not restrict the limits of my warmth and love for people, especially our near and dear ones. I do hope the same for you too.

This is possible when the two of us feel *secure* and *relaxed* in each other. If our relationship gets insecure and tense, it will infect and contaminate the relationships we share with others (immediate families, friends, and colleagues). As your fiancée now and as your wife later, I'll always pray to God to help us create a solid relationship in which we will feel secure and relaxed, not insecure and threatened by each other.

Any comments, Boss?

Love,
Vatsala

Dear Deborah,

I have your letter of 3 November. I also have with me a few lines of the message you had sent to Ehud during his stay at the Taj Hotel. He simply tore the page and gave me the lines. You expressed your desire to give me a big hug in thanks for making someone you love so happy. Deborah, you would not be breaking any Indian norms if you gave me a hug. That brief message touched me deeply. I have it with me and I cherish it a great deal.

The process of getting to know Ehud through letters, getting engaged to him, and now waiting for him to enter my life completely as my husband—this whole chain of events, so far, by God's grace, did not have a single stumbling block. Everything has gone on smoothly and without doubts. Besides thanking God ceaselessly, I also need to convey to you that I am deeply impressed with your magnanimity and ability to read me in the right spirit and recom-mend me to Ehud. You have done for me what very few people care to do for anyone, and for this I will always be very thankful to you.

I can understand that if you and Ehud had shared a conventional boss and employee relationship, the association would not have lasted so long. Better opportunities often come one's way and it takes just a little daring to quit one and take the other job. It is not just the post, the assignment, and the paycheck that keep you connected to a company. It is in fact the deep and genuine love, friendship, caring, and concern that you and Ehud share that have kept the two of you together. I can fully appreciate the depth and beauty of this relation-ship. I think both of you are lucky to be blessed with each other's company. I do intend to enrich Ehud's life with my simple love and sense of belonging to him. I pray to God to help me accomplish this holy mission.

I consider it a blessing to have you come forward to welcome me with warmth and open arms into a new and different world. I might need all the help that you can spare, Deborah, for only one purpose, i.e., making His Excellency Ehud truly happy. And you have guessed right: left alone, Ehud and I would need very little else than each other. But in case I find you hovering around, I won't mind. I am used to having four big sisters, so obviously you will quickly be considered my fifth big sister who means only well for me and my husband.

You don't sound like a sentimental mushball to me at all. You sound like a caring, concerned, warm, and practical person with an amazing level of understanding. This is no biased overrating. This is what I can make out about you from your letter . . .

I do consider myself lucky to have found a friend in you. Much love to you, Stephen, and Lilian. Please do make it to the wedding.

Bye-bye.
Vatsala

7.11.95

Dear Ehud,

Enclosed is a note for Dada in reply to his message of blessings and good wishes. Could you please forward it to him? Also, I wanted you to take a look at it. A translation runs as follows:

Respected Dada ji,
Pranam.

Your brief message was as delicious as a prasad. My Holy Mother was delighted to read the same. Your friend* has mentioned that you will be coming to Trivandrum. It will be nice if your wife can come too. In my family, everyone speaks Hindi, so you won't have a communication problem, and also, we will try to take care of you as best we can. Therefore I think you may not find any inconveniences in a Trivandrum trip.

Since I do not have your Bareilly address, I am sending this note to your friend and requesting him to pass it on to you.

Please convey my Pranam to everyone at home. God willing, we will meet soon. Looking forward to your blessings,
Vatsala

*Your friend, i.e., Ehud. I am not supposed to call you by your name. My culture says so!

Ehud, I think it is appropriate to reply to his message of blessings and best wishes. He is a senior person whom you hold in high esteem. He has taken pains to write to me and tell me how happy he is about this development in our lives, even though he has yet to be introduced formally and in person to me. It would be a gross impoliteness on my part to simply receive his message and keep quiet, therefore, even though I do not have his Bareilly address, I thought I must write to him. I'd also like you to take a look at what I wrote. For this, what better than trying to route my correspondence via the high office of my Big Boss.

Ehud, it goes without saying that people who are near and dear to you are also the same for me. I intend to stand united with you in this regard, and present a common front. However, though "united we stand," it is obligatory on our part to act as *filters*, and to keep out those contacts and relationships that eclipse our personalities. We should be able to detect unhealthy, harmful associations. Our contribution to each other's lives should be to *supplement the process of positive growth and development* and disseminate the harmful and negative associations. All this is to be done with strict adherence to nonviolent, peaceful, and democratic manners and means.

I guessed love is contagious and have found it to be truly so. You do love one person and slowly you do realize that he/she walks into your life with an assortment of people he/she loves deeply, and you cannot help but love them all. I think this is how one's world grows and expands. But for this strong adhesive and cohesive power of the human psyche, the world would be teeming with dissatisfied, lonely, lost, and sad souls, who cannot find peace anywhere with anyone or with anything. Thank God we are sensitive and alive enough to need, feel, and respond to love.

Yours,
Vatsala

October 31, 1995

Dearest Vatsala,

It was 30 hours from getting in the cab in New Delhi to the joyous, unbounded, exuberant welcome of Ngurra. I was delighted to have Deborah greet me at the airport in Boston, and we had two and a half hours of driving together to get caught up on my experiences in India and the ins and outs of Inner Traditions over the last two weeks.

I got home at 8:30 in the evening, immediately took Noogie for a walk, and before bringing my bags in, unpacking, or anything else, I popped my videocassette into the player and got to see your radiant face once again. I'm now four days closer to being back in your arms, and life in Vermont is taking on a completely new meaning. As I walk through the mountains and gaze upon the natural beauty, it is with you in mind that I see all of this anew. I think only of how to share these wonders with my beloved, weaving you into the story of my life.

I trust you received my and Dada's letters, sent to you as I was leaving the Oberoi. Dada was simply overjoyed at our betrothal. He was all full of enthusiasm for the qualities we'll both be bringing to our marriage. He says he is now coming to the United States only to spend a little time in New York and in our home. He wants to teach you painting and pass on to you his knowledge of ayurveda. He's really relishing the idea of playing Grandpa to our kids and bouncing them on his knee.

Everyone says that I'm beaming, and I know why. The love that has been unleashed inside of me is just bursting out of every cell of my body. I'm feeling fulfilled, happy, and peaceful in the knowledge that I have found completion in my beloved Vatsala.

With all my affection and unending love, I remain yours now and forever,

Ehud

9.11.95

Dear Ehud,

Your letter of 31 October has come. I was in the fourth floor
doctor's restroom, taking a five-minute break to sit quietly. Earlier,
during such breaks, I used to pray for the sick children and poor
parents in our hospital. Now, during such breaks, all I can possibly
do is think about you, about us. And while coming down to the lab,
something tugged at my heart: go see, there is a letter from Ehud.
Promptly, your letter was handed over to me by the receptionist.
Is that telepathy or what?

I think, Ehud, we both are badly in love except that instead of
falling in, *by God's grace* we have raised ourselves to the sublime
purity and spirituality of loving another human being.

It makes me absolutely happy to know that you are beaming,
Dear. For the same reason, I am glowing too. If you have found
fulfillment, happiness, and peace in the knowledge that your
completion is in me—*I thank God for this grace. I thank you for
this feeling.*

I am happy.

I love you absolutely.

Yours,
Vatsala

*Shiva linga at Chitrakoot.
Since the earliest times,
the Sanatana Dharma
has included the worship
of the sexual organs. Here
the lingam of Shiva is
garlanded with flowers
and rose petals as an act
of worship.*

Dear Ehud,

Your birthday is approaching and I am full of best wishes for you. I do wish you a very happy birthday. Hope you like the card.

When we were talking in the airport lounge just before your departure to Delhi, I was *thrilled* to learn that you do believe in the fact that togetherness between parents and a new baby helps. Yes, it certainly does. We as a young family will learn the art of growing around and with each other without overshadowing anyone. I had often read in novels and leading magazines, and also seen in films how, in the West, babies just out of the hospital maternity room are placed, *with all associated luxuries and risks,* in a specially built and designed nursery at home. This idea, besides a few others such as using bottles to feed the babies, just did not appeal to me.

In my family, I have seen important days celebrated with a quiet and peaceful prayer at home. We haven't been party animals (not that it is wrong). Take, for example, birthdays and wedding anniversaries: we assemble in our pooja room, pray together, *thank God* for His kindness and mercy, and *thank our parents.* Then a brief pooja is done, raising the prasad to the deities, which is then shared among us, maybe with a few neighbors and friends. This tradition has taught me that everything, every event, and every moment in life originates from God. To God it must refer from time to time, and to God it must return for eternal peace. Then, every special event becomes an occasion for special thanksgiving and special remembrance of the role of the Divine in our lives. The same is done when we pass exams, get jobs, receive a hike in pay. The same is also done at mealtimes. Food is always offered to the gods first. If all successes and failures are celebrated and regretted at the feet of God, the practice teaches us the importance of God in our lives and the futility of giving undue pampering to our individual egos and personalities. Also, when a family always gathers around, and gets together in the pooja room, prayers and thanksgiving become *habit* and it remains no longer a dictation from the culture/religion which must be followed whether one likes it or not.

Similarly, in a family, children tend to learn from the religious preferences of the parents. I have a severe cardiomegaly (generous, big heart) with regard to religions, and so far in my meager contact with non-Hindu faith, I haven't found a single "bad" aspect in any religion. Therefore, in my future household I intend to maintain an atmosphere where all religions are accepted, respected, and considered as equally efficient road maps leading us to God or to a way of life that understands the limits of man and the limitlessness of nature and of God. I do not want the next generation to grow up believing "might is right." They should be open to adventures in religion, philosophies of life, and food, and in living their lives in general. They should be taught to *search and find goodness* in every aspect of life, including all religious doctrines and faiths.

Last evening, Amma and I started our preparation for the wedding. I unearthed my collection of sarees and listed the accessory garments that are needed. List is long. This evening, Amma and I will go shopping for the accessories. With Xmas, New Year's, and Pongal approaching, the tailors will be very busy. It's better if I get started now than wait and lose time. When I was trying on sarees, Ehud, I felt conscious of the fact that for the first time in my life I was preparing to meet *my man*. This awareness about the purpose of my preparation filled me with new energy and enthusiasm. I felt distinctly happy and hoped you would feel happy too to realize that you are always in my thoughts no matter what I am up to. All my activities now have a distinct, definite direction that is *you*.

Despite all the new energy that fills me while I prepare myself for you, in a part of my heart there is a growing concern about my kid—who other than Amma? She is trying to take the event with courage, and in a sporting spirit. It is I who am feeling terribly upset about having to go away and leave her alone. I do console myself by saying that when Junior Ehuds prepare to arrive, we can ask Amma to come and spend some time with us and teach me her art and science of handling babies. She is very fond of stitching outfits for babies. All her kids and grandkids have grown up wearing outfits made by her, and I want our juniors, too, to have that privilege. More than this, I want her to come to our household, sanctify it with her prayers, and see for herself that we genuinely love each other and are happy to be together. I truly want her to see this and be happy at this stage of her life.

Ehud, reading about my attachment to Amma, are you getting worried that the obstetrician forgot to cut the umbilical cord connecting us? Being bound by an umbilical cord is a sign of total helplessness and a completely parasitic relationship of total dependency. Presence of such a bond in an adult, albeit symbolically, is a psychological indicator of immaturity, insecurity, and a tendency of avoiding responsibilities/commitments. Fortunately, I am confident that my relationship with Amma is not of the type mentioned above. I think I am quite mature, secure, and confident, with a good degree of self-esteem and willpower, and I have never avoided a responsibility or a commitment. And when I still am so much attached to Amma, it is just because her package makes good sense to me. You do know that I am cold, rational, logical, non-emotional, and analytical about studying any package, and if I like one, it does make sense to me (or I would not have cared to continue an association). For me she makes solid good sense. And I will consider it lost time and a lost opportunity if because of being away from her I am not able to practically extend love, caring, warmth, and concern for her. It is like being married to you and taking a long leave from being a wife to you. I want to live each waking and sleeping moment with you because I care for you too much to waste my time in being away from you. I see it as something very different from selfish possessiveness and parasitic dependency. It is the heartfelt need and longing to be together, not a tendency of grabbing, owning, and possessing.

I am glad that, mother-in-law jokes aside, you are already looking at her the way I do. This I consider as my blessing and your magnanimous gracefulness. If you had pulled out a sword and declared battle on mere mention of her name, I would have felt torn into two, a part of me with my husband, whom I love, and a part of me with my mother, whom I cannot help loving so naturally for what she is as a human being. That could have been a very painful, sorry affair for me. I am glad that you are already considerate to the one and only member of my family who matters to me most.

Vatsala

My dearest Vatsala, fiancée, beloved of my heart, my true wife:

God bless the day I found you
I'll build my whole world around you
Now and forever, let it be you.

This tune has been running through my mind today, and although you won't know the melody or the lilting quality of the vocalist, I'm sure you'll appreciate the words. Since our engagement, I have vowed to keep you at the center of all my feelings of devotion, putting your welfare and happiness before my own. This vow and devotion is our marriage contract. As far as I'm concerned, you are already my wife, and will be treated by me as such. All the rest—the marriage ceremonies, the friends, the relatives, the licenses, travel visas, etc.—are but a public representation of what for me is already a fait accompli (I know this time you get the meaning . . .)

Your packet of letters arrived, and I have read them with the greatest joy. I'm truly in awe of the way things are unfolding, and thank God for the grace and blessings that have been bestowed on us. The way you are experiencing our coming together as described in your letter is so harmonious with my own feelings and sentiments that I start to wonder who's writing to whom. Who is really speaking here, and who is listening? Before I started writing, I thought to myself, *I really don't have anything to say. Vatsala has already said it.* I even for a moment thought I might not be able to write a letter, wondering what I could add. However, as my friends will say, I'm not one to be at a loss for words for long. So I'll take this opportunity to express my unbounded joy and love for you, and my commitment, absolute and forever, to cherish and keep you near, to protect and honor you.

I marvel at the consistency and determination that is expressed in the path you've chosen to take in this life. To wait all these years without compromise for the right man is a tribute to the veracity of your commitment to your ideals and values. I feel privileged to be able to honor those values by giving myself to you totally and without compromise.

When I enter you, it will be as an act of worship, to reach that most secret and sacred place at the center and core of your being, and unite it with that of my own. As with all things in life, it is our intention and attitude that raises or lowers the experience. I feel, as I know you do, that it is our work to sanctify our relationship in the most sublime manner we are capable of and, with God's grace, create that atmosphere in ourselves that will attract a being in harmony and concert with our own spiritual values.

To call life into this troubled world is indeed an act with profound consequence, not just for us as individuals with all the responsibility, work, joy, and activities it entails, but also, how will this new life affect and contribute to the decline or renewal of the world we will be leaving as our legacy to our offspring?

As I mentioned on the phone—although I don't know how well my words came through the intermittent loss of connectivity—I do not see your finding sacredness in our relationship or in a stone, for that matter, as a cultural hang-up. Unless, of course, you will allow me to be hung up as well. In the mineral or stone, we have the earliest, simplest form, and hence the form closest to God. So we start out with the stone, and we end up on our return back to the Creator with man. Everything has an inside, even the stone. Consequently, our worship impresses the stone as much as it does the man. True devotion inscribes the stone as it does the bone in man. From that inscription, the blood is generated and from that blood, the whole human form. So from the field of the mineral to that of the biological to that of the electromagnetic, and on to the universal field of consciousness—all is imbued with sacredness. And in my view, it all is deserving of our feelings of devotion, thanksgiving, and remembrances of God.

I think you'll find it interesting that in the Judaic tradition, marriage is considered the completion of our contract with God and is the most sacred of institutions. Judaism does not provide for any celibate priest caste, and the most wise and most spiritual in the traditions have always been married men and women. Judaism, like Hinduism, sees the need for the human being to complete all stages of life, from that of child on through householder and husband, through the final stage of death and liberation. The *Talmud* (a sacred book of commentaries and collected wisdom of the Jews) says that as soon as you are born, you should prepare to die. Now the meaning here is not morbid, but rather, that death should be the measure of your deeds on earth. If on the day of your passing, you are not reconciled to your acts in the world, then you should have been thinking about this simple statement of truth earlier on.

The sacredness of family and spousal relations are at the core of the Judaic teachings, and as such, are in complete accord with the Brahminical point of view. It's been truly enlightening to me to observe the incredible similarities between Jewish teachings and Hindu teachings. I have yet to discover any substantive point of dissension between the two views. Quite to the contrary, I find them complementary and supportive of each other.

The way we've come together certainly is imbued with spirituality and cosmic proportion. I could not have dreamed, imagined, or made up such an encounter. That we have been drawn together through such a great distance and from such different cultures is truly extraordinary and most definitely sacred in my heart. I will always endeavor to keep this sacred quality alive and present in my interactions with you and our family. Further, I see the sacredness of our relationship as forming a foundation from which we can give to others something of that spiritual quality that is flowing through our relationship. To be able to give freely of these qualities will only enhance and enrich these attributes in us. Already, and quite miraculously, I find myself deepened and broadened by my union with you. I already feel that I'm more than I was by myself, and am certain that the two of us will be far greater than the sum of each of us alone.

As I write you, I realize that I'm one month closer to being united with you. It's now just three short months until I arrive in Trivandrum. I've been thinking quite a lot about this time away from you. At first, I was wanting to find some way to change things and get you here immediately, but realizing that that impatience in me was bound to be met by a lot of resistance by the U.S. government, parents, airlines, hotels, office, friends, etc., I concluded then that the timing was absolutely right, and in fact, arrangements are flowing quite nicely and naturally.

However, I'm still left with this period of time without you. What does it mean? How should it be put to use to enhance and further our togetherness? Each evening after work, I come home and reflect upon you (I also turn on the video and see your image), our life together, and my feelings about that. I'm finding a great joy in doing this. It is allowing me to purify my mind and open up channels of receptivity to you. At the same time and for the first time, I'm feeling such a sense of trust, nurturing, and confidence in you that some of the very delicate and sensitive feelings of spirituality, devotion, and inspiration that are kept deep inside of me and protected from the outside world are emerging. Memories of childhood and childhood innocence are returning. The feelings of peace and love that were so exuberantly and abundantly present in me as a child are returning to me as a man, and for this, I'm truly grateful to you.

I'm delighted with your attitude toward Deborah's involvement in our relationship. I could not ask for a more understanding, loving approach than the one you have taken. It is absolutely what I would have hoped for, and shows me that those who are close to me will also be close to you and that the circle of love will expand as we come together.

Everything I have written you is the unedited, unadulterated, stream of consciousness that comes out of me when I sit down to address you. Nothing has been changed or altered whatsoever. However, Deborah has played another, more significant role in this correspondence: she has been present as the spirit of the feminine. Consequently, when I'm writing, that spirit which you both share is in the room, and I'm inspired to address it. Hence, if there is any inspiration in what I say, credit goes to Deborah and her unconditional love and affection, unencumbered by the complexes, neuroses, and hidden agendas so common today. She has been midwife to this correspondence, and I, like you, shall be forever grateful and thankful to her.

However, as it is natural for a husband and wife to have correspondence that is for our eyes only, please simply draw a sign at the top of any letter or any page of a letter that you wish to be "for my eyes only," and I, of course, will keep it for myself only.

Wedding plans and activities are moving ahead smoothly. Ramakrishnan has taken on the full responsibility for making all arrangements for the wedding hall, temple, food, priests, etc. We've discussed a budget and I have authorized him to move ahead based on this budget. Now, I know we're stepping a little outside of the modus operandi here, where the wife's family makes all arrangements and all payments. However, as they say in Australia, "No worries, mate." As I said on the phone, I relieve you of all worry or responsibility in this matter and take it upon myself, with Ramakrishnan's help, to make the wedding a festive and tasteful event which can be enjoyed by our families and friends in India and those who come from abroad.

Now there might be some feelings of concern from your brother or parents about me picking up the costs. Know that for me this is not an issue and does not reflect in any way whatsoever on my feelings toward your family. I'm more than happy to be able to contribute in a way that helps realize an event that will mark one of the happiest days of our lives. If your family feels the need to have some financial involvement, what I suggest is that they talk to Ramakrishnan and pick some piece of the puzzle to handle—for instance, flowers, dessert, whatever would feel appropriate and would not burden their finances. Keep in mind that none of this is of any importance to me. The only thing that matters is your happiness and good feelings around this event. In that, I am at your complete service.

I'm sending this letter to you by Federal Express so that we can shorten the time between letters. I've filled out an airbill. Make a copy of it for your reference and simply use it as a guide anytime you need to send me anything. If you use this system, there should be no expense to you. They should pick up and deliver, simply by you phoning them and instructing them to do so.

Please also feel free to call me anytime you wish, the same way you did last time. I'm sorry if I didn't sound terribly coherent, as I was just about going to bed. I was, however, very, very happy to hear from you, as I will always be, and you needn't worry (this is an order from Your Boss—don't worry), so just call whenever you wish. Also, don't be concerned about the expense, as it is much less costly in the U.S. system than in the Indian, and I can certainly afford to be on the phone with you for a half-hour without concern for the cost.

Nevertheless, I still prefer corresponding, as writing approaches much more closely the intimacy and quality of communication we have when we're together physically. Your letters are a joy and inspiration, and a constant source of nourishment.

I send you my deepest feelings of love and devotion—you are at the center of my life's breath.
Ehud

Ehud,

The enormity of the decision that we have made shakes me up from time to time. Two chronically independent and self-made people have decided to let go of their independence, have found that despite so many years in this world, their capacity to love is intact, and they have committed themselves to each other. My God, my God. The meaning of this commitment in my eyes is incomparably larger than marriage. One can be married and have no commitment, have commitments but not be married, have commitments and be married too. Fortunately, we are stepping into the last category. We are committed to each other, and by the grace of God we shall be married soon.

Then Ehud, I must let the previous stream of thoughts come to a halt and respond to the letter that has just arrived. How should I respond? is the question. To the love that you have so beautifully expressed in your letter, a response in printed or spoken words is rather an insult. The only way in which justice can be done to such true and original feeling is by merging myself with you, physically and mentally, never saying a word in the process. Sometimes the power and intensity of a simple hug can tell you a lot more about how much I love you than all these confessions spread over so many pages. I am happy. Gradually, we are inching our way toward the world of touch and physical expression of what we feel for each other. Waiting is long and 90 days seem too many, but they will pass. Let us have patience . . .

These 90 days are like the Roza of Moslems, Lent of Christians, fasting of Hindus. Please excuse my ignorance, but tell me what is the equivalent ritual in Judaism? This fasting is meant to purify our minds and thoughts, and to help us realize the role of God in our lives. This waiting time is meant to make us search our souls and ask why we are doing what we are doing. If our answer is that we are taking each other's help in relocating ourselves to our core, then well, dear, let this answer sink deep into the subconscious mind . . .. patiently we shall wait; the days of self-examination shall pass.

You know by now that I am as much a physical person as one with a religious and spiritual bent of mind. It goes without saying that besides these very refined anticipations of marriage, I am anxiously looking forward to walking into your arms and staying there. I will never tire of giving and taking hugs and kisses, and making passionate love and cute babies (in my eyes, all babies are cute—no matter how, why, when, where, or to whom they are born). To summarize, you are likely to have a hectic time having me as your wife.

I don't know how to thank you for all the pains you are taking to make our marriage a festive and tasteful event for our families and friends. Your concern for my feeling good around these events is touching me deeply. Your picking up the bills is of course the most unnatural, abnormal event in an Indian context. In India, who ever heard of a bridegroom willing to spend to take a woman in marriage? I am indebted to you for this generosity, spontaneity, and concern and care for my family. May God bless you for all the help you are extending.

Not long ago, I was feeling terrible about not being able to take the arrangements in my hands, about having to depend on you, Ramakrishnan, and Anna. I do not often blame myself (I never, ever blame anyone else), but I was feeling quite helpless because personally I was not doing anything other than preparing myself to be your bride. Everything else was being done by you, Ramakrishnan, and Anna. Your attitude that you have mentioned in your letter of 13.11.95 has relieved me of this feeling of anxiety and helplessness. (Do you have a remote-control switch or something, Boss?)

I do not see you as someone different from me—a stranger, a not yet fully known man, a newcomer to my life. I do not even see you as a boyfriend, a fiancé. I see you as my own image. I don't feel you are someone else, someone different from me. It doesn't hurt at all, anywhere, to put myself completely into your care. It all seems the natural order of the day. It is better that this feeling is already born in me. It feels great to learn new lessons about your generosity (which I will never take for granted, never demand, never exploit, and never take advantage of, it is my promise to you, Ehud).

As your wife, I hope to be at home for you and our kids. I don't intend to take a job. This simply means that I will totally and for all practical and theoretical purposes be depending on you for all my needs and sustenance. And this also means a big financial commitment for you. If a feeling of resentment at having to depend on you for everything kept nagging me, if I continued to feel awkward at having lost my small earning capacity and the freedom to use it as I liked or deemed fit, it would not be a healthy trend. On this front, I must unlearn the lessons that I learned out of necessity and circumstances.

I have been too proud, too independent, to accept help—at least in terms of money. It made me feel small when I had to take money from my family for my studies. Of course, from 1965 till 1987 (through schools, colleges, and universities), it was my family that supported me because my scholarships were pitifully small . . . My family sacrificed a great deal to see me through expensive colleges and universities. They never grumbled—that is their helpful, generous spirit. In 1987, when I was selected for a national research fellowship, the sum was not big, but the first thing that I did was to stop accepting money from home. I imposed strict discipline on my eating, dressing, and spending, and tried to live on what I got from the fellowship. This put me into big trouble at times. But I learned to survive with Rs. 10 or 15 as my pocket money from the 15th to the 30th of many months, and never to write home asking for money, never beg, borrow, or steal, never run to the bank before the 1st, and never delay payment of any bill. This strict disciplinarian economics taught me how to stretch a rupee to its maximum and squeeze it for all it was worth. This also taught me to be wise in spending, honest in earning, and never to waste anything. It taught me to train my mind to be content with what I have (this is an easier way to peace), and never to crave or let my mind be polluted with competition, greed, overambition, or lust. I learned how to make a pair of new dresses look new for years. I learned to ignore hunger, pain, small illnesses, and temptations, and to keep all my mind and energy focused on only one aim—I must complete my studies well, I must not let my tyrannical professor ruin my life, I must get my degree, I must be successful. My disciplinarian measures taught me to respect poverty. (I do not love it, do not desire a lifelong association with it, but it has served its purpose: it has taught me what I must learn from a practical encounter with it, and now I won't feel bad to have to let it go forever.) Poverty is not a curse. It is a great opportunity to learn about life, about material and spiritual forces that affect life and people. It teaches various aspects of human behavior and psychology—all depending upon whether one looks at it as a teacher or as a messenger of death (and with the latter attitude, poverty is what else but a curse?).

With these measures in force, I could save money for my thesis, and extend help with money, clothing, and food to a fellow student who had no other means of getting money. I also managed to buy lavish gifts for Anna and Banu for their weddings, for my parents' wedding anniversaries, and for Amma's birthday. Getting this job at CTH added fire to my fuel of independence and made me even more disciplined. Whenever possible, I would pay for the lab tests for very sick kids of very poor parents. (For want of money should medical care be denied?) Whenever possible, I extend a hand in giving, not taking, help.

With you as my husband, these attitudes of mine will have to change radically. I will be depending on you for everything from a handkerchief to socks. Initially, it will be difficult for me because I am not very comfortable being so desperately dependent. But you have so gracefully assimilated me into your system that this giving and taking seems like child's play. Well, Captain, as usual you are leading the ship. I will unlearn quickly what I learned out of necessity (but I will never let go of the education that my experience gave me), and let you take pride in spending for yourself, which means your wife and kids. On my part, I can assure you that I will always respect you for the support you are giving as the man of the house.

I will obey your command, and never again worry about calling you anytime I wish. But what would you suggest to cure the longing I feel, on hearing your voice, to run into your arms? Talking to you on the phone plays havoc with my memory-recall system. I feel more lost than before. I do get vexed for having to wait so long, and my wisdom in viewing this waiting period as a time for self-examination vanishes as quickly as the phone connection. With this unique problem that I face regarding speaking to you on the phone, I will avoid calling you as much as I can and use the telephone only for emergencies. FedEx is fine for me. It lets me take liberty with what and how much I write. It lets me tell you I love you without the phone attendant listening in. It lets me tell you how prayerfully I am waiting for our merger. Could I ask for a better mode of communication? Of course, the best is to live in our home and spend each moment together.

Before I close, I must tell you that I am wondering if Noogie watches the video with you every evening. He probably does not have color vision, but his eyes can translate all colors to shades of gray, and I think all that he sees on video, he can recognize if he sees it in person. This is my layman's hypothesis, and may scientifically be right or wrong. According to this hypothesis, if he sees me every evening on the video, his culture shock of seeing me in person will be less profound. Initially, like any other human being, he is going to resent having me in the house because he might see me as someone who takes away some of the undivided love and affection he is used to. Till he manages to develop some fondness for me, this resentment is likely to stay. Only when he sees that his boss loves him as dearly as before (even though he has one more person in his life), is his resentment likely to lessen.

I've been trying to see my entry into our home from Noogie's point of view. I really don't know what I can do to make him feel less threatened, and to make it easier for him to have me in the household. Is there someone like a canine psychologist who could be consulted regarding the psychological trauma a four-legged member of the household feels when a new member joins the team? I will certainly take time to adjust to Noogie. As I have said before, I have never moved closely with pets. But I don't and will never resent Noogie, simply because I have learned how dearly you both love each other. How will Noogie learn that I love you too, and, because I love you and belong to you, he should not resent me? Do canine and human logic see eye to eye on this ground?

The major worry of a woman who is about to get married is usually how she is going to adjust to her husband, his world, and the in-laws. I have absolutely no problems in these areas of human interaction and relationships. However, I am beginning to wonder how Noogie and I are going to learn to adjust to, respect, accept, and love each other.

For me, a dog is not oh-just-a-dog. It has as many feelings, sentiments, emotions as any human being, and many times, an animal's feelings are purer, less selfish, and more genuine (only they don't have the ability of human beings to brag about it). As decent, civilized human beings, we should treat nonhuman life forms with as much sensitivity and kindness as we treat humans.

Somehow, Ehud, get Noogie to watch me on the video every evening, freeze a frame, call me aloud by name, and show him . . . "See, Noogie, this is Vatsala . . ." He is likely to get used to watching a different shade of gray and new contours and hearing you call an alien name in the household. Maybe these well-intentioned exercises will help him accept me into his fold.

Now Ehud, don't laugh about these propositions and possibilities, and don't tell me not to be silly. As human beings, sometimes we notice others' fears, pains, sufferings, and traumas. Most of the time we are so miserably self-centered that we intentionally or unintentionally ignore them. With an inborn, built-in mechanism of insensitivity to other human life forms, often man tends to take nonhuman life forms simply for granted. I don't wish to do this. As I don't want to hurt a human being, so I don't want to hurt a fly. And on this ground, I am very happy to be a vegetarian. Well, this is my combined extract from Hinduism, Brahminism, Buddhism, and Jainism, all of which teach *ahimsa*, i.e., not hurting any life form. Hurting anything is called *himsa*. Transferred into my relationship with Noogie, I want my entry into the household to be painless, fearless, and smooth for him. Please, Ehud, if you can make that happen in any manner, I will be grateful to you.

The way it is raining now, it seems as if the clouds have come to stay. Will the Blue Dart (FedEx) man come to pick up the letters, I wonder? Maybe the yoga class in the evening will get washed out too. On rainy days like this, my ever-green dream is to stay at home, feel warm, cozy, clean, and comfortable, munch my favorite snack, read a nice book or paint something or simply catch some sleep. Rains . . . well, I have seen plenty, but those dreams of staying home when it rains never came true. I always just had to go to school or to work. Watching snow in Vermont will be a new experience for me. And you are my teacher of how to survive such a cold and crazy winter, OK? It amazes me to realize that soon my adaptation skills will be put to the test in the snow-covered land of Vermont.

Ehud, I am ready to face the challenge head on, be it Noogie or the snows of Vermont.

Vatsala

November 20, 1995

Dearest Vatsala,

I'm very much enjoying receiving your letters. They have become a source of respite in the evenings, a way of staying in touch and hearing your voice inside me. I've read over many of the letters a number of times, and I really feel connected to you in the process.

I'm delighted that the yoga sessions are going well. I'm very pleased that you've increased the sessions to two a week and that you're making good progress. I've been watching the video that Desikachar gave me of his dad, and it's truly an amazing piece of work. We're both very lucky that you're taking yoga in this school, as you're getting exposed to an authentic tradition in a place that is full of good energy.

I trust the rains have subsided and you're feeling better. Please, for my sake, take care of yourself and don't overdo it at work. The main thing now is to keep your energy up and your health in good shape. There are many changes coming in our lives, and in order to make these transitions successfully, it is very important to keep rested and healthy.

VISA:

We sent your and my photos along with the application to the Immigration and Naturalization Service. They then review the documents and give an authorization to the State Department for the visa. What's really happening here is that they're preapproving you for naturalization and immigration to the United States, and not just approving you for a visa. This means that when you get here, it will be a relatively quick matter to obtain permanent resident status for you as my wife. This process should take about three weeks. Deborah will be calling into them regularly to make sure everything's on track.

As soon as they give their approval, the State Department will issue you a packet with various questions and a list of requirements, which will probably include a medical exam, etc. You will then submit these documents, and they will then give you an appointment to get your visa. Our understanding is that this will happen in Madras, but we will know for certain once we get through the Immigration and Naturalization process and have approval. I don't anticipate any problems here, and you shouldn't worry, as we're on top of things.

WINTER CLOTHES AND WHAT TO
BRING ON THE TRIP HOME:

As you know, we will be going from Trivandrum to Madurai and then directly to Vermont. So whatever you wish to take with you on this trip back home should be included with your luggage going to Trivandrum. You will be allowed two suitcases on the plane, plus a carry-on bag. Anything else could be shipped, although it will take six to eight weeks to get to us.

In your checked luggage, you should include all your best sarees, a few of your nicest pajama outfits, any woolen sweaters, undergarments, and toiletries. We will be met at the airport with a winter coat for you, and whisked off to our home. Within a couple of days of arriving in Vermont, we'll go shopping and get you properly outfitted. So get ready for the shopping spree!

The only thing I'd like you to buy now is a pair of boots that would be suitable for walking in the snow. If this represents a problem, then simply send me a tracing of both your feet and I'll have a pair available when we land at the airport. Again, don't worry about whether these are the ideal boots or if they will stand up to the conditions here—you just need them for the first couple of days until we go shopping.

UPWARDLY MOBILE:

In keeping with your career trajectory, I'm hereby promoting you to the position of my wife and, with God's grace, mother of our children. This is a full-time position with excellent benefits and a loving Boss. As your new home has four stories in it and will soon have children, there will be many opportunities for you to be upwardly mobile!

It gives me no end of delight and pleasure to know that you are happy and contented to take this position with all its responsibilities and joys. I will do everything within my power to help you succeed in this challenging new role. Along with this work, I very much encourage you to give alternative medicine serious study. I would ask you to focus on two areas: family health issues and longevity. Dada knows a great deal about both of these areas and is happy to share this knowledge with you. In addition, we publish a number of excellent books on this subject and I have friends who are practitioners who could also provide guidance.

The decisions we'll be facing around the health care of our children will be extensive, and our convictions and values will be tested in this area. We will need a thorough and comprehensive knowledge of the issues. For example, I've had to face a number of issues just around how to treat Noogie, even though he's extremely healthy and the vet says that I should keep on doing whatever I'm doing. For instance, all vets say that dogs must take heartworm medicine. This medicine is very powerful and has side effects. Yet almost all dogs are on it. I have instead consulted with a homeopathic vet, and am giving Noogie a homeopathic prophylactic against heartworm. The vets all recommend removal of the dog's testicles both as a preventive measure against prostate cancer and as a way of making male dogs less aggressive. I haven't done this. Noogie is a gentle and sweet dog, and this has been achieved through good nutrition and a loving environment, with good contact with other humans.

So you can see that, in our household, there will be a real need for in-depth health care knowledge in order not to be swept up and into the allopathic treatment modalities. As we are both having children late in life, it is essential that we be able to keep up with them 10 to 15 years from now. This can be done through good habits, proper nutrition, yoga, and the application of herbal and ayurvedic remedies in support of longevity. There's a lot that can be done to keep one's energy level and endurance high—high enough to run around and play with your kids without feeling exhausted.

Add all of this to your painting, which I very much want you to pursue—for yourself, as well as with our children—and catching up on your reading, and you'll have more than a full-time job. You can leave the worldly matters to me. I'll take care of the foreign office; you take care of the home office.

I think you should put your CV and letters of recommendation in order, as I would like to have a copy, and I think you should as well, by way of a summary and completion of that phase of your life. Also, if sometime after raising children you wish to write, having your credentials documented could be of use.

I, too, am delighted about our honeymoon plans. It's a wonderful example of our compatibility and shared values. Our home is actually in the middle of a resort, where people from all over the world come to take their honeymoons and vacations. I can think of no more wonderful way of spending our first two weeks of marriage than in our home, where I will be able to gradually and gently introduce you to life in Vermont. I look forward to spending a wonderful, peaceful time with you in front of the fireplace, enjoying each other's company without the intrusion of the world.

As far as I'm concerned, visits to India will be very much a part of our life together. As you know, I'm starting a business in India, we have family and many friends in India, and I have a deep longing to be in India. So I think it's fair to say to your mother and family that a once-a-year visit by us to India is part of the plan. We will of course have to take into consideration pregnancy, kids, etc., but nevertheless, we will try to get to India once a year. So please tell Amma not to despair of losing a daughter, but rather to focus on gaining a son.

Please, don't you worry about any restrictions on love. For love to flourish, it must be unbounded. As we are graced with a deep love for each other, for that love to be healthy we must share it with others, with our children, with our parents—all the people who are important to us. Let our love be a beacon illuminating all around us, and in so doing, causing our own faces to shine.

I am your refuge, your abode, your safe haven. I am the rock on which you can stand in the secure and relaxed certainty that I am immovable in my love for and devotion to you. Your sentiments with regard to security/insecurity, relaxation/tension are at the core of what makes for good relations. They should be the bedrock of our relationship, of our children's experience of us, as well as the way our friends and loved ones experience us. There can be no substitute for these basic fundamentals.

I've seen it over and over again in my experience of life—people being insecure with each other, having low self-esteem, in turn creating unbearable tension which inevitably leads to conflict. In this world where nothing is certain, to know for a certainty that you can find secure refuge in your beloved is one of the greatest blessings that can be bestowed upon us. I feel, as you said in a letter prior to our meeting, "blessed."

I found it truly amazing to receive your comments about "falling in love." After many years of thinking about this subject, I realized that falling in love is a big problem, and the key to the problem is contained in the words themselves. A *fall* is a descent, something destructive, so how can it be linked to love? In most cases, and particularly in the West, people *fall in love*, which means they are attracted to another person, they lose consciousness, and in an unconscious state, experience the currents of love. In most cases, this "fall" is due strictly to sexual attraction; often the lover is nothing more than a projection or fantasy. Some time passes and they recover from their fall, only to discover that they don't know the person they are sleeping with—and in many cases, don't care for the other person, don't share their values, goals, and aspirations. They are unable to support each other and live in peace and harmony. And they fall out of love.

So I also feel graced and blessed as you do: we have carefully and meticulously explored each other's goals and values, aspirations and inspirations, and were diligent in our explorations of each other's psyches. We were fortunate enough to be blessed with the *ascent* to love, loving each other and what we stand for, and looking to support, augment, and enhance each other's lives, and to create one life together with our eyes and hearts open.

My bedroom is certainly big enough and, God willing, so is my heart, so put as many kids in there for as long as you want. I, like you, want nothing more than a happy, peaceful, loving home environment, a nurturing home in which children can grow secure and strong in the knowledge that their parents love them and see them in a good light. I have had the privilege of living with Dada and his family over many months and have seen firsthand the benefits of an enlightened, tolerant, yet religious upbringing. Dada and Pratibha have raised many children, both theirs and their relatives', and in each and every case, have turned out excellent young men and women. So you can be sure of my support and encouragement in your efforts to create a feeling of devotion and commitment to God in our children and in our home. I am 100 percent behind you.

Both in my life and in my publishing work, I have embraced all the religions of man, both formal and informal, "civilized" and "primitive." To me, the hallmark of religion is in the behavior and character of its practitioners. I believe in a religion of love, peace, truth, and beauty, and wherever I find the expression of these virtues, I make my altar and express my devotions. Likewise, I would encourage a similar attitude in our home and children, one that I see amply supported by what you've written.

However, in all these years and in all these interactions with leaders of different religions, publishing different religious points of view and experiencing the various rituals and practices, the two religions that I have most closely affiliated with are Judaism and Hinduism. In our home, you will already find the icons of Agni, Ganesha, Shiva, and Kali. I suspect we will draw most heavily from these two traditions in our home, and as I said earlier, these two traditions complement and harmonize with each other very, very well.

I see from your letter that you have a lot of concern around the wedding and how things will turn out. As I said to you on the phone, you are relieved of all the responsibility for and concern about wedding arrangements. I, with the help of Ramakrishnan, will make things happen and will make things happen in a fantastic way. I have already reserved five rooms at the Surya Samudra. Everything has been confirmed directly with them. I stayed in this resort in February—it is first rate, all the rooms are from converted, hand-carved Keralite homes. It sits on a rise overlooking a private beach. It's run by a retired German schoolteacher who is partners with one of my friends in Bombay. The food is excellent, as are the amenities. All our foreign guests will be housed there.

Ramakrishnan is engaging a wedding hall, priests, musicians, and dancers. I am arriving a week in advance of the event, and will inspect all facilities and make sure all arrangements are satisfactory. Our guests will have a fantastic beach resort holiday with great food, music, and dance. Just on this most superficial of levels, I already feel confident that we will be able to give an excellent experience to those who attend our wedding. Add to this the great pleasure of participating in our love for each other in this wondrous event with so many friends and loved ones present—well, I'm preparing myself, as you should, for a great time.

So you're asking yourself, *What does the Boss expect me to do?* I want you to arrive in Trivandrum relaxed, refreshed, happy, and healthy. I want you to give up any concern or worry about the event. I want you to remain composed, collected, centered, and relaxed, so that my

friends and loved ones can have the pleasure of experiencing the beauty that's in you. I want you to pray for our happiness and be that quiet center from which I can draw strength while attending to all the details. I want you to have the pleasure of interacting with my friends during their week in Trivandrum. I want you to beautify yourself, pamper yourself, and feed that feminine spirit in anticipation and expectation of our coming together.

I send you my undying love, devotion, and sincerest wishes for your happiness.

Ehud

A stone icon of one of the divine couples, a theme throughout Hinduism.

Dear Ehud,

I have received your letter of 20.11.95. The courier boy came in like a wet crow. He had got caught in the rain. I offered him tea so he would feel better before he resumes his next delivery, unmindful of the torrential rains. That is quite a sense of duty, isn't it?

Oh, what a letter. At the end of it I felt like a baby . . . like a flower. How meticulously you have looked into each and every aspect and suggested what could be done. At the end you have even asked me to beautify myself, pamper myself . . . Very few daughters have such a reassurance, such a guidance from their fathers. A wife getting these from her husband is a much rarer event. And see, we are such a rare duo. I am flying, Ehud, feeling so light, so secure, so protected, and so heavily pampered by you. I will make a spot diagnosis . . . you are suffering as much from a premarital paternal instinct as I am suffering from a premarital maternal instinct. Of the two of us, who is luckier to get whom, God knows. All I know is that I certainly am lucky, absolutely lucky to have you. For me, you are many of my relations rolled into one. I certainly did not expect this. I did not think I deserved a man like you. Well, I daydreamed about it and felt that I needed such a person. God has been boundlessly kind and generous and loving. He has made my daydreams come true. He has given me you. What else do I care for?

Love to you . . .
Vatsala

chapter 9

THE COLOR
OF ABUNDANCE

November 30, 1995

Dearest Vatsala,

Your letters are such a source of nourishment and healing that I can't adequately express my appreciation for your marvelous communication skills. I'll save the expression of my true appreciation for the night of the 22nd.

I am you, you are me, we are altogether, as the song goes. You have found your world and I have found mine, and neither of us need seek any longer. With this God-given foundation, it is now up to us to build, grow, and become more than we are individually. We have been blessed with the physical, psychological, and spiritual basis for *sadhana*.

In Judaism, the "90 days" would fall in a shorter period of time: *Yom Kippur* is a day of fasting and atonement at the end of a ten-day period of introspection that marks the beginning of the Jewish New Year and is devoted to our relationship with Divinity.

Please stay in my arms always and forever. Let's marry the physical and the spiritual, as we marry ourselves, and let our passions flow through and into each other, right to that core and center of which you so beautifully speak. I can't wait. Yes, I do have a remote control and it's programmed to operate heart to heart. I'm glad to see it's working, and relieving my beloved Vatsala of pain and worry.

I'm very happy that you've understood correctly my attitudes about money. The father of a friend of mine, who was at that time in his 80s, came to visit me in my office one day. He is a man who had made an extraordinary amount of money. While we were sitting and chatting, he turned to me and said, "Ehud, money is like manure. If you pile it up, it stinks. But if you spread it around, it makes things grow." This, of course, made a very strong impression on me because of its simple wisdom. I have always kept this idea alive in my mind, and have tried to be true to it to the best of my abilities and means.

I was very moved by your recounting of life at school and its hardships, how you conducted yourself and managed your small resources, and the lessons you learned from this. This experience and what it has formed in you will be very helpful to me in more ways than you can imagine right now. As I was growing up, my parents decided to emigrate from Israel to the United States with their three-year-old son and hardly any belongings or money. However, I never felt deprived of anything, as there was always a great deal of love in my home and support for me as a person.

I started Inner Traditions with very little money, but a lot of luck. In growing the company, I have had the opportunity of interacting with people from all walks of life, from the extremely wealthy to the very poor. I can tell you with certainty that it is much more difficult to produce healthy, well-balanced offspring from a home of wealth than it is from one of poverty. This is not to suggest that a lack of financial means is anything to be promoted, but children who have grown up never knowing if they were liked for their money or for themselves, never knowing if they can trust the intentions and expressions of affections of others, and finding more often than not that they're being taken advantage of and exploited because of their money can be quite unhappy and dysfunctional.

I feel privileged to have started out with just my own creativity and imagination, and after 20 years have worked up to a point where I no longer have to struggle to meet my basic needs. However, I have not lost contact or understanding with people who are still struggling with the most rudimentary of financial needs. One of the great joys of working at ITI is helping the individuals who work here, often young, to move forward financially and gain their own independence and sense of security.

This shouldn't give you the impression that I'm wealthy—certainly not by American standards, where the wealthy have their own helicopters and multiple homes—but I am, as my horoscope says, wealthy enough to feel good. But not enough wealth, as Dada says, to make me a prisoner and a slave to my money. I've also realized that the issues and concerns people have around money are largely the same, whether they have very little or they have a lot. It's just a matter of how many zeroes are behind the number.

I've been able to build Inner Traditions and provide good wages for 30 employees and their families by being very, very careful about how I spend, why I spend, and on whom I spend. I've been very fortunate in having the support of Deborah, Patty, and others in the company, who've taken on board my attitudes about spending and have supported me in managing the finances of the company with a single voice. And that voice says, *Don't waste, don't spend foolishly; this money is an expression of our hard work and should be treated with respect and used wisely.* They know, as we all do, that what doesn't get wasted or spent foolishly can return to all of us and our families.

In reading of your experiences, my heart leapt, saying, *Thank God, thank God. Vatsala and I will act as one in the management of money, in relationship to home, children, and others.* You will be called upon to shepherd financial resources, just as I am. You will have money to manage the household, to spend on yourself and the children as you see fit. It doesn't matter that this money comes from "me," as in truth, I'm just the conduit, I'm just a channel for "spreading it around."

Equally important to me is your obvious predilection for philanthropy and giving to others. I want to encourage this trait, and hope that we can set aside some money to be given away on a regular basis.

As to dependency, we're both desperately dependent here, needing to be with each other, to love each other, passionately and with abandon, to share each other's company, to be fellow travelers. It's one of the great mysteries of life, this complete and utter attachment, dependency, and need for connectivity with another. At the same time we've both learned to be independent and detached in order to be effective and dynamic in our endeavors, we have been storing up a great deal of love and devotion to give to another person. Now we've both found this person and, boy, I'm depending on you in a very big way!

I'm glad you're not traveling around, not exhausting yourself with activities, and instead keeping very focused on us. I'm glad that you're making the transition out of one life into your new life gradually, gracefully, and without stress or conflict. May this trend continue.

I recently gathered with my parents and sister to celebrate my niece (soon to be your niece) Sarah's second birthday. Noogie kept running up to her, licking her up and down, and creating a wonderful, hysterical, happy scene. My mother had just returned from being with her sisters in Israel for one month. As I may have told you, my mother worked as a baby nurse in Israel before we moved to the States when I was three years old. Her favorite baby, Danny, is now a very prominent figure in Israel, and she was invited to the wedding of his daughter. At that wedding, she was introduced to the prime minister of Israel as "Danny's other mother." He very charmingly told Danny how lucky he was, and of course made my mother feel quite grand.

I took the opportunity of this family gathering to announce our engagement to my parents. This was received with a lot of enthusiasm and many questions. I satisfied their curiosity, and we've received the blessings of my parents. My mother wants to correspond with you, and asked if you would send her a letter.

If you're wondering what to write, you're always safe in telling my mom how great I am, as she already thinks I'm God's gift to humanity and you'll be supporting her view . . . If you want to send the letter to me first to look at, fine, but I'm also quite happy and confident to have you write to her directly.

During the weekend we discussed travel plans, and it was agreed that my parents would not fly to India as my mother suffers from a swelling of her legs when she's in a hot climate, and my father thought it would be unwise to make the journey. (He's quite fit and would love to come, he confided. However, he doesn't feel he can leave my mother behind. I agreed, it wouldn't work.)

My sister, however, is definitely coming, and it turns out that another very, very dear friend and former colleague, Leslie Colket

Blair, will most likely be coming. I've also just learned that two of my best friends in Germany are planning to come. I'll fill you in with names, CVs, and all pertinent details later, as everybody's plans become more firm.

You don't have to "access" me. I am always there. Just put your mind to me and I am with you. I will be sending you, with another letter, exactly where I will be throughout all my traveling to you. While I'm traveling, you will be able to reach me by Federal Express, by fax, by telephone, no problem. I will be sending you details on how to do this, and you will know my whereabouts every day and every hour of the day. So have no fear, my beloved, I am with you and connected forever.

The snow is glistening, the last rays of the sun are making the outlines of the mountains iridescent. Noogie is pulling at me, saying *C'mon, Dad, let's get out there and run around.* I'm saying to him, *Noogman, I am writing my beloved.* He says, *Well, where is she? Bring her along.* I say, *OK, I'll just do that, but it will take some time.*

Until that time, I send you love and thanksgiving from the center of my being, the place where you live.

Ehud

8.12.95

From: Dr. B. R. Vatsala
To: Mrs. Helen Sperling

Dear Mrs. Sperling,
Hope this letter finds you well and happy.

I have been told about you. I have seen your picture. Even though I have not met you personally as yet, I do feel good about writing to you. Call it chance, luck, or grace of God, I got to know your son in April of this year. From then on, there has been a gradual buildup of a relationship based on understanding him as a person, as a man. He has told me about his work—publishing books—and I can't but admire the consistency, perseverance, determination, and sharp business acumen that he has displayed in his 20 years of association with books and writers.

My interaction with him is, however, outside his business world, as it comes into the field of friendship. This friendship has now seasoned into mature and secure love that is about to graduate into marriage and domesticity. I look at him as a person who, by God's grace, is my husband-to-be. I fully trust his ability to be a good husband and, later, a responsible father to the kids. What I mean to say is that it has been a wonderful experience getting to know him.

As he has discussed with you, we are going to be married on 22.2.1996. I would be very happy if you could make it to the wedding. But I will understand if long travel and the hot climate here in India cause you concern about your health. Once with Ehud in the U.S., I will try to call on you as soon as I can, and then we will have a heart-to-heart talk on any topic you like. You can tell me all about your life and your son.

I do believe mothers can make or break their children. In making Ehud the kind of man he is, Mom, you have done a remarkable, excellent job. It is only natural for you to feel proud of the work you have done in your lifetime.

In starting my life with Ehud as his wife, I will carry with me the deep sense of commitment that my culture and especially my family have instilled in me. It will be my top and only priority to fill his life at home with peace, goodwill, happiness, and love, all of which he so richly deserves. In being successful in my mission, I will always need your blessings and best wishes.

I do look forward to being with you and sharing a wonderful relationship with you as your daughter-in-law. I will be obliged if you please pass on my best wishes and greetings to Mr. Sperling (senior).

Thanking you,
With regards,
Vatsala

Dear Ehud,

Feels like heaven, to be back to the office after a hectic trip to Madurai, to rush through the trivial routine and then settle down to my favorite routine, i.e., writing to you. A phone call from Anna on Saturday made me decide I must visit him. I reached there Sunday morning and am back to work today, Tuesday morning. We had many rounds of discussion about our wedding. And you know, whenever the word *wedding* is mentioned, you see the word *money* trailing closely behind. In terms of community-based practices, the two words have become intertwined forever.

Do you mind, Ehud, if I get into a long discussion-mode? We met on 19 October, 1995. On 20 October we decided we would like to go ahead, get engaged, and be married. Prior to this momentous decision, all that we had was a correspondence in which even the remote possibility of marriage did not surface.

Somewhere along the line, and much before our personal meeting, I did discover that you are my man. Thank heaven, God gave me the right sense at the right time. It was so natural, so easy to tell you "I love you" when we met without escorts. I did not have to struggle or search for these words; they came on their own because they have been there since my discovery of you. Your defenses, too, were not long in melting away. We got along as if we were drawn together by a strong unifying magnetic power.

It has been one of the most wonderful experiences of my life . . . getting to know you, loving you, feeling all that I feel for you. It is so nice to realize that there is so much love in me waiting to be given to you. This feeling has no parallel and I have felt blessed all along. The whole experience has become tastier because I know that a similar feeling of unexplored, rich love waiting inside you is struggling to find a direction, a way out . . . and you have discovered too that you can channel all that love to me. By God, I am lucky.

It strikes me as certainty, in this world where uncertainty is the only certain thing, that what we feel for each other is not accidental, not our own planned design; rather, it is the way God wants it to be. Then, yes, I need all the love you are capable of giving. I will never hold back whatever love I am capable of giving you. This is so beautiful, mysterious . . . so wonderful. I never want it disturbed. It is something like the peace that descends on man after his complete surrender to God.

Since we never really got around to discussing marriage in our correspondence before our engagement—how it should be conducted—I never got around to telling you my views on this issue. When you told me how you wanted it to be held, I took a pause, checked my feelings for you, and found that I love you more than I don't love the extravaganza around weddings. Then I decided I would simply come along because you like it this way.

In keeping with my individual background of very little money, no savings, and a salaried lifestyle, I understood that in a marriage, how it is held is not important. What is important is one's motivation and what one makes out of it at the end. The end product is important. Every event in a marriage—from beginning to end—has become a mockery of culture. Without realizing the need, meaning, and purpose for which a tradition was invented and continued down the ages, people simply follow it because they don't know what else to do. And this is why a traditional wedding, held at great cost with lots of effort and attention to cultural details, does not make any sense to me. Money spent on one-day merriment can be used for loftier and humanitarian causes, like seeing intelligent but needy kids through schools and universities by giving them scholarships. In these so-called culturally approved, community-based marriages of today, *spending* is the key word. In this Indian patriarchal society, this spending is senseless, endless. And then, too, so many marriages flop.

As revolutionary as I happen to be, I decided long ago that if I ever met the man I was searching for, if I ever decided I was going to marry him, it would be in my working civilian clothes, without any jewelry or makeup, without noise or crowds. My wedding would be held in a marriage registrar's office, followed by a simple home-cooked lunch with close family. This procedure would cost me what I could spend from my salary, without borrowing from the IMF, the UN, and the World Bank. Also, this would be in accordance with my simplistic lifestyle, and definitely my Mr. Right would not be offended, because his value system would be the same as mine. Because he, like me, believes that how a marriage is conducted is of little importance—what a couple do *after* the marriage, what they make out of a wedding, is more important—are they able to achieve the unity of man and woman which is called the union of Shiva and Shakti? Are they able to stick together through rain and sunshine in life? Are they able to make their home a temple of love, devotion, caring? Can they create a good life and a good family situation for their kids and aging, dependent, and needy relatives? These are important to me, and I am marrying in order to achieve these goals. Any amount of dollars and rupees spent by anyone around the marriage ceremony makes no sense to me.

With you, I am sure of what we are heading for. The more I make contact with you, the clearer it becomes that we are destined to be man and wife. What we want to make out of our wedding, what we are prepared to put in to make our marriage a stable, lasting, successful, fruitful, and loving relationship, is also very clear to us both. I am sure of these, about you, about myself too. There is not a single doubt.

Then the question comes to mind—should I come along, cooperate, let you pay for and manage the whole event as you like, or should I put my foot firmly down, scream, Enough is enough! and say, "Ehud, I am at the extreme end of simplicity. By God's grace I am not influenced by social and cultural pressures, and would not buckle and cow down to the demands imposed on me by modern-day misinterpretations of my culture and tradition. By God's very divine grace, I am not suffering from greed, lust, or endless wantings. And if you ask me what I want, I will tell you that I want to go for the simplest of simple weddings. In my heart of hearts, I realize that I am your wife—it is true whether one priest says it or ten, whether it is said in the civil registrar's office in India or a rabbi's office in the U.S. For me, our life after the wedding is most important, because I see the wedding as a step to a long and challenging road, and not a stop."

Well, when I looked at the intensity in your eyes, I decided to let you be the boss. And I did not say a word about how I wanted to get married. All that mattered to me was that you should feel happy, fulfilled. You want the wedding in a particular manner and I want this for you. Later, I learned about how you look at money. I knew very well that neither my family nor I could ever conduct a wedding as you desired, but your outlook toward the event and the budget removed all my fears, apprehensions, and concerns. I learned that you are going ahead with the plan because you want to make our wedding a festive, joyous, and tasteful event for our families and friends. And even when you learned from Ramakrishnan about my family's inability to foot the bill, you did not get disgusted. Your attitude toward the whole event, your reaction to my family, made me feel absolutely proud of you. And I said to myself . . . *This is my man . . . I just need to flow along, I need not push him around, I need not poke him awake to convey what I mean; I simply go along, and God, how blessed I am, I love him, he cares for my well-being, he loves me too. Everything else that I have or don't have doesn't matter. To me, he alone matters, and that is all.*

In sharing with my family your views toward the whole event, in telling them in the subtlest terms how you and I get along, I grew much closer to you. Do you want to know how close? I think it is simply crazy, but it is perfectly normal and natural too! Appa has a bedroom for his own use. Anna, Manni, and Asha retired to theirs. Here I was in the living room, alone on a makeshift bed. The quiet of the cool night descended on me. I did feel very distinctly, very uncomfortably cold, and alone. Something like being left out. And we had till then spoken intensely about you. My heart simply cried out. Quite easily, quite naturally, I wept . . . because I could not push aside my need for you. It seemed the most natural thing in the world to be with you, love you, let you make love to me, curl up by your side. It seemed absolutely unnatural to be in this cold room all by myself, feeling the chill breeze rustle through the sheets. I would have given anything to touch you next to me, elope with you that very moment. Then it occurred to me again how special our relationship is. If you look carefully, Ehud, it has everything in it . . . good manners, courtesy, friendship, fun, understanding, romance, needing, giving, love . . . the emotional, the spiritual, and also the physical. The best aspect of this relationship is how we are opening up to each other to be explored, to be shared. What else is this but magic?

Are you wondering why I marked this letter with the "For your eyes only" sign? How the wedding should be conducted is the only point on which our views have differed grossly. I want this difference to be buried right here between us without anyone getting any hint of it. As two adults, we are bound to have different views on a topic. These differences should not divide us. We have to examine the difference, learn each other's minds, respond carefully, and then do what is right and what should be done. Regarding the events around our wedding, I am with you. I want only your happiness.

I also trust you enough to tell you that I need you. I am happy to realize that you won't take advantage of this expression—that my need for your touch is alive and I am not a cold and dead log of wood. Then there is this concept of mine that what is private between us must be given the dignity of remaining private and personal . . . hence the sign "For your eyes only."

Bye and much love to you.

Vatsala

15.12.95

Ehud,

Boss, the letters exchanged between us will be more than a foot tall, when piled up. Any scholar researching the development of love and affection between people from two different cultures, religions, skin colors, social and personal backgrounds, and continents could produce an excellent hypothesis/thesis based on the material in our letters. For quite some time, I have been thinking that once I'm with you, I won't give up writing to you, and you just said today that you want it to continue. In fact, it will be interesting to study our responses to each other when circumstances change and distances vanish.

Just now, there is an addition to my table. It is a slide projector. Why I got it from the auditorium is that not just the auditorium but the entire visitors' area in the first floor is flooded with kids and parents who have come to attend a free heart checkup week. The hero of the show is a young doctor, a cardiothoracic surgeon who has just returned to India after a degree and dollar-gathering spree. He is trying to bring some glamour, style, standard, and quality to patient and parent care in the cardiothoracic surgery superspecialty. He is doing rather a good job and the press folks—reporters and photographers—are here, trying to get him to say something.

Well, I have been successful in retrieving the projector from the auditorium, and installing it right on my table. Having accomplished this, I go for the ward rounds. There are three kids with culture-positive typhoid fever, one newborn baby who is passing dysenteric stools, two kids with *Pseudomonas sepsis*, one boy with a head injury who is like a zoo—literally, because all specimens from him are growing many organisms—and there's a little girl undergoing skin grafts. She has been doing well for the past 20 grafts, spread over many months, but during the current session, I believe all is not well with her.

In my daily rounds, if the kids are not sedated and sleepy and are able to talk, I do play and talk with them, meanwhile assessing the damage done to them by the bugs. I try talking to their parents too. There are times I see the stress and the strain a kid's health can cause to parents, testing their relationship as husband and wife. I see how unpleasant it is to fall sick and foot the medical bills, how cold, frightening, impersonal, and mechanical the hospital-based professionals can be. The nature of our jobs tends to make us see a problem in terms of numbers or statistics, and to say to parents, "There is only a 10 percent chance of a child with typhoid fever developing *Acalculus cholecystitis* requiring surgical removal of the inflamed gall bladder . . . there is only a 24 percent chance of a neonate with hospital-acquired septicemia dying of infection." During the next day's rounds, we discover that the child about whom we were speculating and playing a numbers game has unfortunately come inside this 10 or 24 percent. Now, here, statistics have no meaning to the parents. It is their child, and the doomsday prediction made in some textbook has been 100 percent correct and applicable to them. When their child is suffering or is no longer with them, it doesn't matter to them that the 90 or 76 percent of children with a particular illness do get well and get to go home. Their child is not coming home and that is final, irrespective of the statistics and what the doctor says.

Rounds over, back to my office, I unwind. It is day after day, the same routine—watching the comic and the tragic drama unfolding itself on all floors of this hospital.

My tiny office is a world of its own. Here, patients and parents don't queue up and create a scene trying to see the doctor first. We try to maintain a humane, peaceful, calm, antiseptic, efficient environment where academic fervor and a personal warm touch are alive. It is a far cry from the rest of the hospital, where the people live on the edge, each nerve strained as if it will snap any minute. Tension . . . tension . . . tension. In comparison, my sparsely furnished, utilitarian $15 \times 10'$ chamber looks like an oasis, a piece of heaven. Add to that the rest of the department, which is manned by the politest of people I have ever met.

And this is what makes me count my blessings. If I were one of the medical doctors here, or anywhere else, I could not have managed to have a stretch of a few undisturbed quiet hours each week to devote to our long-distance love affair. Thank God. Thank God, I happen to be a nonclinical scientist specializing in infectious diseases. I'm in the middle of a much-envied, upwardly mobile career in a hospital, have an enviable posting as head of the department, and am given the freedom, time, and authority to manage my department, research activities, and academic exercises. Once I'm through with my duties as an attending microbiologist, here in the same hospital in which the drama of life and death is unfolding every minute, where nerves snap every second, tempers fly like sparks, careers and people and lives are made and demolished, I can be in my small, clean, quiet, systematic, well-organized office and simply do anything that I like—maybe even writing I LOVE EHUD, a thousand times or more.

I think I have made the best use of my God-sent freedom: I scrutinized my past and present and tried to glimpse a trajectory of my possible future 10 years from now. I tried to figure out what I had been wanting and "needing." I examined my priorities, ambitions, plans, hopes, dreams, fears, and failures. I tried to take a break from chasing and kicking the ball in order to *stop, stand still, and take a real look at it*. With session after session of deep contemplation, I have come to a conclusion about what I, as a person, as a woman, *need*.

My decision to marry you is the result and the outcome of those deep, unbiased contemplations in which I examined myself most ruthlessly and mercilessly through an electron microscope.

Having made my decision, now I feel like a mountaineer who has scaled the peak, flown his flag, and is descending to the stability of the ground. I feel like a seafarer who has been to the rough and high seas and has been fearing a shipwreck, but luckily has been spared the tragedy and is heading back to the shore, to the inviting arms of the soil, the earth. Bye-bye, mountains, bye-bye, seas. *I am going to where I belong*.

In going back to the stability of the base camp, I am full of thanksgiving, full of awe and wonder at the way God has been so kind to me all along, to the extent that He has assured me a warm welcome home. After my trip to this career, I am not returning to an empty house. In the home I am heading for lives My Man, and, thank God, he is equally looking forward to appointing me his wife and mother to his kids. I was led to him by the merciful hands of Destiny.

Well, Ehud, I am full of thanksgiving for everything that God has given me and also for everything that God, in His infinite wisdom and compassion, has denied me. No complaints, no grumblings, no demand, no unhappiness, no dissatisfaction . . . simply, truly, completely, and only thanksgiving . . . for God's blessings, His graces, and His love.

I have the happiest of memories from my years at home. Amma was never a career woman. For her six kids she was *always there* to open the door and welcome them anytime they came home (we never violated curfew hours!). I do not recall a single day (except those in the recent past when she went to Madurai during Appa's accident) when I had to walk into an empty home to talk to the walls. She was always there. We could run into her arms with the happiest news of our lives, or we could lean on her shoulders and shed a few tears of frustration. She never encouraged weeping in defeat. She consoled us with her love, and with her touching words of wisdom, caring, and encouragement, she could rekindle our sporting spirits. My God, she was always and ever there. This, however, I can never say for my father. He was too busy helping everyone outside his immediate family, and, as a result, he never had time for us. It was always, ever and only, Mom.

A few years ago, I would have wanted more than being at home, cooking food, making babies, and being a wife to my man. If I had met you then, I would have critically analyzed the package you are offering and said, "Well, thank you, but I am looking for something else." A few years ago, you too would have been in a different set of circumstances, managing a life, a stressful business, and living through a marriage that shook with every jerk. You wouldn't have been what you are *now* like I wouldn't have been what I am *now*.

Timing is important in life. And every event occurs precisely when it has to. I never regret that I did not meet you earlier. Rather, I am quite happy and thankful to God that I have met you *now*, and that we have a future together. It is true also that we will be taking on the role of parenting quite late in life—so what? We are both ready and prepared for this, in our *minds*—and the body simply must obey the commands of the mind.

Just now, I hear a pager summoning Dr. So-and-So to so-and-so floor; surely a child is gasping for breath and the doctor is having coffee downstairs or is reading in the library for the forthcoming exam. I watch my technicians trying to draw blood from a perfectly healthy looking little boy—he surely is in the wrong place and has been dragged here because of excessive parental anxiety over the couple of sneezes he might have had in the morning (this is called single child syndrome!). I am winking at him and he is issuing a flying kiss in my direction—kids do this with such pure innocence. Life goes on and on.

Love,
Vatsala

Beloved Vatsala,

This Saturday we had our first big snowfall. It literally snowed from 7 in the morning to 7 at night. Noogie and I, of course, went out in the storm a number of times and frolicked. Noogie just adores the snow— he rolls in it, eats it, and runs after snowballs that I throw into the air. One of his most favorite things is frolicking in the snow. Me too.

The storm left about three feet of snow, and Sunday morning the sky was exquisitely blue with not a cloud in sight. Noogie, Morgan, Willow, Pepper, and I rode off into the fresh powder-like snow. It was quite fantastic and exhilarating. The horses have specially designed snowshoes to give them traction and protect their feet. They love getting out and galloping in the cold weather—no insects to bother them and no heat to exhaust them. They were exuberant and so was I. If you can imagine us charging through virgin snow, with the dogs jumping like rabbits through the snow, sinking down and then jumping back out, snow flying everywhere . . . Not a sound except the hooves beating the snow and the breathing of the horses and dogs. Just a quiet, perfect stillness, punctuated by our party's forward motion.

It was a great antidote to my experiences earlier in the week, when I traveled to New York for our spring sales conference. That evening I went out to dinner with my parents and some colleagues to celebrate my birthday. My parents are very excited about our upcoming marriage and can't wait to meet you. My mother has gotten books about India from the library and my father has searched the computer banks at the library (where he works as a volunteer in his retirement) for information on the history of the Jews in India. Apparently, there were large communities in South India, as well as in Bombay and Calcutta. This lasted up until the 1950s and the formation of the state of Israel, when many of the Jews in India emigrated.

I read this material—it's quite fascinating. I was unaware of all of it, with the exception of the synagogue and community in Cochin. Apparently, there is a 2,000-year history of cultural harmony and exchange between the Jews and Hindus on India's soil. I look forward to us carrying on this tradition of felicitous relations in our own household!

MAN'S BEST FRIEND IS YOUR BEST FRIEND:

As I mentioned, Noogie has all this breeding in him that makes him extremely, highly intelligent, a friend of mankind, and particularly gentle and affectionate with children. Since he came home at eight weeks, I have raised him according to the teachings of the Monks of New Skete, a Trappist monastery that raises German shepherds to support the activities of the monastery. They've written a book called *How to Be Your Dog's Best Friend*.

Noogie is constantly meeting new people and his reaction is inevitably one of affection and acceptance. In turn, his experience of humanity is one we can only dream of. All his interactions have been positive; he has never, thank God, encountered anyone who has treated him badly or abused him in any way. Consequently, his first reaction upon meeting a stranger is, *Oh, a new friend—a new possibility for fun and affection. Let me go immediately and say hello.*

I must admit, dear Vatsala, that when I read your letter about your Noogie concerns, I had a big, hearty laugh. Not because I thought you were silly—quite the contrary, I respected your concern for Noogie's and my welfare, for how you might fit into this relationship, and your sensitivity and perception around what was obviously in your mind a point of concern. I laughed simply because of the absurdity of your apprehensions, given the reality of what you can expect from Noogie.

WHAT THE BOSS'S WIFE SHOULD WEAR:

I very much want you to maintain your traditional cultural modes of dress and comportment. I do not want you to be "assimilated" into the Western world, adopting our dress styles, makeup, and fashions. Having said that, I also recognize that you will need to adapt to weather conditions and other lifestyle issues that will necessitate western dress. So here's how I see this working: wear your sarees both in India and in the West when we are with other people, and give me the pleasure of seeing you in a saree when we dine at home. At other times, when at home, wear whatever is comfortable and suits the task at hand. When we are traveling, comfort is the key and you should definitely wear your suits. Please just bring with you the sarees you really like and that suit your taste. When we're together in

Trivandrum and also in Madurai, I will happily go shopping with you, and we can add to your saree collection so that you have a wide enough range that you really like and that I like to see you in.

Yes, you should bring your jeans from school. Inasmuch as you have mentioned it on the phone to me a number of times, I assume that you feel a little bit of concern that you've gained some weight around your waist and you no longer fit into these jeans. I suggest that you ask your yoga teacher about what exercises you can do to firm up, tone up, and reduce the waistline. That, combined with a healthy and vigorous lifestyle in Vermont, will get you back into those school jeans, I'm certain.

When you get to Vermont, I'll take you out and buy you more jeans and the kind of winter clothing you'll need for enjoying the outdoors here. As far as the cold goes, please don't feel any concern about this. Our home is centrally heated and is always warm and comfortable. In addition, we have a wood-burning stove and I very much enjoy coming in from my walks and warming my behind in front of it. If you're missing the heat and humidity of Madras, you can step into our own little steam bath and it'll be hot and humid within minutes. Turn on the shower, and you're in monsoon!

Our car is also heated, including the seats. So hardship is certainly not part of the picture when it comes to being in Vermont. You will, however, need to acclimate yourself to the cold for playing in the outdoors. With the type of clothing we will buy, your upper torso will be impervious to the cold (no sarees for the outdoor activities—it will be all western garb). You'll only feel the cold on your face and a little bit on your hands and legs. This, of course, will happen only if we're out for some extended period of time. I suspect we will gradually introduce you, with short periods of exposure for a few weeks, until you're fully acclimated. Once you are, I'm sure you'll find the winter an exciting and beautiful experience and will cherish it as much as Noogie and I do.

Attitude, exercise, and the proper attire are the key to enjoying this spectacular season. Keep in mind that we'll be arriving toward the end of the winter, and within 60 days, the snows will be receding and Vermont will be bursting with new life, followed by the flowering of our gardens, the return of the birds, the bears, and other wildlife coming out of hibernation, and the long days of summer, when the sun doesn't go down until 9 at night, and the sweet smell of the gardens and the forest embrace you.

I of course received your birthday card and the enclosed letters, which I very much enjoyed. I can smell the roses, even though they're just printed. I thought the choice of roses particularly appropriate, as the rose is an anagram for Eros. It's also a symbol of the *yoni*. Often when I'm in my study reading your letters, I'm filled with warmth and yearning for you, and quite independent of my thoughts, I notice that my *lingam* has raised its head and is standing erect in anticipation of your embrace. I am so longing to lie in our own bed of roses with you.

AMMA:

It would give me great pleasure to have Amma stay with us for some time, and make clothing for our children. The image of this, described in your letter, was delightful, and you have my full support. I also want to have the opportunity to get to know your mother better and to show her firsthand that her daughter has arrived in a good home with a loving and supportive husband.

From the start of our correspondence, I recognized the unique and special nature of the relationship between you and your mother. I recognized it as being a healthy relationship. Most women that I've encountered here in the West grow to maturity without having reconciled their relationship with their mother. In fact, there's a famous book called *My Mother, My Self* that describes all the symbiotic and destructive relationships between mothers and daughters. Most women here in the West are still in a constant battle with their mothers, even when they become mothers themselves. So I'm well aware of the inherent dangers of an unhealthy mother-daughter relationship. I have never, for a single moment, seen your relationship with your mother as being anything but constructive and healthy. In fact, it was your positive assessment of that relationship that greatly encouraged me in further developing my relationship with you. So you can be confident of my support in your relations with your mother. She will always be welcome in our home.

DISEASE AS METAPHOR:

Man in the modern era has seen and continues to see periods of plague, famine, and pestilence. The great Austrian philosopher Dr. Rudolf Steiner predicted prior to his death in 1920 that mankind would be seeing strange and unusual diseases and epidemics in the latter part of this century, and that these unknown-at-that-time diseases would be a metaphor for the state of man in the world.

There is no separation between man's inner nature and the world outside of man. As we pollute and destroy, degrade and degenerate, we can expect our internal chemistry to be reflective of the external environment. Polluting our rivers pollutes our blood. Polluting our air constricts our vital breath. Reducing the diversity of God's creation reduces our collective spirituality.

I of course respect Pasteur's work and his accomplishments. I recognize that little bugs exist and are coursing through our bloodstreams. However, are they the true causative agents? How is it that different ages of man see different diseases prevalent? Isn't it extraordinary that in an era when exponential growth is the mantra repeated in the Church of Progress, that man faces cancer, a disease where cell growth becomes exponential?

So what to do?

Change the dream. Change the imagination. Seed future generations with virtue, the teachings of the ancients, a respect for all life, and aspirations toward the good, the true and beautiful. This is our task—in our marriage, in our work in the world, and in how we conduct ourselves in our relations with others. I'm truly moved by the great depth of feeling you have for others and their suffering, and look forward with anticipation to a union that will support and enhance these qualities and their expression in the world.

On other fronts, I received seven packages of wedding invitations in nine different styles from Ramakrishnan. I'm enclosing an example of each of the nine, just in case you haven't seen the full range. Krishna has also told me that his mother and sister will be taking charge of the food preparation for the wedding, and that his father will be taking charge of the priests. He has also engaged a Bharat Natyam dancer and musicians, at my request. In addition, he has engaged a small temple/auditorium/kitchen complex in a Brahmin colony where his sister lives.

I was just about to pick up the phone to call him and, lo and behold, the phone rang. With an absolutely perfect, crystal clear connection, as if he were next door, Krishna and I were chatting away. He's assured me that all preparations are in order and things are moving along quite well. We discussed the venue and the schedule of events, spanning the 21st and 22nd, and I'm very pleased with the arrangements. He was in good spirits, and is very much looking forward to the event and all the fun and activities around it.

Of course, what I'm most looking forward to is bringing you home and spending my life with you. It's only 30 days till I start my journey back to you, 45 days until I'm in India, and just a little over 60 until we are united once again and forever. Until then, I send you my love and my prayers that God will keep you safe and well.

Ehud

P.S. Just heard from Immigration and Naturalization that you've been approved for a visa. Next step will be your visit to the consulate. I will write or phone as soon as we have the details.

24.12.95

Dear Ehud,

Last evening I visited a stationery store to get some cards. For you, my obvious choice was a picture of Radha and Krishna. Lord Krishna is described as an incurable romantic. He befriended and entertained women of all ages untiringly, and had them twirling around his little fingers.

This demonstration of the human tendency to love, represented by a god incarnate, helps us humans to understand that we do need and are capable of giving and taking love. I would like to see you as my very own personal Krishna. However, I do not want you to befriend all my contemporary women as Krishna did. That is to say, I am possessive about my man. I would certainly like to see that our friendship and interest in each other as man and woman never deteriorates into a boring and stale routine. Just as you do, I realize that the warmth and affection we feel for each other is very much a viable key to a rich storehouse containing a deeper sense of belonging and love. I would like this bright spark to mellow into a stable, energizing glow that continues to illuminate and enliven our lives even after we move away from youth.

For Mama and Papa Sperling, I see the New Year as similar to dawn and dusk. A dawn says, Hello, here is a new day. A dusk says, So what if night is coming, it is not going to be here forever. At the end of the night, there is always a new day coming. Let us keep up hope; let us look forward. No matter how old they become, a new year marks for your parents a new set of days to live and be happy. I wish them both good health and happy times ahead.

I understand that Deborah is visiting India for the first time. I want to tell her that cows have been with us since the days of Krishna and even before. They continue to be with us, making our street scene complete and giving it an aroma that only the holy cow can give. Here a traffic cop and signal are important, but both can at times be ignored and violated. A traffic island created by the cow to feed her calf or just for her own recreation, rest, and relaxation, is, however, never ignored. The army trucks as well as the latest models of Mercedes-Benz meticulously avoid bumping into a cow. The pedestrians stop by a cow, touch her, do namaste, and convey their religious feeling to the divine animal. No matter how much Deborah has read or heard about India, the only thing that can prevent her from succumbing to culture shock on seeing India for the first time is a strong sense of humor—the only prophylactic against the surprises that only India can give to her visitors. This cow card is to wish her a Happy New Year and welcome to India.

For celebrating the New Year, I am planning on taking Amma and my niece Rina out to the beach. These kids are at two opposing ends of age and both enjoy outings, but it is difficult for me to manage both alone. One tends to run while crossing the road (Rina) and one hesitates to cross even when the signal urges the pedestrians to cross (Amma). One runs on the beach picking up sea shells and frolicking in the waves . . . the other likes to sit quietly on the sand and reflect on the continuity of God's work, the beauty of the eternal waves, and the grandeur of nature. Between the two of them, I somersault from being playful to philosophical and the reverse. I love them both. I also love the somersaulting if that can help in keeping them both happy and keeping us together.

That's all for now, Ehud. Love to you.
Vatsala

December 26, 1995

Dearest Vatsala,

I was very happy to speak to you last night and hear your voice, and even receive an "I love you" surreptitiously when no one could overhear. It's interesting how this visa process is unfolding, and I'm glad that you are now no longer stressed and concerned about the possibility that we might be detained in India for a while after the wedding. Although we both very much look forward to the extreme simplicity of a honeymoon in our home in Vermont, it looks like the powers that be are conspiring to cause us to roam around and have an extravagant time together in India!

I was happy to hear your enthusiasm around this probable adventure. Photographing the culture and lifestyles of South India and then coming home to Vermont to paint them sounds like an absolutely wonderful way to transform what at first appeared to be a source of conflict and stress into a venue for artistic expression. This ability to move and flow through and around and above life's obstacles is a basic necessity to a successful life together. I'm glad to see that we can dance this dance together.

PAST-LIFE NOSTALGIA:

Many years ago, during my first trip to India, Dada said, "I've got to take you to Baba Bhoot Nath in Lucknow—he's a mind-blower." I said, "OK, let's go." We got to Baba Bhoot Nath's ashram and he couldn't immediately receive us, as he was taking his once-a-month herbal mud-bath. He was then in his 80s and there was a special ayurvedic mixture that was buried in the ground for a year, dug up, and then smeared on his body. After we waited for about two hours, he received us in his audience hall with a long line of people behind us waiting to see him. He was covered head to toe in mud, including his long hair. He was quite a sight—I liked him immediately.

He looked at me and pulled out a big syringe-like device and completely drenched me in rosewater. I thought this was a pretty outrageous thing to do to someone he had never met, but again, I liked it. He then said to me that I had met and become intimate with three saints in my life but that I wasn't much impressed by saints. I said to him, "That's right. I'm a man—I've got a life to live. How is being impressed going to help?" He laughed and said, "That's right." He then materialized a ring—mind you, he had nothing on his body except a loincloth, and nowhere to hide this ring—so he produced the ring and some cloves and gave them to me. I thanked him, but was obviously not impressed. He laughed again and proceeded to give me a detailed description of my life up until the moment of meeting him. That was certainly impressive, as he had no way of knowing any of this information.

I said, "This is interesting, but I already know all this, having lived through it." He then said, "But did you know you were a sadhu in your past life?" I said, "No, I didn't know it, but so what? That was then, this is now." He said, "Yeah, but you've got to stop being nostalgic for the sadhu life."

I thought this was quite astute, as I'd always imagined myself as dropping out of society, rebelling against the established order, and being a revolutionary, but only in my inner nature. I imagined myself getting a job where I would work in the forest by myself, where I'd have little to do with the world, where I'd spend my time by myself reading and cultivating myself. Baba Bhoot Nath said, "Yeah, past-life nostalgia. This life, you're meant to work in the world. You need to act. Your actions will then have influence all over the world."

He then sent everybody out of the audience hall, took me into his private shrine room, blew a conch shell, initiated me, and gave me mantras. He and Dada then had about a half-hour of conversation

about me, of which Dada only translated about five minutes' worth. Baba Bhoot Nath predicted that I would have a much closer association with India than I imagined, and that I would have educational work to do in India.

I've certainly given up the nostalgia for my past-life lifestyle and have just accepted that in this life, my actions and my activities will be wide ranging and impact many people. His predictions are also becoming quite true—I'm starting a publishing program in India, and

Baba Bhoot Nath, the mindblower.

I can imagine no more intimate contact with India than is embodied in my marriage to you.

LESS IS MORE:

If it were possible and appropriate to operate strictly out of my needs and desires with regard to our marriage, this is how it would have taken place: On October 20th, I would have said, "Thank you very much" to Ramakrishnan and your brother for facilitating our meeting and exchange. I would have then turned to you and said, "Woman, follow me."

We would have gotten into a car and driven to a remote forest. I would have taken you into that forest to a place that had a sense of presence—a stream, a waterfall, a place with Shakti. I would have then drawn a circle on the ground, disrobed, and asked you to disrobe. I would have invited you into the circle and there, dressed in the garments that God created for us, I would have pronounced my undying and unalterable devotion and love for you, I would have pronounced my commitment to honor, protect, and hold you as my dear wife and companion for life, I would have asked God to sanctify and bless our union. I would have then turned to you and asked you to speak from your core about your commitment and devotion. After this exchange of commitments and invocation of the blessings and protection of God, I would have asked us to sit down opposite each other in the circle, look into each other's eyes, and in the moment that we lost the sense of our separateness, I would have embraced you and consummated our marriage before God.

In this extreme simplicity, I would have been completely satisfied and content that our marriage had taken place in the most sublime and beautiful traditions of mankind, as marriages have been taking place since the beginning of time. I then would have taken you with me back to Vermont, we would have immediately started our life together, working on Junior Ehud and company, and we would now be returning to India together for the Delhi book fair and to visit with family and friends.

MY CIRCLE TRAVELS IN THE FOUR DIRECTIONS:

When Dada had my horoscope done, it said very clearly that my name is a good name and that it would be known in the four directions. It also said that I am a person with the power "that makes things possible." In other words, if something needs to happen, send him in and it will happen. I've come to see this is true, and I also accept this role and just let things happen around me.

You are now part of this game, and you can see how it's starting to unfold in our first public event together. The felicitous effects on our friends and families are apparent, and the story continues. My very dear friend, and soon to be your very dear friend, Leslie Colket Blair, will be attending our wedding. She worked for 10 years as the editor-in-chief at Inner Traditions, and just recently retired to get married. She was there for me during the good times and the difficult times, always a true friend and supporter to me, as I have been and continue to be for her. In our 10 years of working together, we did not once raise our voices to each other or express any bad feelings, nor did we ever have an argument. Never once!

Leslie has been talking about and wanting to come to India for years, but has never been able to make it happen. Now it's happening. Why? Because of our wedding. The stories and effects of our wedding plans as they relate to the other guests coming from the West are also fascinating and worthy of telling, but I'll save that for another moment.

I think you will understand by now that you'll have to look somewhere else to find a difference between you and me. This virtue and shared family value of extreme simplicity is one that I fully support. However, your past life is past and your palette has just been increased by one color—the color of abundance. The techniques and virtues that you've developed as an artist must be maintained. However, you need to master the new palette. Introducing this new color allows for a whole new range of expression, but does not in any way alter the fundamental values and principles from which the artistry operates. I am with you in this 100 percent. I need nothing but you. All the rest is theater.

THE WEDDING SCHOLARSHIP TRUST FUND:

In reading through your views on the wedding, it occurred to me that one element in my design was missing and I thank you very much for bringing it forward. It's evident that the wedding will do a lot to create good energy, happy feelings, and good experiences for our friends and family. It will also provide sustenance for the merchants and vendors who supply the goods, as well as for the priests and for the upkeep of the facilities, of the temple. However, there is nothing in it that is philanthropic, where we're giving to people who we're not associated with, where we're simply giving without any payback.

So, on the first anniversary of our wedding, I will give you the same amount of money that I gave to Ramakrishnan to set up our wedding, for you to give away as scholarships. My only proviso is that the recipients have no knowledge of where the funds have come from. If the recipients know that you and I have given them this money, then they will be thankful to us. If they are thankful, then we have received a benefit, and consequently, it is not philanthropy, but a charitable exchange: we give money, they give praise. If we give without any recognition, then we are giving freely and with no expectation of a benefit to ourselves.

So you have a year to identify whom the recipients will be, and to find a technique for making the grants anonymously. I will, of course, be happy to help you in any way I can, but look to you to take the lead and responsibility in this matter.

The certitude that is growing in our relationship, the inexplicable and mysterious way in which we so naturally and readily flow into each other and act with one voice, is truly amazing and, for me, shows God's grace. It is the fire and light at the core of our experience of each other. It is so precious that I, as you, do not ever wish it to be tampered with or disturbed. Rather, I wish for this fire to be fed and protected so that its light is constant, even, and clear, so that its warmth expresses itself in our home, in our physical coming together, and in the spirit that shines from our eyes out into the world.

I love you, I love you.
Ehud

chapter 10

THE BIG
GAMBLE

1.1.1996

Dear Ehud,

What a nice way to begin the day . . . speaking to you for a long time, the realization that you are changing my life, its direction, its course, its *manzil*, and immediately after the call receiving two FedEx packages from you. I tell you, Ehud, the New Year and my birthday are both beginning on a happy note. Let me also tell you that *manzil* is a word from the Urdu language. Its equivalent in English is aim, goal, or target. But none of these three English words have the dignity, depth, and beauty of that word *manzil*.

You are my manzil. This does not mean you are my goal, aim, or target. Manzil is the end point of a journey, the point where one always wanted to be; one feels a strong sense of belonging to that point. One does not belong to an aim, goal, or target because they are calculated ambitions, but one can feel an affinity with, a oneness with, and a sense of belonging to one's manzil because it is a natural end product of a journey.

As I have told you before, my prayers are unusual. They do not fit into a specific religious dictation, and are said at the most unusual places, just anywhere, anytime. No matter what I may be doing at a given time, my mind is beaming out a humble prayer . . . Mostly those prayers are . . . *God, please put me and everyone else on the right track leading to the manzil that you have for us in your mind.* There is always a manzil for every person and there is always a right way to reach it. In our confusion we might lose sight of the apparent, but that does not mean the apparent does not exist. Therefore, instead of asking God this, that, and the other, I always request that He help us in our life journey, staying on course and reaching our manzil. My faith says this is what the living God does to people . . . holds them by their little finger, lifts them up at the times of distress, leads them on to their manzil. And everyone is traveling to somewhere, searching for something. I am traveling to you, I am searching for you. To this living God I have dedicated our lives. This is my offering to God for the New Year.

I recall that I responded to your ad because it was direct. I had been screening ads for years in search of Mr. Right and had become sick of the typical ones that mention birthstar, age, height, weight, color of hair and skin, preferred color of the applicant, pay, job, education, property, and then the most important American connection— mentioning visa status. It is like saying, Here is a man . . . he has two eyes, two ears, two lips, two hands, two legs, and he has the most important organ that makes him think he can buy and sell females in exchange for peanuts. These copycat, traditional ads talk about everything that must be there for a person born to human parents, raised in a family, educated enough to subscribe to and read a newspaper and run an ad in the matrimonial column. It says nothing about the way by which he can distinguish himself from the crowd and be himself. In other words, these ads say nothing about the nonmaterial backbone that a person needs to be himself and to be a true, genuine human being. Because your ad told about you and not just about your height, weight, and color, I wrote a reply. Do I know what you need? I hope God helps me in knowing this. Knowing what you need and giving you that is my prime duty as your wife.

That was nice of you to tell me to look elsewhere for discovering differences between us. Why should I spend my time and energy in finding out about the differences between us? Instead, why not spend whatever time I have in discovering what is common between you and me, making the bond stronger, and seeing how best we can stay united? Differences, if any, have no business poking their noses in our affairs. Love to you.
Vatsala

Dear Ehud,

In your letter that arrived on New Year's Day, I read with interest how you have been busy changing the lives of people who touch you. Some people are specially sculptured for this role, and God gives them all the opportunity and means to bring about positive changes in the lives and journeys of people around them. You are one such person and I cannot but appreciate and enumerate the changes that you are bringing to my life.

I often regarded males as essential evils. The types of male speci-men I saw around myself filled me with revolt. A man was either a bully, a bulldozer (who never cared for anything or anyone), or he was a spineless worm, a shapeless jelly (without any sugar at all), always needing a skirt to hide behind, its frills. With this observation, I could only agree with you when you say that women are born, men are made by culture, experience, and action. All three are lacking in the males I've seen around myself, with a very few exceptions.

My contact with you has made me see the other side to the male species. Honorable males are not many, but you happen to be one of them. This should not be taken as flattery. I just need to admit that you are different and are fully made. There is no trace of the bully, bulldozer, worm, or jelly. Instead there is a man who means what he says, who is warm, caring, considerate, kind, gentle, loving, and very lovable, who is man enough to defend and protect a woman, care for her, and give her a sense of pride and security. This is an unusual combination, and this finding about you has changed my views about the male species . . . it is not an irredeemably gone case, mutants are possible, and there is still a possibility for finding a mutant who is a man or a gentleman. The total merger that I have been speaking about is a concept that has got much to do with my finding you to be a gentleman. It never fails to strike me how lucky I am to have found you.

My individual preparedness was there. I was beginning to feel the need to begin a family. Here comes a man who catalyzes the whole process of transformation and makes it possible. The man who is bringing in this change is you. You are not asking me to continue with my career. All you are doing is appointing me to the position of your wife, saying that it is a full-time job with a very loving boss. If a man insisted on me continuing my career, my desire to be a full-time wife and mother would have been of no consequence. I was willing for a change . . . you are making that change possible.

I have always loved painting and drawing. Apparently, you are very keen on assisting me in pursuing these hobbies. Earlier I had no time or resources to indulge in artwork, but with the changes in living environment that you are bringing in my life, artwork seems like a possibility.

I have always loved the smell of books—or else how would you expect me to spend years pursuing an academic trail? Here is a man whose lifetime is devoted to books. He understands the value of time spent in reading. He is taking me into a home that is full of books. I can spend long hours reading for knowledge and pleasure, to my heart's content—without fearing the library fine for returning the books late.

I grew up in crowded, polluted Indian cities where people ooze out of every possible hole. While living in these unplanned, haphazard, unnatural concrete jungles, a part of me was always with nature. I could never ignore the beauty of a tiny wild flower whose common or scientific name I never knew, that somehow escaped getting sunburned and managed to raise its beautiful head amidst the chaos, litter, filth, and toxic waste dumps that mark the footpaths. I could always appreciate its instinct for survival, its tenacity and resilience, and its ability to make a dirty spot beautiful. Quite a winner, you little fellow! While breathing in (or, to say the truth, stopping breathing) whenever a vehicle blew its exhaust fumes right in my face while I stood in the middle of the road trying to cross over to the other side, I imagined and dreamed about long walks through clean, pure countryside, green forests supplying oxygen, beautiful sunsets and sunrises, gentle and rolling slopes of mountains . . . I visualized myself amidst the splendid beauty of an unpolluted, quiet, serene, gentle countryside blessed with immense natural beauty. While dreaming these situations, however, I could not give up whatever I was doing and run. Well, here comes a man who enjoys living in such a countryside and is making it possible for me to join him and live a new life amidst the beauty of nature. Restoring me to nature is the big change you are bringing to my life, Ehud.

Exercise . . . call it lack of will or privacy, I could never stick to an exercise schedule. Add the fact that obesity was never my problem. But I always dreamed of being physically fit, athletic, and able to live a hard, rugged life. Ehud, I know you are a yoga enthusiast, and I am looking forward to letting you bring this change in my life . . . making it possible for me to stick to a walking and yoga schedule when I come home to live in Vermont.

Dressing up . . . who ever saw Vatsala caring to dress for an audience? I always wore what felt practical and comfortable, and what I could afford within my shoestring budget. My views on animal testing done for the evaluation of safety of cosmetics conveniently kept me out of the theatrical possession and display of cosmetics. No makeup has ever touched my skin. This wasn't self-denial. I simply was not born with any inclination for pampering myself. I have been happy being a plain Jane and have never been tempted with all that glitters. And since jewelry seemed like a statement of one's wealth and an attempt to draw others' attention to oneself, I decided they were not good for me. Your outlook on these issues is different, though you do seem to like me without ostentatious costumes, jewelry, or makeup. You are changing not my views but my approach to these issues. I will indulge in them just a little . . . with an aim not to impress others but to be suitably dressed for an occasion. This is a big change in me.

In fact, your enthusiasm for taking me saree shopping is infectious. I have been searching hard and haven't found a single streak of resistance or revolt rising in me. It seems so *natural*, so spontaneous. Your motivation and generosity, and the pains that you are taking for my sake, are all that I can see. Saree shopping is just an act—what I really love about it is your *intention*. You are being a husband in its fullest, truest sense. I love you for this.

Well, Ehud, by the grace of God, you will be able to bring all these changes. In thanksgiving and gratitude, all I intend on doing is to try to be a good wife for you and fill your life with simple, pure, gentle love. If I am successful in doing just this, I will consider myself someone who has passed the examination that I consider the marriage to be.
Love to you always,
Vatsala

Dear Ehud,

A quick walk to the consulate . . . to be told right at the gate to
get lost, by those bloody, impolite pigs who work at the consulate.
How I feel like thrashing them! And then I recall your soothing
words to me on the phone . . . they are troubled people . . . if things
don't work out, don't worry . . . I will take care of it . . . I recall all
the soothing words I have heard from you so far. I don't fail to realize
that I am lucky—very lucky. Hundreds of people receive worse treatment at the consulate gate. The mantra the staff are trained and paid
to repeat is "Throw these swarming Indian pigs out . . . they should
be treated like sick and sore street dogs . . . don't let them feel welcome and at ease in the consulate . . . or else the entire America will
be filled with 900 million Indians and there will be no place for the
Americans to live." And the Indians employed by the consulate do
this job of ill-treating other Indians so well, with such appreciable
dedication. Not all the visa aspirants have an Ehud across the globe
who is offering to help. I have Ehud. Because he is my manzil, I will
bear all that I must, with courage, conviction, hope, optimism, and
undying faith. I will spend the rest of my life with Ehud. The bark-
ing, howling, rude, horrible monsters at the consulate are only steps,
they are not stops. I won't stop at a step and be deflected until and
unless I reach my manzil.

Back at the hospital, I try calling the consulate number, only to be
told most impolitely to call later. The phone is slammed down.
Should I get the bank draft ready and get medical tests done? Seems
like a good idea, and I take a quick run to the bank, get a draft made
for the visa application fees, and call the doctor's office to get an
appointment for Wednesday.

While sweating my way to the bank in the hot midday sun, I can't
help thinking what I would give to get over with these irritating hurdles and be with you. Each day I live here away from you is a day
spent on my pilgrimage to you. What will I do when I finally reach
you, Ehud? I can't imagine as yet, but I surely feel that I will be filled
with peace, happiness, satisfaction, and a deep calmness. I will try to
transmit these feelings to you as best as I can because in my presence
I want you to feel peace and happiness. I am aware that like any

other normal woman, I'm curious and enthusiastic about the physical closeness with you, but I'm sure in my mind that I'm not marrying you just for that purpose. Our manzil together as man and wife is to primarily experience the calmness, peace, happiness, relaxation, and warmth that are possible between two people who genuinely and truly love each other. These experiences can create a very spiritual dimension in a household. In that spiritually charged environment of our home, we will also indulge in expressing ourselves and our tender feelings physically. Then Ehud, physical love becomes one of the many expressions of the greater love that binds us. It ceases to be the end, it becomes a means to an end. This also says that in our home we need not prove ourselves to be superman and superwoman. You are you. I am I and in our love that has spiritual, metaphysical, psychological, emotional, and physical dimensions, we are together, we are one.

Vatsala

Dear Ehud,

This morning your call again filled me with new energy. I respect your idea of spending our honeymoon in India if I don't get a visa before our wedding. We could spend our time in very special settings such that we can fully enjoy the magic moments. On this issue I think I have a special wish for you. I wish that the magic time of the honeymoon should expand and stretch itself across the entire length of our lifetimes. Is it possible? Whoever heard about a honeymoon lasting a lifetime? Age, commitments, the drudgery of routine, kids . . . everything takes its toll, reducing the sweetness and brightness of a honeymoon. Can ours be an exception? The challenge for us is to prove that ours is an exception. How to do that?

My formula is that I will never stop seeing you in a positive light, never stop loving you in my mind, never overlook the fact that you are a very special gift to me from God, never take you for granted, and never forget all the reasons for which I should be grateful to you. This attitude is, I believe, sufficient to make me love you with fresh energy for a lifetime. The same applies to you if you choose to behold your wife in the attitude I just described. This formula, I hypothesize, will make sure that the magic time of the honeymoon continues to extend itself to cover our lifetime.

Love to you,
Vatsala

While the letters were being exchanged back and forth between Ehud and me the U.S. government shut down due to a budgetary crisis. I continued to visit the gates of the U.S. consulate to inquire about my visa application. The U.S. happens to be the favorite destination for almost all Indians who are ready to try their luck in a western country, and therefore, you can always find a spiraling, serpentine queue of hundreds of visa applicants who are braving all kinds of weather conditions just to get inside the gates of the consulate. The consulate staff, from the very bottom to the very top, however, are very well paid and very well trained in the disgusting art of treating the visa applicants like scoundrels and wayward, sick dogs, and rejecting ninety-nine out of every hundred applicants for the flimsiest of flimsy reasons. During my few visits to the gates (I couldn't even get through the security staff at the gates to ask questions of an officer inside), my spirits were drowning in deep frustration and despair. It was past mid-January, and I was afraid that if I kept trying on my own, I might not even succeed in *entering the gates* of the consulate, let alone getting my visa application approved. And the very idea of proceeding to get married without a valid visa to travel with my husband was very frightening to me. At all costs I wanted to avoid being left behind, waiting for the consulate staff to approve my visa application whenever (or if) they liked. They had to do it *now*, when I needed it. Of course, Ehud was the only refuge to whom I could turn for help, and so I sent a fax to his hotel address in Tokyo.

19.1.1996

Dear Mr. Ehud C. Sperling,

I am just returning from the impenetrable fort that is the consulate. The crowd is enormous and it is beyond my capacity to handle.

What I would suggest is for you to take at least a couple of days' halt at Madras and HELP me in pushing the papers in. If this is done even by the first week of February 1996, we have February and March to spend here, and by the end of sixty days' time we should hear about the visa approval. Please consider this request thoroughly. Wednesdays, Sundays, and Indian holidays the fort is closed. So between 26 Jan. and 2 Feb., please consider a brief visit to Madras to help me out of this mess.

Thanks,
Vatsala

I began waiting for Ehud's response to this SOS call.

On 26 January he called from Sydney. My spirits lifted instantly. He sounded like a gallant savior who was coming to the rescue of a damsel in distress.

He promptly arrived in Madras on 28 January, and the same day he scrutinized all my application papers, medical certificates, photographs, visa processing fees, and so on, and arranged them very neatly in a file. The next morning, he took me to the consulate. Being a white American, he did not have to wait in any queue, and as he breezed through the crowded gates, I tagged along, despite the security personnel coming after me to prohibit me from entering the compound. He silenced them quickly with a charming smile. "She is with me." Once the application was submitted, there was a painful waiting period for about an hour, and I was called for an interview. During the interview I was asked some very embarrassing questions, and the interviewer seemed neither to listen to nor believe any of the answers I gave. This brief interview over, we were asked to report at the gates at 4 P.M. the same day. When we arrived at the gates at the specified time, we were given a visa stamp on my passport and a sealed envelope that I was told not to tamper with and to submit at the port of my arrival in the U.S. And that was that. This visa, that I got like a piece of cake, would have been totally out of my reach if Ehud had not upset his travel schedule and come down to Madras to help me out.

In our hospital, from 25 to 31 January, a pharmaceutical company was sponsoring "Hospital-Acquired Infections: Awareness and Control Week." I, being the chief of clinical microbiology services, had been roped in as the key figure to plan and organize the event, including selecting speakers and topics to be covered in each day's session. I was scheduled to give the concluding lecture about hospital-acquired infection. By the afternoon of 29 January, my lecture outline, slides, and data were ready. On 31 January, I had lunch with Ehud, and when it was time for me to return to the hospital, I casually asked him, "Would you like to come along to this lecture?" He agreed without any hesitation and picked up his video camera.

When we reached the hospital together (for the first time), I could not help noticing the look of utter astonishment on the faces of my colleagues. They were caught unawares. No one anticipated seeing me walk into the hospital with a stranger, let alone a foreigner—a handsome, young white guy. I clearly read the questions popping out of their curious eyes—Who? Why? When? Where? How? What?

Soon I took Ehud around the hospital to introduce him to my close friends and colleagues on all seven floors of the hospital, and to show him the various wards. I introduced him to all of my assistants as my friend, a book publisher from the U.S., and they all liked him immediately. We both then went into the auditorium, which was jam-packed with in-house staff as well as guests from hospitals around the city; those who could not find seats were standing in the walkways on both sides of the auditorium. I was introduced by the chief of nephrology services as the speaker who needed no introduction, and went on to deliver my lecture.

As was always the case with the lectures I gave, the contents made good sense to the listeners; this was evident from their roaring laughter at my scientific humor, and from the long question-and-answer and discussion sessions, followed by thundering applause.

I was aware of Ehud's presence. I was aware also that this was probably the last scientific lecture I would give in my capacity as the chief of clinical microbiology services of this hospital for sick children. And it felt good to have done this job well.

After the lecture, Ehud complimented me on being a natural, and said, "After you leave, the hospital will get a microbiologist, but they will have a hard time finding—or may never find—somebody as talented and popular as you."

The visa battle over, Ehud returned to New Delhi for the book fair, and I resumed my work at the hospital—and writing my letters.

3.2.1996

Dear Ehud,

The mood of being in transit has come over me. Coming to the department is not like before . . . when I felt like I was being pulled to it. The pulling force has disappeared neat and clean. I am coming to the office to clean up the act of the past four years . . . the act of being a microbiologist. I am doing my best to avoid getting trapped in a farewell melodrama. It is just 11 days more and there is this promise of a phone call from you on Monday . . . a lot to look forward to.

I have been thinking about what you said in the airport lounge. It feels good to be appreciated. As always, I agree, not because I have to as a dutiful wife-to-be, but because I cannot but agree. As a man you have been treating me . . . the woman . . . very well. It has been a good feeling being with you, and for this I appreciate your role as a man. It feels good to have a husband whom I can admire, appreciate, and hold in high esteem both in and outside the home.

Consequently, I've been thinking about slow-release vitamin C. The slow-release mechanism covers my whole life span . . . from now onwards. It is every day, every moment of being a wife to you, being your center of letting yourself go, that I will tell you how grateful, thankful, and appreciative I am for all that you mean to me. I can't say it once, I can't say it a million times and be over with it. I need to live all my moments, every day for the rest of my life for you, and then probably I would have barely managed to let you know how I love you, how I appreciate and admire you, and how much I am grateful to you. So, Ehud, it is a saga for a lifetime . . . expressing my appreciation for you . . . it is for this long that I send you my love.

Vatsala

The days passed very quickly. I was not expecting any letters or phone calls from Ehud, who was at Delhi attending the book fair and meeting Harish Johari in Bareilly. This lack of communication did not upset me in any way. I felt connected to him at very deep levels, and I was amazed at the contentment and peace such a feeling of connectedness brought to me.

In the department I continued as before, and at home I tried to spend as much time as possible with my mother, fully aware that this precious relationship was now going to be tested by time, distance, and the addition of new relationships to my life. I was also fully aware that the deep, spiritual, and pure relationship of love and devotion that I had with my mother was never going to be diluted, no matter how much time or distance, no matter how many new relationships came on the scene. My divine, holy goddess, my dear, loving mother—nothing could ever replace her.

While going through my last working day in as casual a manner as possible, I could not help having flashbacks of the good and the bad times that I had spent in the hospital, trying to make a career and earning my livelihood. I had amply succeeded in both, and the pain that I felt in letting go of both was quite genuine. In the middle of the day, I got hold of a few moments to write one final note to Ehud—from this office, from this hospital, from this city, and from this country. It was the last note I wrote to Ehud before becoming his wife. I posted the letter by airmail to his Vermont address, fully aware that Ehud was not there to receive it, that I would never get a reply, and that, in fact, we might even reach Vermont before the letter did! But it felt good to still be able to write to him despite all the excitement, aches, and pains of leaving my familiar environment and relationships, and taking long strides toward new horizons.

Outside of my immediate family, I had not informed a single human being about my marriage, and had not sent out a single wedding invitation. All of my relatives, friends, colleagues, and neighbors in Madras were in total darkness about this marriage. I knew that these people would be hurt, offended, angry, and insulted when they learned about it later. But I did not feel guilty at all. I had my own reasons, and very strong ones at that, for keeping my wedding a secret, quiet event.

I felt sure about Ehud and his suitability for the role of my husband. This assurance was based on the eleven months of correspondence that we had exchanged. I had grown to accept all the contrasts that we had because I was convinced that the compatibility between us was of such a high magnitude that in comparison, the differences were pale and insignificant. But what about my colleagues, neighbors, friends, and acquaintances? If I let the news out, how was I going to handle their intense curiosity, comments, criticism, opinions, suggestions, expectations, well-meaning advice, jealousy, and sense of outrage? Most of them were not the kind who would hear the news in a noninvolved manner and say, "Oh, well, congratulations." They were the kind who would come up with thousands of questions, whipping up embarrassing personal details about me and Ehud (though we did not have any skeletons in our closets).

If I dared to release the news of my wedding, the curious newsmongers would want to know how much money I was going to spend. This could be easily gauged by asking a few friendly, simple questions about 1) wedding venue; 2) number of invitees; 3) amount of cash dowry; 4) number of silk sarees; 5) gold and diamond jewelry items; and, finally, 6) if the boy was living abroad, who was providing the travel expenses. And then the "worth" or the "market value" of the bridegroom would soon be determined by asking a new set of questions about his 1) education/degree; 2) profession; 3) employment; 4) salary; 5) family background; and 6) status of relatives.

Although I could easily provide answers, I was not willing to discuss these questions in a public forum. The news was too sensation stirring. I was not in the least prepared to receive this kind of attention. If I did not disclose the wedding, I would not have to face any questions at all. I chose the latter course of action in order to preserve my privacy and sanity.

The society in which I lived would not care to respect my unconventional actions and my strong belief that the dowry system should be totally abolished. At work, even though my colleagues were all highly trained, educated professionals (mostly doctors, professors, scientists, nurses, and researchers), they were steeped in the traditional, orthodox way of life, never deviating an inch from the norms set by our ancient Indian society. If I were getting married to an Indian man selected by my family, the same curiosity would be there, but to a much smaller degree. But I had initiated a relationship on my own *and* decided to marry a westerner. This was simply an outrage. According to the social order prevailing in my community, everyone would join me when I celebrated and rejoiced, but if I fell apart, who would come to my rescue? I didn't need greedy participants and passive onlookers. So let me rejoice on my own, let me pull myself together on my own if I fall apart. If I never announced the marriage, I would be able to resume my old life from where I had left off. Only I would know the scars I had received.

I had another reason for keeping quiet. When Indian men and women move to the West in search of education, jobs, and better material life, they are subjected to extreme cultural, social, political, and racial situations. Some of them realize the value of their Indian heritage and become more deeply patriotic and religious. They invariably come back to India to marry a person whom their family finds and chooses. Some Indian men who cannot resist the pressure try to mold and adapt themselves to prevailing local conditions. While working to excel in their professions, they adopt the western lifestyle, values, food habits, and dress code. They also take advantage of the freedom of sexual experimentation. Nothing wrong, they are trying to assimilate, you can say. But trouble arises when such men are pulled back to India by their families and made to marry innocent, never-married girls whose parents have provided huge sums of dowry.

Most of these unfortunate girls never get visas enabling them to join their husbands in the U.S. Some of these Indian men are married to American women, and simply lied to their families that they were still bachelors. The alert hawks at the U.S. consulate dig out this truth in no time, and since polygamy is not legal, the girls are denied a visa. If the men have just been experimenting and cohabiting with women in the West, they do manage to get a visa for their new Indian wife. Yet when the girl goes all the way across the Atlantic with dreams in her eyes, she soon discovers that the man with whom her family had arranged a wedding at great expense has a steady partner and maybe even kids. Frequently, once this truth is unveiled, the man starts ill-treating the wife. More often than not, these women are not fluent in English, don't know how to drive and find their way around the city, don't have a job permit, don't have friends, relatives, and social contacts, and don't have the big chest and white skin seen so frequently in the West. Unable to relate to her wayward, abusive husband, this is now a destitute woman in distress. If she is smart enough, she can try to find her way to the societies for battered Asian women that provide temporary shelter, jobs, and help in obtaining divorces, as well as assistance in obtaining citizenship. If all else fails, they can attempt to deport these women back to India.

Many such horror stories reach the Indian press. Maybe out of a hundred, ten marriages fail; out of one hundred failed marriages, news of one reaches the press. But that is enough to put fear, suspicion, and rage in the minds of Indian girls and their families.

Having witnessed the destruction of the life of a close friend of mine this way, I had some degree of apprehension and fear of the path I had chosen to take with Ehud. The ghosts of "what if" sometimes haunted me. In our correspondence, I had seen only the very best of Ehud; he seemed like a perfect gentleman. But what if things changed once I married him? What if some long-suppressed monster in Ehud came alive and tormented me? What if I experienced a total and irreversible culture shock and in no way could adjust to a life in the West? What if everything conspired and worked against me, and I wanted to get back to my old life and start again? What if Ehud soon got fed up with me and sent me back to India? What if I turned out to be one of that ten in one hundred women whose marriages to western men failed? What if . . . ? What if . . . ? What if . . . ?

To counteract these "what if" ghosts, I thought I must take precautionary measures. While going on such an adventure in a far-flung place, it did not seem wise to burn my bridges. So I figured I must retain my family and home base, must not resign from my job, and must not tell anyone I was getting married.

I had discussed all these "what if" situations with Ehud. He could understand that I was adventurous enough to poke my hands into the hot water but quite frightened of getting burned. He knew that my fears were real to me, although he was sure that none of them would ever come true. He was kind and supportive enough to come along with me on my "what if" trip and confident enough to let time dismantle each fear one by one. He knew me better and had more faith in me than I had in myself. And he knew himself well—all he wanted to do was give me a good life filled with love and security.

13.2.1996

Dear Ehud,

Today is my last working day at the Childs Trust Hospital. Needless to say, I am nostalgic about my stay here and the people I met en route. The medical director who had interviewed me for this post resigned three years ago for personal and health reasons, but he has just returned. From the moment he decided to hire me, he was my ardent admirer. When he rejoined CTH a couple days ago, he showed immense pleasure at seeing me still working here. Today I met him at his office to tell him officially how happy I was to have him back at CTH. I then presented him with a copy of my annual report. He was floored: "You have been consistent, unrelenting, thorough, and lucky . . ." was all he managed to say. Then he assured me that he would fight with the management to raise my pay to triple what I am getting now. I took his assurance quietly, but said to myself, *Sir, thank you, but my life has taken a new turn now . . .*

I hoped that he would not change his opinion of my performance as soon as he learned the real reason of my visit. My hands trembled as I tried to pull the leave application out of my file. Many doctors have run crying from his office because he berated them for asking for a couple of days' leave, and he tore their application into shreds. He firmly believes that only imbeciles take leave. All those who take leave are traitors to the hospital and their patients; he himself comes to the hospital 365 days a year, year after year, and is fond of taking a midnight round of the wards (besides morning, midday, afternoon, and evening rounds). During his rounds, he closes leaky taps, switches off unnecessary lights, pulls up errant staff, and comes down heavily on anyone found gossiping or stealing a few seconds of nap time during their 24- or 48-hour duty. He is a total, unpredictable terror.

"Sir . . . in fact, I came here to give this application."

"What, Doctor, asking for a pay raise?" He chuckled while taking the application from my hand. As his eyes moved down the page, his chuckle was quickly replaced by hard lines around his mouth. His blood pressure must have gone up at least ten points.

"I can't accept this nonsense, this is not right, you *cannot* do this to the hospital and to your poor patients, you *cannot* leave the department to the mercy of the gods. This is grossly irresponsible behavior, Doctor, and I *cannot* give you such a long leave. No way," he bellowed.

"Sir, I fully agree with your views, but I request you to consider the fact that during the past four years of working at this hospital I have not taken even a couple of days of vacation. If you have any doubts, Sir, I could bring in my duty roster for you. And this is an emergency situation. My father, who is 82 years old, has summoned me to come and see him. I cannot refuse him. And, Sir, I would be ever grateful to you for sanctioning this leave application."

He did not seem to have listened to my pleading at all. His silence hung heavily in the office. I felt like I was suspended in the air, his waves of anger and frustration swinging me like a pendulum.

"Have you arranged any replacement?" he asked.

"Sir, since this is a short leave, I have scheduled my assistants to run the daily show, and if they run into any problem, I have asked them to seek your help or meet with the pathologist, who has offered to see them if they have any problems."

This was followed by another, longer bout of very tense silence. He was mumbling under his breath, perhaps cursing me.

"I sanction this leave only on condition that you will find a regular replacement," he said, signing the application and handing it back to me.

"Sir, the pathologist, who also has good undergraduate training in microbiology, is as good a replacement as any," I said.

He angrily snapped back, "Don't give me that crap story. She is not at all like you." He got up to get a glass of water. "I did not expect this from you, Doctor. I always believed that you were one of the most devoted doctors around here."

"Sir, I must thank you for this observation and also for granting me leave."

I made a very quick exit from his office before he had a chance to change his mind.

Back in the lab the scene is charged with emotion. It is not just me, but many people who trust their intuition. These colleagues of mine . . . I'm a fool if I still believe that they have not guessed what is cooking. This morning Shankari, who had worked the night shift, was leaving as I came in. Since she is the senior-most assistant here, I have practically handed over the entire department and the staff to her care. While saying goodbye, we hugged. Wiping a tear from her eye, she said, "Ma'am, I don't think you are coming back." I can't deny the truth of her intuition, though I can't say, Hey . . . You figured it out right . . . !

I'm planning on walking up and down the stairs today, covering all the floors. There have been days and days I have walked the stairs of this hospital, paused to catch my breath, looked down a corridor and prayed . . . *God, please help, please lead me on to the manzil that is right for me.* Consciously handing myself over to God, asking Him to lead me on, always took away like magic a heavy weight of worries, planning, wantings, wishings, yearnings, cravings . . . It made me lighter, lively, and filled me with renewed energy that helped me stay focused and take what came instead of clamoring and struggling to be in control. For me, prayer was never a secluded time spent in the company of a visible God locked in His shrine. Prayer for me was a silent monologue with the God who is everywhere and whose detailed scrutiny we can never, ever escape. If that God chooses to become one with our conscience, it does not surprise me, because only when that unification occurs does the mind of an individual become truthful, conscientious. Watching humanity weeping, smiling, puffing, and panting its way up and down the stairs of this hospital has made me a person who is chronically, silently praying, always communicating something to God, and believing that God is nearby and alive, listening and responding.

Overall, the time I've spent here has been very satisfying and stimulating, both personally and professionally. Not that I've never had a bad patch here. But somehow, the good patches smartly outnumbered the bad. Some people did rub me on the wrong side; they got their fingers burned and in due time realized that they were playing the wrong game with the wrong person. I was disturbed momentarily, but not hurt or damaged, by these negative energies.

Our correspondence was born amidst the cheerful and the traumatic times in this hospital. Strange but true. While this "I love you" note is being written for you, on some floor here, somebody's loved one is slipping away into a coma, never to return. But is it not true all over the world? This whole big world is a big cocktail of joys and sorrows. In that cocktail we seek a patch of good times for ourselves. And luckily, away from the publishing elite, away from the mad rush of the hospital, we both have discovered a small patch of good times for ourselves in each other. I feel blessed.

I have concluded my time at the Childs Trust Hospital as smoothly and as best as I can, giving an altered but semitrue version about my exit. This is the least injurious for everyone, as I do not want to drop a bombshell on CTH. My schedule for the day is simple . . . relish every moment, pick up my bags, go home. No coming back. No dramatic farewells.

What next? It is a big gamble . . . this whole life is a big gamble . . . the very process of being born, living, and growing is a process of taking risks and dealing with the unknown.

From the land of the known, I am moving on to the land of the unknown . . . I am nervous, though just a little. The pain of leaving is there too. But then there is also that trust in God, His plan for our well-being. I am nurturing this trust and it has been helping me out of the fear.

This morning, I woke up at about 5 A.M. Instead of springing straight out of bed and getting into the usual rush-rush routine, I lazily rolled to my side, pulled the sheet over my ears to prevent the numerous mosquitoes from getting their breakfast from my blood, and took an extra 10-minute nap . . . Oh, what a luxury! Mother was singing bhajans and prayers in the pooja room. I tried to listen to her with each cell in my body. Soon I will not have the privilege of waking up every morning to the sweet, melodious tune of my mother's bhajan singing. I will have only the memory of her voice. I felt a stab of pain in my heart. Why do we always have to give up something to receive something? Most surely, human lives are governed by strict laws of time, place, and circumstance, and when the time for an association is over, no one can ask for another moment and be granted that wish. Each human being simply has to move on and progress in the spiral of his own life, destiny, and journey. All we can carry with us is a memory of time spent with others. If this is all I can carry, then my load is big—full of very sweet memories of being the last-born of this mother, being raised and nurtured by her with total love, and, in my adult life, having her as a close friend, confidante, counselor, critic, and admirer. With her growing older, I am giving back to her what I received so abundantly—love, friendship, admiration, care. My only regret is that I will never be able to give her all I want and need to give her. She is "Janani," the sacred, feminine creator, the mother. She will always be way ahead of me, above and beyond the game of giving and receiving.

Then, dear Ehud, no more letters from this hospital laboratory. And my dear hospital, bye-bye . . . sure, you will do well and find a good replacement for me . . . sure, life will go on. And let me move on to the unknown with only one medicine in my emergency kit . . . *total trust in God.*

I love you, Ehud.
Vatsala

PART III

Manzil

chapter 11

FOR SEVEN
LIFETIMES

O n 15 February, 1996, Ehud and his friend Payson Stevens
came to pick up Amma and me at Trivandrum airport. As
soon as I saw Ehud, the pain of leaving, my fears of an
unknown land—all the worries that I carried with me—dissolved and
vanished. I felt as if no care in the world could touch me.

When we arrived at Ramakrishnan's house, his mother, brother,
wife, sister, niece Sharada, nephews, and sons Kartik and Giri welcomed us. We dropped off our bags and had tea together. Ramakrishnan's sister and her family lived right across the narrow street
in the predominantly Brahmin colony, which also contained the
wedding venue and Ganesha temple.

Almost everyone around us were Brahmins. Their unique way of
speaking Tamil, their ceremonies and rituals of greeting and hospitality, spoke loud and clear about their caste. It amazed me. Only a few
decades ago, the very *idea* of mixing and mingling with non-Hindu,
non-Brahmins would have resulted in expulsion from the caste. Yet
for decades now the "Brahmins-only" enclaves where non-Brahmins
could not even walk the streets had been over for good. And here
they were, gathered in an astonishing display of acceptance, generosity, warmth, and friendliness to do the most unimaginable of all
tasks . . . getting their Hindu Brahmin girl married to a foreigner. In
doing so, their deep-seated feelings of kinship and extended family
came forth.

Ehud whisked me away to Surya Samudra, the hotel where he and his friends from abroad were staying. The car sped along the coastal road and arrived on a hill overlooking a small cove on the Arabian Sea. Each hand-carved wooden home displayed elaborate motifs, designs, and stories from local Hindu mythology.

Ehud showed me into his room. Laid out on the bed were five bridal ornaments: exquisite bangles, a necklace, earrings, girdles, and ankle bracelets. A headpiece, finger ring, and five different hand-woven pure silk sarees with intricate embroideries and fascinating colors were also laid out. Together, these items represented wealth that I had not seen in all my life, nor could have earned working two lifetimes at my hospital.

I turned to Ehud and said, "You know, I am not marrying you for this."

He laughed. "I'm very happy to be giving you these, as you have no desire for them nor any expectations around them. I have no need to impress you, so this gift is freely given and freely received."

When I asked Ehud why he was giving me such a lavish gift, he explained that Dada Harish Johari had suggested that according to my horoscope, emeralds and diamonds set in gold would make the most appropriate ornaments for my wedding. Dada had further explained to Ehud that in Indian weddings, it was traditional for these five ornaments to be offered by the bridegroom to the bride, and that there are spiritual and occult reasons for adorning the bride in jewels and gold. To the groom, the bride represents Lakshmi, the goddess of wealth and good luck, and adorning her is a way of expressing devotion to the goddess and blessing the household. The placement of ornaments stimulates *nadi* and *marma* points on the bride's body, and are thus essential for her health, fertility, and longevity.

This explanation from Dada helped Ehud change his view about jewelry, which, in his experience, was worn like a trophy to display wealth. And the two of them put their heads together to acquire the precious gems (a rare matched set from a maharani's necklace!), design the jewelry, and commission a jeweler in Bareilly to craft the entire set by hand. What I saw before me at the Surya Samudra that day was the result—except for the silver anklets, which were a gift from Pratibha, Dada's wife. In Indian weddings it is considered very auspicious for the bride to receive jewelry worn by a senior woman for her own wedding.

Later that evening, I was musing over my first encounter with this immense display of gold, silver, diamonds, emeralds, and silk when I realized that in this lovingly and painstakingly assembled set of adornments, one item was missing. It was the *mangalasutra,* the most essential item in the list of jewelry worn by a Tamil bride.

Dada, a North Indian, had overlooked the fact that in South India, no Tamil wedding can be performed without the mangalasutra. In North India, the wedding ceremony is completed by application of *sindoor,* or red vermilion powder, by the bridegroom on the bride's forehead and the parting in her hair. In South India, however, the wedding could not be completed without the bridegroom tying the mangalasutra around the bride's neck. In our particular community—shaivait Brahmins from the Madurai district in Tamil Nadu—our mangalasutra consisted of two gold medallions engraved with the icons Meenakshi and Sundareshwar (incarnations of Parvati and Shiva, the cosmic couple eternally wedded and totally devoted to each other). These medallions were held in place by four gold beads on a thread smeared with sacred turmeric powder. With the wedding only a few days away, how could we find this piece in time?

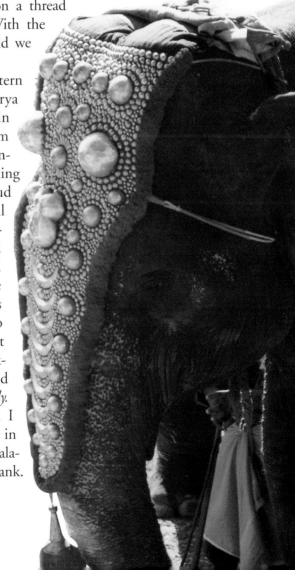

The following morning, all the western guests arrived and were taken to Surya Samudra. Two elephants decorated in traditional Kerala style welcomed them to their unconventional lodgings by sprinkling them with rosewater, instantly washing off their jet lag. After breakfast, Ehud announced that we would take them all shopping to pick out sarees for the wedding festivities. While the guests hurried to get ready for this adventure, I grabbed this time to tell Ehud about the absence and importance of the mangalasutra. His face took on an intensity I was coming to know. It was already 16 February. The next day would bring Shivaratri and the weekend and so most of the jewelry shops would be closed. He had to do something *quickly.*

Over the next few days, Ehud and I went in and out of scores of jewelry shops in search of the specific design of the mangalasutra medallion, but drew a consistent blank.

However, our luck held true. On the morning of 19 February, an unknown jeweler from an obscure part of Trivandrum appeared at Ramakrishnan's sister's house. He had heard of our urgent search from some of his jeweler friends and had come looking for us.

The very next morning, at a *subhamuhoorat* (predetermined auspicious time when all sacred and good activities can be started), this jeweler appeared at Ramakrishnan's house with his creation. He also brought a priest along with him who infused the medallions with life and longevity, chanting verses from the Vedas and invoking Shiva and Parvati. This sacred emblem of matrimony was presented to Ehud for safekeeping.

Later that evening the wedding party decided to go temple hopping to see the colorful Shivaratri celebrations. As we drove through the streets of Trivandrum, we could see long processions of heavily decorated elephants, their sedate *mahouts*, or trainers, urging and prodding these beasts to move on toward temples where, to the ear-piercing sounds of drums and hair-raising chants of *"Aum Namaha Shivaya"* by tens and thousands of men and women, offerings were made to Shiva with prayers seeking his protection.

At the largest Shiva temple in town, devotees crowded every square inch of ground. Ehud got out of the car and signaled me to join him. Out of the earshot of the others, he explained to me that Ramakrishnan had informed him that the priests he had engaged to perform our wedding had just told him that they would not conduct a Vedic marriage for a non-Hindu man and a Hindu girl. They had never done such a thing before—the wedding venue had never been used for anything other than a Brahmin wedding—and they would not risk their priestly careers on such an unorthodox alliance.

I was shaken by this news. Here Ehud had traveled all the way across the globe, four months of preparation and eleven months of correspondence had gone into the precipitation of this wedding, and in the end it was not going to happen. Yet Ehud's demeanor was quite relaxed and calm. How could this be?

Dressed in the traditional outfit of *kurta* pajama, Ehud could easily pass for a fair-skinned North Indian and enter the sanctum sanctorum where the sign proclaimed "Hindus Only." I wondered at how easily he floated between one world and another. He took my hand and boldly entered the temple, yelling *"Jai Shiva!"* The feeling of devotion was extreme, as was the crowd's pushing and shoving, which literally allowed one to pick one's feet off the ground and be carried around the shrine. It occurred to me that in this atmosphere, how could one be concerned about one's personal and minor problems when all around you the call was for Shiva . . . Shiva . . . Shiva . . . Talking about this moment later, Ehud and I realized that we shared the same feeling as we stood in that throng in the temple. With our wedding only one day away, it was totally out of our hands to materialize a priest—even though we were surrounded by hundreds of them. We would have to trust a power beyond ourselves.

I was jostled, pushed, and shoved in the procession. My mother joined us in the temple, and as I protectively held her sweaty, wrinkled hand in mine, I recalled how as a little girl I had held her hand tight and stepped around the Shiva *linga,* my young mother chanting and prompting the little me to chant "Aum Namaha Shivaya" and circumambulating Shiva late into the night until my legs ached and my eyelids glued together in small stretches of sweet sleep. When I could no longer carry on walking, she sat me on the lawn outside the temple and told me the story of Shivaratri:

One day while a young boy was hunting, a bear came out of the woods and lunged at him. Afraid for his dear life, the boy climbed high into a vilva tree. To keep himself awake, he began plucking leaves from the tree and dropping them down, chanting "Aum Namaha Shivaya." As the night wore on, the bear got fed up and went away. In the morning when the boy came down from the tree, he found a Shiva linga below the tree that he had not seen in his panic the night before. Apologizing for his sin of not saluting Shiva, he prostrated in front of the Shiva linga and begged to be forgiven.

At this moment, Shiva appeared in front of the boy. "You have chanted my name all night long and laid vilva leaves at my feet and remembered me in your hard time," he said. "I bless you with a long life and remove your fear of losing it. Live happily and have no worries." The boy, enchanted with this divine visitation and blessing, made a temple around the Shiva linga and spent the rest of his life in Shiva pooja.

"Live happily . . . have no worries . . ." These words came alive to me, and I could hear their echo in the story told to a small girl by her mother, a story told to all children by their long-gone ancestors to strengthen the memory of their history, culture, tradition, and genetics, a story of faith that, no matter what, God is kind and will help . . . *have no worries.*

When we all emerged from the shrine, Ehud looked very calm. I wondered, Why? How? Was his faith in the Vedic belief "what has to happen will happen" the same as my own? Could his faith in God be equal to mine?

We did not discuss our feelings, nor did we comment any further on the difficulties we now faced. Seeing that Ehud was somehow fully engaged in the present moment, it occurred to me that this problem, as with all other problems, would bring its solution in its own shadow. Finally the only thing we have and can share is the present moment, which right then was supercharged with high-voltage currents of pooja and *bhakti* (devotion) for Shiva.

Henna designs on the palms of western women.

The following morning, 20 February, the women guests and I visited an artist who painted elaborate henna designs on our palms. While watching the creation of these ancient designs, which are done preceding all happy occasions and are believed to be auspicious, I thought again about Ehud, who, though burdened with a seemingly unsolvable problem, had chosen not to worry his guests with the situation. Surely, this strength and confidence, which had carried us so far along this road toward our union, would overcome these obstacles now. Every time I looked at Ehud's calm and majestic profile, I could see the letters I'd been reading all these months start to come alive. I clasped my hands together tightly, as if some of Ehud's courage would flow into me.

Ehud also wanted henna designs on his palms, so after the other women and I had been decorated, I collected a little henna paste and headed to Surya Samudra with my mother. Carefully, I shaped the dye paste into a Star of David on Ehud's palm. It was late in the evening and with the henna drying, Ehud was unable to feed himself. Amma—this ever-shy, quiet woman—offered to feed him. This was the most unorthodox and unconventional thing she had done in her entire life.

Amma feeds Ehud while his hennaed hands dry.

Left to right:
*Invitation card
for the wedding;
Invitation in Tamil;
Invitation in English
with schedule of events.*

Text visible on invitation cards:

Sri Ramajayam

Srimati. Narayan... Ammal
and
Sri. B.S. Ra...
request the pleasure of
with family and frien...
of the marriage o...

Sowbhagyavati...

Chiranjeevi. E...
On Thursday, t...
at the Brah...
Vinayaga Na...

With t...
DEBORA...
ROBERT...
B.R.BA...
R.RAM...

The Preamchid.

AN INVITATION

I crossed the barriers
of nationality, language and religion
and found a woman in India
to share my life with.

Her name is Dr. B. R. VATSALA and
she is a microbiologist by profession.

I am marrying her on the 22nd of February '96
at the Brahmin Community Center, Vinayaka Nagar,
Trivandrum-18, India, amid Vedic chantings in
a traditional Hindu ceremony.

I request you to attend the function
and bless our union with your participation.

EHUD C. SPERLING
President,
Inner Traditions International
One Park Street Rochester
Vermont, USA 05767

(Programme Overleaf)

Prog...

21-2-96 WEDNESDA...
5 p. m. Devotional Music Re...
6 p. m. "Baraat" Bridegroo...
7 p. m. Solemnising of the be...
8 p. m. DINNER.
9 p. m. Bharata Natyam Recita...
to
10 p. m

22-2-96 THURSDAY
7 a. m. Breakfast
8 a. m. Vedic Chanting.
9 a. m. The "Fire" ceremony
10 a. m. The tying of the auspiciou...
signifying marital bond.

Traditional clarinet-based...
on the occasion. The food

11 a. m. Blessing ceremony, (Throw...
12 noon LUNCH.

In between spoonfuls, Ehud described his day at Ramakrishnan's house, where all the frantic last-minute preparations regarding the flowers, musicians, and artists were being worked out. Ramakrishnan, this man in his fifties, this husband and a father of two young boys, had gone to his mother— the source of security and comfort throughout his life—to confide in her about this devastating problem with the priests. His mother, a very orthodox, conventional Tamil Brahmin well versed in the cultural practices and sacred traditions of her community, chided her son for not having told her earlier about the dilemma.

Only the day before, I had heard her tell Ehud how much she appreciated his love and respect for our culture, his intrepid crossing of the boundaries of race, culture, and religion to give a good life to an Indian woman, and his agreement to marry according to the sacred Vedic rites. Even though it was unconventional, she decided to participate in it fully, and encouraged all her neighbors and her entire extended family to do the same. She told Ramakrishnan that she would, that morning, visit a very old retired priest known to her in a nearby village temple. This priest, well over eighty years old, had stopped practicing, had gone into seclusion, and was living a life of saintly austerity.

The old priest listened to our story. He reflected for a while and said that this marriage would be good for the *Sanatana Dharma,* the eternal religion. In his long years, the priest had seen vast changes in the cultural fabric of India. The British had left. A secular republic had established itself after a massacre in which millions of Hindus and Muslims had been killed and made homeless. Many young people were rejecting the age-old traditions and practices that he had grown up with. He saw in our marriage an opportunity for the Sanatana Dharma to reassert and establish itself in a new form in a new land. Just as Hinduism had transformed itself many times before by embracing and finally absorbing alien cultural and religious trends, and had emerged strengthened and rejuvenated, so too did he feel that this alliance between two cultures and two religions would enhance each of them. He told Rama-krishnan's mother that he would gladly come out of his retirement and perform all the Vedic rites himself. Our interreligious, cross-cultural, international wedding had his complete blessing.

Ehud told us all this as his hennaed palms dried. As my mother handed him yet another pinch of *idlis* and chutney, I saw that a few lines and wrinkles had disappeared from her face. When Ehud and I looked at each other, he swallowed his idlis quickly and we said together, "Jai Shiva . . ."

Western women dressed in India's finest sarees. From left to right:
Maria, Barbara, Debby, Sara, Deborah, Leslie, and Maura.

On the evening before the wedding, to the sound and spark and light of firecrackers, the bridegroom's entourage, or *baraat,* consisting of Ehud's sister Debby, Ehud's friends, and many neighbors, assembled in front of Ramakrishnan's house. The entire community spilled out into the streets to watch this gathering and to admire the adventurous spirit of the foreigners in embracing Indian cultural etiquette. Children from the neighborhood were thrilled to be dancing close to Ehud. A group of traditional village musicians arrived from Ramakrishnan's ancestral home in Tenkashi, a little township hundreds of miles away on the border of Tamil Nadu and Kerala. Their long trumpets and large drums had preceded the baraat in weddings for as long as anyone could remember. Their spirited enjoyment of the event radiated out from their instruments and filled the entire neighborhood. Ehud commented that if this kind of racket were taking place outside his boyhood home in New York, certainly the police and fire brigade would be called in to control the mob. In India, such festivities are part of our very life and landscape.

Deborah Kimbell, Leslie Colket Blair, Debby Kanig, Barbara, Sara, and Maria Theiss, and their friend Maura were draped in the silk of India's sarees, and they were a delightful sight. After an afternoon of being fussed over by Vijaya and Ramakrishnan's mother, sister-in-law, and niece, they wore flowers in their hair, *kumkum* on their foreheads, and beautiful glass bangles on their wrists, and they carried ceremonial plates filled with *paruppu thengai,* coconuts, flowers, sweets, *betel* nuts, turmeric, garlands, and sandalwood paste. They were transformed by the dress and ambiance of India.

I was kept apart from this incredible noise and chaos and was myself being elaborately decorated and adorned, for the first time wearing all the jewelry and exquisite ornaments that Ehud had presented to me. I could hardly hold my head up from the weight of the elaborate floral headpiece woven into my hair.

As the baraat continued its slow march, I was put in a car and whisked away to the wedding venue. When the procession arrived, Ganesha was invoked with chanting, prayers, deep *aradhana* (worship), ringing of bells, bhajan singing, *arati,* and distribution of prasad. The bride's party came to the entrance to welcome the baraat with flowers, garlands, and songs. The priest raised the sacred fire for conducting the ceremonial rites of betrothal.

According to the traditional practice, Ehud's party and my party were seated on opposite sides of the ceremonial sacred fire, with the priests in between. I was surprised to see not just the old priest (who looked sixty, not eighty!), but *five* priests, each one chanting and conducting the ceremonies with full gusto.

At the auspicious moment, the chief priest inquired of Debby and my father what the purpose was for this assembly. The intention of both parties—for Ehud and I to be married—was recited by the priests in a verse and conveyed to the Agni, the sacred fire, and Agni was invoked to be the celestial witness for this occasion and to bless the couple with a good conjugal life. Having obtained the permission and blessing of the Agni, the priest announced the beginning of the betrothal rites.

My father asked Ehud if he was willing to marry me according to Vedic rites. Then Payson (who was officiating as Ehud's brother) and Debby asked my father if he was willing to give away his daughter as a wife to their brother. When both parties agreed, the priest announced the sacred betrothal to the guests. Anna offered gifts of *veshti, angavastra,* and jewelry to Ehud to welcome his decision to marry me. Debby applied sandalwood paste and kumkum on my forehead and wove flowers into my hair, inviting me to become her brother's wife and part of their family. This concluded the betrothal ceremony.

The guests and our families rejoiced, congratulating one another, and I was blinded by the cascade of flashing lights coming from scores of cameras. The ceremony was followed by a sumptuous feast South Indian style. All the foreign guests were amazed at this indigenous technology—food is prepared on a wood fire, served on banana leaves, and eaten with the hands. The banana leaf plates are fed to the cows and goats, and there is no china and cutlery, no need of biohazardous washing agents, no use of electricity, and no waste.

Five priests officiate the wedding. These Brahmin priests are trained since childhood in the spiritual and religious functions that are a part of Hindu cultural and social life.

In the midst of the rich and delicious feasting on this warm evening, the guests were shaken from their reverie by the sounds of a new pattern of drumbeat. The temple lights were dimmed and strong lights shone on the stage where our betrothal had taken place. A young woman appeared, clothed in classical costume and adorned in jewelry. Her beautiful face, full lips, sparkling teeth, exquisitely expressive and thickly kohled eyes, flower-bedecked hair flowing down to her slender waist, and shapely, firm, strong legs all spoke loud and clear that she was a dancer with years of dedicated training. As it turned out, she was the founder and director of the most renowned Bharat Natyam dance school in Trivandrum. Her mother, a woman in her fifties, sang the first song—an invocation to Shiva in the form of Nataraja, the originator, creator, and perpetuator of all classical dance forms. And as the dancer's feet and ankle bells brought her mother's song to life, I saw that the chief priest's eyes were closed, his lips quivering with the beats of the invocation. As the pearly drops of sweat ran down his forehead, blurring the sacred ash lines, I could not but recall how Shiva had helped me by coaxing this priest from his retirement. In my heart, I did a salutation to this priest and bowed to Shiva.

Intense applause brought me out of my reverential communication. The dancer was on to her presentation of Meenakshi, a human incarnation of the goddess Parvati, who was famous for her beautiful round eyes and invisible third breast. This breast was intended for nurturing the entire universe (Parvati is also known as Annapoorna, the universal mother who nurtures the entire creation) and could not be seen by anyone other than Shiva, her eternal companion and husband in all her incarnations.

Parvati, Shiva's wife, presents him with soma, the divine elixir, in my painting.

Meenakshi was raised in the palace of her father, King Pandiyan of Madurai, with all the pomp and gaiety befitting a princess. As she grew up, she made it known to her father that she would marry only the man who saw her invisible breast and hence recognized her as the universal mother. After several failed attempts by different suitors, Meenakshi began a fast with a determination to end it only when Shiva appeared before her and married her. Moved by Meenakshi's love and devotion, Shiva incarnated as Sundareshwar, a very beautiful prince to whom the third breast was visible. King Pandiyan recognized his daughter and son-in-law as incarnations of Parvati and Shiva, conducted their marriage under a *kadamb* tree, and built a temple around the tree to commemorate the union. Presently known as Madurai Meenakshi temple, it is one of the largest and most ancient temple complexes in the world. As per the traditions of my shaivait clan, the wedding that was to take place the next day was a reenactment of this story of remembering, celebrating, and worshipping this primordial, everlasting union of Shiva and Parvati, male and female.

I visualized the gigantic temple in Madurai as the Bharat Natyam dancer, accompanied by her mother's beautiful singing, enacted the story of Sundareshwar and Meenakshi. My maternal and paternal ancestors had lived in Madurai, and now Anna and Manni were living there. Manni had asked Meenakshi at the Madurai temple to help me find a suitable husband. As a sacred offering every morning, when she lit the sacred lamp in her family prayer room, she deposited a coin in a *kalash*. After the wedding, my husband and I were required to visit the Madurai temple, convey our gratitude to the goddess, and empty the kalash into the temple offerings box. I could almost see Ehud and myself prostrating at the Madurai shrine, and I prayed, *God, please help this happen, please help us all the way.*

I smiled as I listened to the story-song and saw the dancer bring Shiva and Parvati to life. When she completed her performance, she turned over the stage to a troupe of violinists, percussionists, and a young boy who enchanted us with Karnatic songs. He invoked Ganesha, the remover of all obstacles, and then sang about Shiva and his powers.

As the audience was drawn into the mysterious depths of this boy's beautiful voice, the Trivandrum municipality decided to turn the power supply off. Well, without the amplifiers and electric lights, we heard the real voice of the singer and realized how pleasant, vibrant, and alive it was. The room illuminated by candles, the boy singing ancient songs composed by the saint and musician Thiagarajar, I lost track of time and place. Everything merged into Shiva . . . my fears, worries, "what-if" ghosts, they had no more energy and stamina to harass me . . . The people, the festivities, they could not make me nervous and anxious like a bride . . . The dark, flowing tresses of Shiva devoured the darkness around us and everything, every feeling, everyone was drenched in the energy of Shiva . . . Shivamayam . . . Shivamayam . . . Shivoham . . . Shivoham . . .

The wedding ceremonies started before the crack of dawn, around 4 A.M. Sharada, Vijaya, and Manni dressed me in the saree that Ehud had given me on the day of our engagement. Again I was made up, my hair decorated with flowers, and I was taken to the wedding venue. The priests had already raised the sacred fire, which my mother and father nurtured with offerings of ghee and puffed rice. My father chanted invocations and prayers for the successful completion of the greatest sacrifice of his life: giving away his daughter in marriage for the continuation of the Sanatana Dharma.

As I came in, I offered my salutations to the Agni, my parents, and the priests, and sat next to my father on the wedding altar. The priests and my father initiated me into a ceremonial fasting ritual with a *sankalp,* or prayerful determination, that I would break the fast only when Ehud married me. I meditated on the meaning of this fast. If Ehud decided not to marry me, I would refuse all food and water and ultimately die. A vow witnessed by Agni is taken with an uncompromising attitude of do or die. With closed eyes, I prayed to Agni and to all the gods.

My prayers were interrupted by a loud thud: a delivery boy threw a bundle of today's newspapers with such practiced precision and force that it landed sharp at the feet of Ganesha. Was this a ritual for the boy, offering the bitter-sour prasad of the daily news to the central deity of the wedding venue?

The sun had not yet risen, but its blazing brilliance below the horizon was enough to illuminate the city, which was starting to move and swing to the sounds of temple bells and morning invocation chantings. The temple priest picked up the paper and began to read. With a wide grin, he approached the wedding altar and poked one of the assistant priests in the ribs. The priest took the newspaper and burst into a giggle in the middle of his chanting. He tapped the chief priest, who with closed eyes was chanting blessings for

Trivandrum's largest newspaper featured an article about our betrothal ceremony on its front page.

successful completion of my fast. Undisturbed, the chief priest went on chanting the blessing. When he finished, he looked at the assistant priest with questioning eyes and was handed the newspaper.

I knew very well that everyone in Kerala could read and write; it is the only state in India with a literacy rate of 100 percent. But what could possibly be so compelling that it needed to be read in the midst of a wedding ceremony? The priest handed the paper to Appa, and raising his folded hands above his bowed head and doing a *sashtang namaskar* to Agni, he began muttering, "Yes, Sanatana Dharma is victorious again. Now everyone can see that a peaceful merger of two religions and cultures cannot destroy basic Hindu beliefs. Hinduism is a loving, forgiving, all-embracing, universal religion. It is not a set of archaic beliefs practiced with total exclusiveness by a handful of fundamentalist fanatics."

What was going on? Silently, my father handed me the paper and I was touched by a 220-volt current. So that was the reason for all the exploding flashbulbs: Ehud and me, on the front page of the number-one newspaper in Kerala! The entire story of our courtship and alliance was described in Malayalam.

The faces of my dear friends and colleagues danced on the tips of Agni's mighty flames, asking why I had not told them about my wedding. I could feel the pain I had inflicted on my most beloved friends: Shankari, Sheela, Lissy, Clara, Seema, Venugopal, Padmapriya, Shyamala, Mary Babu, and scores of senior colleagues and mentors with whom I had shared years of daily headaches and heartaches. For an instant, I thought that this Malayalam newspaper might not reach Tamil Nadu, but no, about 90 percent of the nurses in my hospital were from Kerala, and would certainly read this paper.

I tried to chase these disturbing thoughts out of my mind and focus once more on the priests' chanting. They were invoking Agni, Ganesha, and all other gods and goddesses to witness the wedding that was about to take place. As the flames continued to rise higher and higher and I wiped tears of heat, smoke, and shock from my eyes, I said to myself, *It is now all up to Shiva. My intentions were and are good. Shiva, if unintentionally my words and deeds have caused any pain in the hearts of people whom I have loved dearly and held in high esteem, please forgive me. It is all up to you now to bring healing into these hearts.*

As I began my fast, I knew that Ehud and his friends were arriving at Ramakrishnan's house. His forehead, biceps, forearms, and chest would be marked with three horizontal lines—shaivait marks of wisdom, indicating knowledge of past, present, and future. He would be given a walking stick, representing the measure of wisdom that he could lean on during his journey through life, and a book of sacred scriptures. He would begin a fast and then be initiated into the Brahmin sect, and given a sacred thread to wear across his chest. Thus dressed up as a Brahmin who is about to renounce the world and go off into the forest in search of wisdom and enlightenment, according to the wedding tradition, Ehud would be handed a small cloth parcel of cereal grains meant to nourish him on his journey. A black umbrella placed over his head would protect him from all evil influences along the way.

As the sun reached its full illumination over the city, I watched Ehud and his procession move slowly up the street. Many new faces joined in as the group passed the homes of friends and neighbors—at Indian marriages the whole community is welcome, and it is sometimes hard to tell who are invited guests and who are curious onlookers swept into the excitement. With the sounds of trumpets and drums approaching closer, my parents and the priests assembled at the gates of the wedding venue. They stepped out in front of the procession and my father spoke the traditional words to Ehud.

Ehud and I on the ceremonial swing.

"My beautiful, well-brought-up, and cultured daughter is on a fast, and will not give it up if you don't marry her. You need not go to the forest to do *tapasya* and gain wisdom. If you marry my wise daughter and settle down in grihasthashram, you will—by experience and by virtue of a family life lived well—gain all the wisdom that you are seeking in the forest by giving up worldly life."

With delight, I heard Ehud say with certitude that yes, he would take the beautiful, wise daughter as his bride. The bridegroom and his entourage were greeted with arati, songs, garlands, and flowers, and I was brought to the entrance to welcome the bridegroom with *varmala,* a garland. This varmala was exchanged back and forth between the two of us, and we were led to a ceremonial swing, which was rocked gently while the women around us offered joyful songs in Sanskrit, Tamil, Telugu, English, German, and Hebrew. Language was no barrier to this flow of feelings.

Ehud and I proceeded to the wedding altar, where the priests again raised the holy fire. My father washed Ehud's feet while my mother poured sanctified water as a purification of his thoughts and realignment of his priorities, so that he should not have any regrets or nagging doubts about his decision to get married to me.

Opposite: My father, assisted by my mother, performs the ritual washing of Ehud's feet.

Next, the priests assembled the mangalasutra medallions on a yellow thread. With chanting to invoke the blessings of everyone present in the ceremony, the priests placed the mangalasutra on a silver plate with fruits, coconut, flowers, kumkum, and turmeric powder and circulated it among all family and guests. Having received everyone's goodwill, blessings, and prayers, the plate was passed back to the priests.

I was taken to a dressing room while the blessing of the mangalasutra medallion was going on. Manni and Vijaya draped me in the nine yards of red silk that form the saree worn traditionally by Tamil Brahmin brides. With fresh flowers in my hair and a fresh garland, I was escorted back to the wedding altar and seated next to Ehud, who was listening to the priests chanting the Vedic wedding vows in Sanskrit:

"O Bride! You resemble the goddess Lakshmi, you are beautiful like the moon and you have doelike eyes. You have immense wisdom derived from reading the scriptures and following the life of discipline, purity, and austerity. I pray, be my mate in living a life as directed by the Vedas. With your wisdom and my hard work we can create a happy life of stability, peace, and prosperity. Our household will be blessed abundantly by the Sun, Nature, Wind, Rain, and Earth. With your kind nature, you can bring happiness to all lives associated with our household. I assure you that in our household, truth will reign supreme in all actions, words, and thoughts.

"I will provide you with all the necessary comforts, healthy cattle for milk and agriculture. You can bring stability to these livestock by looking after them as your children. In times of sickness, emergencies, and problems, I assure you of continuous support. I will cherish and protect you to the best of my knowledge and ability, as an earthen pot protects the lamp, because, O Bride, you are the light of my life and my household. This holy fire, which represents the continuity and brilliance of the Sun, who sustains life on Earth, is the witness to my sacred vows. I promise to abide by these holy vows.

"O Bride, please agree to be my wife and assist me in creating a household that will perpetuate Dharma, promote learning of the Vedas, have respect for knowledge and wisdom, honor Brahmins and scholars, and respect the holy and wise men. This household will have children who will follow the Vedic path and become great men. With these holy vows, O Bride, I ask you to be my wife and assist me in living a life of austerity according to Vedic traditions."

Opposite: *Debby accepts me into her family by placing rings on my toes.*

The meaning of these vows took me back to the time when people were true to their word, and marriage was based on promises made and kept. A strong current of joy and elation flowed through me, kindling a deep-seated sense of devotion to my relationship with Ehud. No legal documentation would be necessary to validate our marriage after these vows. Our marriage would be binding for seven lives. I could visualize Ehud and myself having not just seven lifetimes together, but asking God to give us an extension for several more.

As I reveled in the beauty and depth of these vows, I was urged to sit on the lap of my father. My mother stood beside him, assisting with the ceremonies. This tradition is rooted in the words *kanya daan,* meaning that the bride's father has faith in the holy vows and is willing to give away his daughter (kanya) as a holy offering (daan) to the worthy and deserving bridegroom.

Ehud tied the first knot of the sacred mangalasutra around my neck, signifying the permanence of the wedding vows. Guests threw rose petals to bless the union. As the drumming and chanting grew in intensity, I felt light. I did not experience the physicality of this once-in-a-lifetime moment. I could not feel Ehud's touch on my neck when he tied the sacred first knot; it was as if my soul were outside of my body. In this trancelike state it occurred to me that this marriage was not the marriage of Ehud and Vatsala; it was about being married to and united with the eternal mate.

Immersed deep in these feelings, I closed my eyes tight shut and gave my life up to God—*God has brought me to this state of union, and my life is no longer about me, about my aspirations, dreams, and wishes. It all about you, dear God; it is from you, to you, and because of you.*

The second and the third knots were tied by Debby. By tying these knots, she took on the role of her mother, accepting me as a member of her family and offering me the honored position of daughter-in-law. Ehud led me seven times around the sacred fire to offer prayers and thanksgiving to Agni. I stopped at a grinding stone—symbolic of continuous gastronomic activity in the family—and Ehud slipped a ring on the second toe of both of my feet. Debby did the same. I was now a permanent part of their family.

The ceremony complete, Ehud and I prostrated ourselves before the family, guests, and elders to convey our gratitude. After another big meal, at which Ehud and I broke our fasts, the wedding party gathered at the entrance of the venue and formed a procession. I stood by Ehud's left side, the side of his heart,

Opposite: *After the wedding ceremony, Ehud and I offer our humble salutations to all the elders, guests, and relatives.*

Ehud holds all five fingers of my right hand, representing that my five senses are devoted to him for our lifetimes.

and extended my right hand to him. Ehud took my hand in his right hand and held all five fingers in his grip. With this gesture I surrendered my five senses to my husband; from that moment on, all my senses would be satiated totally by Ehud. Thus, like Parvati, who finds her completion in Shiva, I would not have to search for anything or anyone else. At the touch of my husband's hand, a few words floated in my mind like fireflies in a dark summer night . . . *God, please help us . . . please be with us . . . please show us the right way.*

By the time our processions reached Ramakrishnan's house, only close friends and family were with us. Quite spontaneously the whole crowd started dancing to the musicians' tunes, Indians doing moves from popular and present-day Indian dances, and westerners doing God only knows what. While this hoopla was going on, I realized for the first time that I was now married to Ehud.

I scanned the room, relishing the sight of our loved ones enjoying themselves. "Do you know those two strangers?" I nudged Ehud. He looked at the men I was pointing toward and said he had no idea. In the meantime, one of them jumped onto the windowsill and with one hand pulled out a camera, shooting wildly. "Let them get their photos," Ehud said, laughing.

We left the celebration and changed into our everyday clothes. With no dress rehearsals, no fittings at the tailors, and none of the other preparations typical of western weddings, he had performed flawlessly in this Vedic ceremony. No one would have known that he was a westerner until this moment, when he appeared in his American jeans.

Outside in the courtyard Ehud's car and driver waited to take us to Surya Samudra. The luggage was already loaded, the engine running. "Get in quickly, let's get away without those long, drawn-out farewells so typical of Hindu and Jewish partings," said Ehud. *"Chalo!"* he told the driver. But before the car could move, someone tapped at the car window. Ehud rolled down the dark glass that shaded us from the hot afternoon sun. With a big smile, the stranger we had just seen shooting photos held out his business card. I took a quick peek and instantly my heart collapsed: it read "Senior Journalist, *The Hindu.*"

The car raced to the hotel, where the entire staff welcomed us with flowers. After spending a respectable period of time with our hosts and well-wishers, Ehud motioned to me that it was time to bid goodnight and retire to the nuptial chamber. We walked up the narrow pathway from the courtyard. As we moved into the room, we could not believe what we saw. It had been transformed. The shutters of the windows overlooking the veranda and the sea beyond were all wide open and strung with flowers. The sea breeze flowed through the petals, bringing an exotic and sweet aroma into the room. All the stone sculptures were garlanded with fresh flowers, and their foreheads shone with spots of kumkum and sandalwood paste. My eyes, moving from flower to flower, finally alighted on the nuptial bed. The staff had painstakingly cut the tops off hundreds of flowers and arranged the petals in elaborate patterns, transforming the bed into an exotic *mandala.*

I thought about the instructions on flower arrangement given in the *Kamasutra.* Ehud had published and distributed throughout India the first complete English translation of this work, and was familiar with the guidance from Kama, the god of love, on the sixty-four arts necessary for a happy conjugal life— from how flowers should be arranged in the bedroom, to how the wife should greet the husband returning home, to all the sexual *asanas,* or techniques, necessary for a rich and varied experience of intimacy. I gazed at the bed, knowing that I would be seated in the center of this floral mandala for my first sexual union.

A conch shell was blown outside our window, followed by the pulse of drums. Ehud opened the door to the veranda and stepped out.

"Come out here, Vatsala, quick, take a look at this," he called.

I walked outside. Against the backdrop of swaying coconut trees, their silhouettes illuminated by the last rays of the sun, six beautiful dancers bowed with their hands folded in namaste to a glowing prayer lamp. Music filled the air as the dancers performed Radha Krishna *leela*, the enactment of India's divine lovers. In this story Krishna is a desirable young lover who enchants Radha and the other *gopikas*, or milkmaids. With their sinuous bodies and beautiful costumes, they try to entice him away. The dancers' facial expressions and fluid hand gestures radiated erotic energy.

The sky grew dark and the stars of the Southern Cross were fully visible. Behind the dancers, hundreds and hundreds of tiny lights moved and flickered. The fishermen of Kerala were out on their nightly vigil: standing on their log boats with a lantern and a single net, they sought their livelihood. Their lanterns seemed like earthly reflections of the stars.

I turned to see how my Krishna was reacting to this extravaganza. He sensed the moment as being full and simply extended his right hand, into which I placed my right hand. His grip was firm around my fingers as he led me to the nuptial chamber, closing the door on one life and opening the path into a new world.

✻✻✻

Waking up the next morning in each other's arms, we felt complete and at peace. We knew that my parents and my brother's family would be waiting at the breakfast table to bid us farewell, so we dressed quickly. With a long look back at our flower-bedecked room, I followed Ehud out to the dining room. Ramakrishnan was ready with a stack of newspapers, each carrying an article about this unusual alliance between an American Jewish book publisher and a traditional Tamil Brahmin girl. This story had captured the imagination—as well as the headlines—of practically every major newspaper in Malayalam, Tamil, and English, including the *Hindu*, Tamil Nadu's largest English-language paper, in which I had first seen Ehud's matrimonial advertisement.

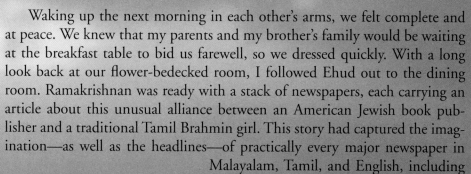

I was an unknown figure here in Trivandrum. But what about the neighborhood where I lived? What about the hospital where I worked? I knew the shock that these newspapers would cause in Madras. Almost everyone I knew subscribed to these papers.

THE ⬤ HINDU

India's National Newspaper

Printed at Madras, Coimbatore, Bangalore, Hyderabad, Madurai, Gurgaon, Visakhapatnam and Thiruvananthapuram

THIRUVANANTHAPURAM, FRIDAY, FEBRUARY 23, 1996

A marriage that crossed cultural barriers

From Our Staff Reporter

THIRUVANANTHAPURAM, Feb. 22. Amid Vedic chanting and the traditional 'naadaswaram' recital, Mr. Ehud C. Sperling (42), an American publisher, today tied the auspicious chain on Dr. B. R. Vatsala of Madras, at a ceremony held at the Advaitha Hall, Karamana.

"I crossed the barriers of nationality, language and religion and found a woman in India to share my life with" Mr. Sperling said.

For him India is a home away from home. Attracted by the Hindu culture, philosophy and religion, he has been visiting India every year for the past 17 years.

His company, the Inner Traditions International has brought out over 400 titles, mostly on subjects related to India.

Born in a Jewish family, he is settled in Vermont in the U.S. His decision to choose his life partner from India was not an impulsive one. On March 4, 1995, he advertised in the matrimonial columns of The Hindu with the help of his friend, seeking "an Indian bride, prepared to spend the rest of her life with a foreigner, who staunchly believes in Indian culture and tradition."

He chose Dr. Vatsala, a microbiologist by profession at the Child Trust Hospital in Madras, after visiting her family in Madras in October '95.

It was Mr. Sperling's suggestion that the marriage be conducted in the Vedic tradition. Thiruvananthapuram, as venue, was also chosen by him, for he was enamoured of the ambience, culture and the verdant beauty of this city.

His sister Ms. Deborah Kang, cousins, friends and a host of other relatives also attended the function.

Though the couple proposes to leave for the U.S. Mr. Sperling has plans to buy a house in this city as his vacation home.

The American, Mr. Ehud C. Sperling, and his Indian wife, Dr. B. R. Vatsala, (both sitting) after their marriage according to Brahminic traditions in the city on Thursday.

മാതൃഭൂമി

MATHRUBHUMI, THE NATIONAL DAILY IN MALAYALAM

PUBLISHED FROM KOZHIKODE, KOCHI, THIRUVANANTHAPURAM, THRISSUR, KANNUR AND KOTTAYAM

Regd No.KL /TV (N)243 Thiruvananthapuram Thursday February 22 1996

ആർഷസംസ്കാരം തേടി; ആത്മസഖിയെ കണ്ടെത്തി

To our amazement, the story of our wedding appeared in major newspapers in English and in many different Indian languages.

Well, I could not have created more sensation if I announced that I had single-handedly thrown the Brits out of India and gained independence. Friends later told me that they had seen the hospital administrator reading the paper, holding his drooping head in both hands. A few moments later he was beside himself, waving the paper in the air and running down the corridor toward the administrative offices to break the news. In the laboratories, the staff huddled together and read the articles aloud. In the library, the doctors split into groups for and against me and fought vehemently with each other about my story and my secretiveness around my wedding, and tried to prove me guilty or innocent. No one who knew me could believe that, without letting out as much as a whisper, I had taken such a bold stand.

Close friends, especially my six assistants in the department, told me about their joy and hurt on learning about my wedding. I had given them the worst shock of their lives. They simply couldn't understand why I did not reciprocate their love by letting them participate in my wedding. No "sorry" could get me their forgiveness.

From the first, Ehud understood my anguish over the distress I had caused my friends, and tried to reassure me that I had made the only decision possible. "Your real friends know who you are and will forgive and forget the pain," he said. "What everyone will remember for the rest of their lives is the spicy, juicy story you gave them to talk about."

As the newspapers that would cause such a storm moved from one person to the next, we finished our breakfast. Amma, Appa, Anna, Manni, and my niece were all set to leave. Ehud and I prostrated ourselves before my parents and took their blessings. My father gave Ehud a bone-cracking hug. For the first time in my life, I saw my father wipe a tear from his eye. He said nothing, but looked at Ehud for a long time. I realized then that he completely trusted Ehud to take care of me.

My brother and sister-in-law conveyed their blessings and best wishes. I hugged my mother and father and looked at their tear-stained, sad, happy faces. They all piled into the waiting car, and I stood by Ehud's side and waved as they drove off. I knew I could never completely go away from their lives. I would always be connected to them with a fine, indestructible string of love.

chapter 12

THE RIGHT MOMENT,
THE RIGHT PLACE

I left India for the first time in my life on 28 February, 1996. Familiar world, family, friends, home, job—I left everything behind. On the plane with Ehud I headed toward an unknown land, a prayer on my lips.

Deborah came to the Boston airport to receive us. How different she looked from the last time I had seen her, wrapped in a silk saree, blonde hair shining in the sun, laughing and light as the air around us. Today she wore heavy boots, a coat, gloves, and a thick wool hat. She handed us a pile of clothing that soon sorted itself into hats, down coats, boots, and gloves. Dressed in this Himalayan expedition gear, I must have looked like a polar bear, but the reason became clear as soon as we stepped out of the heated confines of the airport. Oh, oh, oh, oh, was it cold!

The only exposed part of my skin froze quickly in the wind. There was some snow on the ground, and I saw a few small mountains of snow made by the plowing machine. I'd never encountered snow before. I'd only seen it on picture postcards showing exhilarated skiers hurtling down the mountain slopes, and in Hindi movies made in Bombay—somehow the hero and heroine always managed to sing a superb romantic song and dance around in the white powder. I'd imagined that it must be all fun and romance around snow—not that I might freeze, or fall and break my bones.

And then the highway. I just had absolutely no idea where I was being taken. At eighty miles an hour, I could barely see the road signs. And worst of all, for the two-and-a-half-hour journey from Boston to Rochester, Vermont, all I saw on the road was cars, cars, cars, and more cars, and the huge trucks. I counted the wheels—eighteen of them. Enormous! I couldn't help recalling the trucks on the Indian roads, almost all of them with the logo of TATA. Each one in a state of gradual decay, belching out a black cloud of emission gases and displaying colorful messages about family planning, the right age for marriage of girls and boys, some even reading *Blacken the face of those with evil eyes.* The mighty turbaned drivers would whistle a film music tune that got louder the moment they saw a pretty girl trying to cross the road. And occasionally you could also see their helpers and assistants taking a refreshing nap on top of whatever the truck happened to be carrying—fruit, vegetables, cattle for slaughter, hay, bricks, cement, household luggage, even piles of garbage.

Without streetlights, I couldn't see whether the walls near the highway had gaudily painted slogans like "For brides and grooms . . . meet Professor Chopra, The Perfect Match-Maker, Raigar Pura, Delhi," "Easy, quick abortions, same-day discharge, low cost . . . Preetam Pura, Delhi." Were there titillating film posters with the stars posing obscenely, or larger-than-life cutouts of ruling politicians next to defaced little cartoons of their defeated opponents?

Nobody honked their horns. All the windows were rolled up. There were no cows, goats, buffaloes, litter, or garbage composting into organic manure by the roadside. No bicycle riders, *rickshaw wallas,* no three-wheeled autos carrying ten passengers instead of the permitted three. No bullock carts, no *chai* shops, no houses, no policemen. My supersensitive nose missed the rich aroma of cow dung, which permeates even Parliament Street in our Indian capital city. I could not hear any loudspeakers blaring megabells of film music or religious chanting. But worst of all, why there were no pedestrians, processions, kids running across the road, or public buses with people spilling out of every door and window? Why was this place so devoid of life?

We must have been passing through some kind of no-man's-land. After all, this country had 250 million people. Shouldn't I see *some* activity to suggest that people lived here? Since I was feeling quite embarrassed by my ignorance, I didn't feel like giving a hint of it to Deborah, who was driving the car. Ehud was in the backseat, probably sleeping, and I gradually drifted into a sweet nap.

I woke up to the jerk of the car as it began ascending a very steep, unpaved mountain road. It was dark all around. All I could see were patches of snow glowing faintly here and there. I was freezing with fear. Loneliness gripped me. I imagined lions, tigers, elephants, ghosts, spirits, bandits, and snakes springing out of the darkness. What horror movie had I stepped into?

As soon as the car stopped, Ehud ran out of the car and into the house. He did not say a word, look back, or even close the car door behind him. Deborah got busy unloading the car, and I had just begun helping her when a huge shape loomed up beside me. It was Noogie. He decided that he must examine me, and so he ran in circles, and then he stood on his hind legs: almost knocking me over, he rested his front legs on my chest and watched my face at eye level. He decided he *must* taste me, and he began licking my face, eyes, lips, nose. I was stunned, appalled, and horrified. I had known from Ehud that Noogie was a friendly and gentle dog. But if he were friendly, he would give me a handshake. If he were gentle, he wouldn't jump on me, try pinching off my nose, and lick me. He did the same to Deborah, whom he had known for years. *So this Noogie is different from what Ehud thinks he is,* I thought. *He is more of a monster than a sweet and gentle dog.*

Once we were inside the house, Deborah announced, "So Vatsala, this is your new, beautiful home. Good luck, see you again, got to go now." She gave me a big, strong hug and was gone.

In India, a bride is always welcomed with traditional rituals performed with religious devotion by the family, friends, and relatives. You could always count on curious neighbors trying their best to take a peek at the new arrival; and then there are the children running in and out of the door. Yet here I was escorted into the house by Deborah and welcomed by a dog. A mild disappointment moved over me like a scanty premonsoon cloud.

It was now 1 A.M. We had been traveling for thirty hours. Everything was pitch dark, except a faint glimmer from all the way up in the top of the house. Where was Ehud? He had told me during the flight that although it was a romantic cliché, in the West it was traditional to carry the new bride over the threshold of her new home. While it would be a stark contrast to the floral mandala of our wedding night, I thought it would be amusing for Ehud to carry me into our home after our long journey together. And here, he had disappeared while the car was still running.

I had never felt so alone and so strange in my life. Outside the house it was deep, deep darkness as far as I could see. The city dweller in me was in total panic. I had always lived in houses with my parents and siblings, and later, when I went to the university and stayed in student hostels, I always had some friendly and inquisitive next-door neighbor. Was this man I married a total recluse, living all alone in this Godforsaken place with this monstrous dog?

I climbed the stairs in the direction of the light above. Noogie followed close behind. When I reached the top, a door flew open and Ehud emerged, pale and shivering, and ran up another flight of stairs without speaking or even looking at me.

I was in total shock. I had no idea what to do. I decided to follow Ehud to see for myself what was going on. Noogie forcefully pushed past my legs and disappeared. My knees jelly, I grabbed the rail running along the steps and dragged myself up to the top of the house.

Here was Noogie, sprawled on the bed, his head resting at Ehud's feet. Only Ehud's head emerged from the heavy comforter covering his body. I leaned over and touched his forehead. His body temperature appeared to be about 101 degrees. Ehud opened his eyes, saw me close to him, and began speaking in shallow moans.

He told me that as I was waking up on the steep mountain road leading to our house, he was also awakened by a rumbling in his stomach and an irresistible urge to be seated in his bathroom. The urge only grew stronger as we ascended the mountainside and grew to such an enormous proportion that by the time Deborah brought the car to a stop, Ehud was a man with one single mission in life. He forgot his new wife, dear friend and vice president of his company, all the graces and manners, even his beloved canine companion who he had not seen for two months, and made it to the throne where he reigned for the first five days of our honeymoon. His crazy itinerary—Rochester, Burlington, Boston, Tokyo, Sydney, Singapore, Madras, Delhi, Bareilly, Delhi, Trivandrum, Madurai, Bombay, Frankfurt, Boston, Rochester—had taken its toll.

Although I had done a Ph.D. in enteroinvasive diarrhea and understood his clinical situation well, not in my wildest imagination had I expected to have to revive my training now and deal with a sick husband. So much for a romantic honeymoon. But with a deep belief in the natural healing processes of the body, I applied the ayurvedic remedies that I had seen my mother use at home. A piece of *nayiuruvi* twig tied with a thread around his wrist brought the fever down in a few hours. Repeated drinking of cool buttermilk took care of fluid loss and replenished the population of lactobacilli in the gut. A few spoonfuls of dry fenugreek seeds swallowed with buttermilk worked wonders in binding the stool.

During Ehud's illness, Deborah visited often to make sure that I was all right. A few times she laughed and said, "Take advantage of these days when he is quiet and in bed. Once he recovers, he will be more than you can handle!"

Our honeymoon at home gave Ehud a chance to recover from his bout of sickness, rebuild his stamina, and relax. Once he recovered, he reemerged in full force as my husband, lover, and companion. And, yes, Deborah was right. Ehud is and continues to be more than I could ever handle . . . he is sharp, intelligent, wise, calm, playful, entertaining, humane, jovial, friendly and, at the same time, he is a serious, committed, dynamic, highly charged, and energetic achiever and taskmaster. He moves through his days, day after day, with a unique zest and enthusiasm, a positive and creative urge, and a *mission*.

During our first weeks at home, Ehud managed to arrange matters in such a way that there were no phone calls and no visits. He operated all the appliances in the kitchen and prepared many meals. But soon the outside world knocked on our door, and when Ehud went back to the office, he turned over to me the reign of the kitchen and the household. Alone in the house, another level of my education began.

Ehud's was a modern household, very well organized and full of the best and most complicated equipment. Every time I entered the kitchen, especially, I was swept by panic and an intense wave of nostalgia for my bachelor home with its grinding stone and two-burner gas stove, the bare electric bulb dangling from the ceiling, and the sink's perennially leaky faucet—although the water supply was turned on only for half an hour every other day, when we had to fill every pot and pan and bucket. Everything was so different from my Madras home that I began to feel anxious and frustrated about even the simplest tasks, such as cooking a meal.

Outside, the wind blew hard, and it seemed that every day brought another snowstorm. The entire soundscape was alien to me—piled-up snow from the roof falling with a thud onto the deck, squirrels and chipmunks scuttering across the shingles, temperature variations causing the wooden walls to contract and expand with loud cracking sounds, the heating system kicking in . . . These were not the people-noises I knew: the neighbors' blaring TVs, nonstop yapping and jabbering in the common stairwell, hawkers and beggars pounding on the door, buses and trucks honking more out of habit than necessity outside on the busy road, and in the night the rhythmic sound of my mother's snoring that in a strange way told me *she is alive*.

The new soundscape frightened me. Unable to distinguish between normal, everyday noises and those that might indicate danger in the house, I felt very alone and unsafe. When Ehud returned home for lunch during one of the most severe snowstorms, I confided my feelings of uneasiness. He responded with, "I know. Why don't I leave Noogie with you?"

That day, he returned to work without lunch and without his dog. For the first time since his arrival in Ehud's home five years before, Noogie did not go to the office. He followed me faithfully into every room that I entered, and curled up at my feet and fell asleep when I sat down to read or relax.

I couldn't believe that my new husband was leaving me in the care of a dog. But as it turned out, Ehud couldn't have done any better if he had appointed a twenty-four-hour security man. Noogie—the well-trained guard dog—has become to me what canary birds are to the miners. He is trustworthy and indispensable. If any sound startles him and causes him to bark, I need to pay attention, but if he ignores a sound and continues his nap, that sound is a benign, routine, and casual part of this household and countryside, and something I need not worry about. Looking at Noogie—his ever-happy, exalted, simple, pure state of mind—I often wonder if an "animal birth" is far closer to nirvana (or salvation) than a "human birth."

I became braver and more comfortable with each passing week. Once my fears of being alone in the house faded in Noogie's company, I could spend time enjoying nature, which staged a new play every day.

15.4.96

My Dear Amma,

With your blessing, I am beginning to write a new chapter in my life in the gentle and sweet language of love. As I address this letter to you I notice that the forest outside bears a baby green patina as if an artist has just moved his brush ever so softly over the treetops. Finally, all snow is gone, spring is here, life is back!

Revival of life is celebrated with much joy in the Jewish festival called "Passover." Aba and Ima drove all the way from New York to be with us for this holiday. It warms me up to recount that with Aba and Ima I have developed a relationship of intense love. They both adore me, and every time we meet and part we all have tears in our eyes. Being with them is the closest thing to being with you. With them I never feel that I am from another country, another culture, and another religion. I participate in all the Jewish festivals with the whole family, and am trying to learn to cook Jewish food. My dear mother-in-law is teaching me to bake her family's favorite cakes and cookies. Finding that I am interested in knitting, Ima passed on to me her entire collection of knitting material, accumulated over many years. For me it was like being gifted with an heirloom.

Aba, Ima, Ehud, and the many guests at our home enjoy my old-world and old-fashioned hospitality and the ease with which I spend time in the kitchen. I attribute my attitude toward food, its preparation, eating, hunger, and the grace of the goddess Annapoorna, solely to you, Amma. Whatever I have learned is from observing you. You never "fix" a meal as they call it here—after all, it isn't broken! You prepare it with love, dedication, and elaborate prayers, and always taught us to thank God for every morsel of food on our plate. In my new environment, I am just continuing your tradition of sacred nourishment for the body, mind, and spirit, prepared with all devotion and care.

I have always loved that cooking Indian food is like the thunderstorms of monsoon season—a big bang involving lots of spices, frying, grinding, and roasting. As the sweet aroma of freshly ground spices and finely chopped onions fried gently in ghee wafts through the air, it brings back memories of your kitchen when I was a child. I often feel somewhat perplexed and for a moment wonder where am I . . . in America or in India? Does it matter at all, now that I have finally found my place and am feeling totally at home?

I often miss you, Appa, Anna, my sisters, my country, but it is quite difficult for me to say precisely what I miss—the sights, food, you? It is strange, though, that I don't feel a sense of loss. Is it because all of these elements live in my mind, and are always close enough for me to touch? Is it because the love I have discovered in my new life with my husband has the power to fill my heart and heal the scars of separation? I do not know.

What I do know is that it is 5 P.M. I must go upstairs to my pooja room and light the prayer lamp. Ehud will be home soon, and he loves the temple-smell of incense that greets him as soon as he steps through the door.

I will write again soon. Sending you all my love, and Ram Ram from Ehud.

Your little daughter,
Vatsala

Ehud and I eased into our day-to-day life together peacefully and in harmony as if we had known each other for decades. I did not feel like a new bride. Although I had no prior experience of "falling" in love and experimenting with my sexuality, I did know that Ehud was my husband. I knew his mind well. I had inquired into it, delved into it, and gauged its responses for a year. I knew his aspirations, goals, and values—and I had them in writing!

No, I had not fallen, but I was very much in love with Ehud, and he lost no time in initiating me in a loving relationship—an intimate exchange of energy and feelings. I discovered that I felt at ease, free, and spontaneous in our lovemaking, and often I saw images of Hindu gods and goddesses in my lulled mind. Most of the gods were married; they had one or a few wives. The Hindu religion from which I derive the basic sustenance for my soul and intellect sees the very coming together of masculine and feminine energy as the fundamental tool in the hands of Brahma for creating the entire universe. In our mythology, sexuality, sexual union (in an appropriate time and context), and marriage resulting in a family life and progeny are seen as sacred. Were it not for this innate, fundamental union, the entire creation would collapse.

I had abstained from sexual union all my bachelor life because it would have been out of time and context, but now that I had the right moment, the right man, the right place, and the right reason to give myself completely, I found that I was not held back by feelings of guilt, transgression, sin, or fear. In fact, I felt the contrary. The entire experience of coming together with Ehud was and is a poignant way of reaching out and touching his soul and expressing my feelings of love, respect, and devotion to him, his body, and his being.

Ehud's views on sexuality are consistent with my own. For him, sexual union is like yoga (which, in fact, means "union"), a practice enhanced by physical, emotional, mental, and spiritual discipline. Rather than feeling disappointed or cheated by Ehud's illness the first few days of our honeymoon, I found the romance of waking up with the sun amidst the pristine beauty of the Vermont mountains, practicing *hatha* yoga every morning, and (as Ehud recovered) walking a few miles with Ehud and Noogie, enhanced and promoted a holistic view of sexuality. Every day with Ehud intensifies our coming together and reinforces my belief that the real romance is in living this life together.

We have discovered that sexual union practiced in the context of spiritual and physical commitment has great potential for bringing intimacy, peace, and harmony to the household. Love has many aspects and qualities and manifestations, but all require a committed and devoted heart. Ehud's commitment to me extends well beyond the conventional idea of sexual fidelity. It expresses itself in a desire to nurture and evoke all my inherent potential.

He has encouraged me to start painting again and to begin writing. He has the self-assurance and generosity of spirit to be more interested in seeing me grow, develop, and flourish than in exerting any power or authority. He has emerged in my life not just as a husband and lover but as a father, big brother, and child. In fact, all the familial roles assigned to males are expressing themselves in Ehud. I have found that I am indeed satiated by him in every sense of the word.

Having become an integral part of Ehud's life and landscape, I do not feel like a separate individual anymore. Is this the total union that Ehud and I were talking about in our letters? What a strange kind of merging this is. We continue to live in two separate bodies, but our inner selves apparently have one and the same goal: living a peaceful, happy, and harmonious life, loving and caring for every soul connected with our household.

GLOSSARY

Agni: the fire deity. Since fire is considered sacred, Agni is invoked as a witness to the ceremonies in all Hindu religious activities.

akhada: monastery of the *Naga babas;* also a gymnasium for the practice of martial arts, wrestling, and boxing

alu matar: a curry of potatoes and green peas

Anand Akhada: monastery where Ganesh Baba lived.

angavastra: a piece of fabric draped over the shoulder

Annapoorna: the goddess Parvati in the form of provider of food and nourishment to the entire universe

arati: a ritual of worship performed with lighted camphor and incense, to the sound of bells

asana: seat or posture used in yoga

auyahuasca: the Amazonian wine Netem, the wine of death or communion; a psychotropic plant used extensively in healing or visionary experiences throughout the Amazon rainforest

ayurveda: an ancient, holistic healing system that originated in India

baba: an affectionate way of addressing a senior holy man

baraat: a procession in which the bridegroom, his family, and his friends walk to the bride's house accompanied by musicians

betel: a heart-shaped leaf chewed with betel-nut, lime, and flavorful spices which reddens the tongue, lips, and saliva; a stimulant used throughout India

bhajans: devotional hymns sung in praise of gods

Bharat Natyam: a classical Indian dance form that originated in Tamil Nadu

Bhrigu system: a way of casting horoscopes as prescribed by the saint Bhrigu

bindi: a round mark applied above the bridge of the nose, between the eyebrows at the spot representing the third eye

chai: an Indian style of tea made by boiling together milk, water, sugar, tea, and spices

chapati: round, fresh bread made from freshly ground wheat flour and baked on the stove-top

chillum: a pipe used for smoking plant-based psychoactive substances

chole: garbanzo beans, onions, and spices

Ehud: from the *Book of Judges,* derives from the Hebrew root *Echad* or "one." Means "union with the one."

Ganesha: the remover of all obstacles; a deity with the head of an elephant and body of a human. The son of Shiva and Parvati, he is beloved throughout India. He is the first deity invoked before commencing any activity.

ganja: cannabis indica

ghee: clarified butter

grihasthashram: family life

halwa: a dessert made with cream of wheat

hatha: obstinate or determined; a form of yoga

idlis: soft cakes made by steaming a fermented mixture of rice and lentil paste

kalash: a pitcher made of metal or earth. Painted with sacred markings, the kalash is an integral part of Hindu ways of worship.

Kali: an incarnation of Parvati; ruling deity of the Kaliyuga, the present age (yuga) of speed, destruction, and decline—one of the four great yugas that compose the cycle of time

kalyanam: well-being; marriage

kheer: rice pudding with milk, nuts, and raisins

kumkum: vermilion powder (also known as sindoor), used to create *bindi*

kurta: a loose, full-sleeved shirt that reaches to the middle thigh or knee

Lakshmi: the goddess of wealth

lingam/yoni: penis/vagina

mandala: ritual patterns and designs created in geometric proportions

mangalasutra: an ornament worn around the neck by southern Indian women to signify married status

marma: points along the *nadi* system (energy channels) where life-energy can be activated, stimulated, enhanced, or manipulated

nadi: subtle vessels in which life-force flows within and outside the body

Naga: a monastic order considered to be the oldest continuous religious order on earth. The word means "sky-clad," referring to the sole garment of the Naga *sadhus:* their nakedness. Also the name of a hill tribe and region (Nagaland) in India.

namaskar: "I salute the God within you"; an Indian way of greeting senior or older people by folding the hands and bringing the palms close together

namaste: the same gesture as *namaskar,* used to greet friends and peers

nariyal burfi: coconut candies

nayiuruvi: a wild herb known to bring down fever rapidly when worn externally

palak paneer: spinach sauce cooked with freshly made cheese

paruppu thengai: a traditional cone-shaped delicacy prepared with jaggery, seeds, nuts, and rice puffs; used in pairs during wedding and sacred-thread ceremonies

Parvati: a goddess; wife of Shiva

pooja: worship

prasad: an offering for deities

pulao: a dish made from rice, spices, and nuts

pranam: a greeting when the relationship is highly formal, with the same meaning as *namaskar.*

Ram Ram: traditional greeting of devout Hindus

rickshaw walla: a man who carries passengers on a three-wheeled cycle (rickshaw), a popular mode of transport in India

rishi: a sage who spends his life in spiritual pursuits

rupee: the unit of Indian currency; about $\frac{1}{43}$ of an American dollar

sadhana: spiritual work

sadhu: a mendicant who has renounced the world in pursuit of spiritual life

samadhi: a state of consciousness. Saints and holy men who attain samadhi toward the end of their lives attain the ability to voluntarily release the life-force from their mortal bodies. They are buried in a seated lotus position; their burial site is also called a samadhi.

Sanatana Dharma: the eternal religion

sanyasa: renunciation of the world; the first step to becoming a *sadhu*

saree: a single piece of five-, six-, or nine-yard fabric traditionally worn by Indian women

sashtang namaskar: prostration meant to convey wholehearted salutation to senior people, parents, teachers, wise men, and deities. One lies flat and makes sure that forehead, shoulders, chest, abdomen, genitals, knees, and feet all touch the ground at the same time.

shaivait: followers and devotees of Shiva; a sect of Hinduism

Shakti: another name for the goddess Parvati, who embodies the feminine, creative power

Shiva: god of destruction; one of the primordial trinity that consists of Brahma, Vishnu, and Mahesh (another name for Shiva)

Shiva linga: a phallic icon representing the erect penis of Shiva; worshipped throughout India as a symbol of universal masculine energy

Shivaratri: a festival of devotion to Shiva

Shri Mahant: chief priest

tapasya: penance, with an aim to acquire spiritual insight, wisdom, and grace

Veda, Vedanta, Vedic: refer to the ancient texts, four in number, that are considered to be the foundation of Hindu religion

veshti: a single piece of fabric worn around the waist; its hem reaches the toes